Dirty Diamonds

The Repurposed Life of a Playboy Icon and Cosby Survivor

By: Victoria Valentino

Dirty Diamonds
The Repurposed Life of a Playboy Icon and Cosby Survivor
Publisher: Marissa F. Cohen **www.PublishWithMarissa.com**
Publication Date: September 22, 2022
©2022 by Victoria Valentino - All Rights Reserved
Printed in USA
ISBN 10: 9798813836725
Cover Design by: pro_bookcovers - Fiverr

AFFIRMATIONS

"Victoria found the courage to speak and her story is one of hope, healing, and finding empowerment in one's voice by speaking publicly. Every survivor needs an advocate, someone they can rely on. Victoria Valentino is that woman. She is now helping others find their voices and rise above their own trauma against all odds. Her Story Matters."

—Andrea Constand
Author <u>THE MOMENT</u> - Standing Up to Bill Cosby,
Speaking Up for Women-
Executive Director-Founder,
Hope Healing and Transformation

***

"Violation of the sanctity of the body of another is an ancient and current human weapon of power and dominance. In recent news, sadly, an elder Ukrainian woman raped by invading soldiers sobs and tells a war reporter, "What they did to me… I do not want to live"

Rape leaves a deep and invisible wound that few are able to heal and find pathways to recovery. Victoria Valentino's illuminating memoir Dirty Diamonds, takes us through her journey of rapes, abuse and unimaginable betrayals to her renewal and healing through Nature, its seasons and lessons of healing. Victoria has given a precious gift, a pathway and hope to those who are, or have, suffered abuse. Victoria's memoir stands as a primer for humanity to bring forth change… a call to education, for awareness, understanding and responsibility of our inherited biology. Victoria's courage and vision has brought her to the forefront of leadership... her voice joining the voices of other abused souls to bring forth humanity and justice in the new age."

— Joan Root Ericksen
Artist
Founder "The Sun Foundation"
for Advancement in the
Environmental Sciences and Arts

***

"In her rich, engaging, and authentic style, Victoria Valentino shares deeply personal stories of her journey from objectification toward self-actualization, grace, and transformational healing. She reflects on the trajectory of her life, relationships, and encounters that both harmed and healed her.

As you read of the trauma, betrayal, and violence that occurred in her early life, you'll marvel at her courage and perseverance. Her long and difficult journey has led her to a remarkable life of service to others and to becoming an influential voice for survivors of sexual assault. For decades, her voice had been smothered—even physically damaged. She remained silent about myriad abuses including being drugged, kidnapped, and raped by Bill Cosby. When she finally took the risk to break her long silence, she claimed her power—her power to inspire and influence others, and her power to raise awareness about rape culture.

As she poured her heart into writing this book, she relived, confronted, and exposed very painful memories of a range of abuses in order to help others learn from those experiences.

Victoria's message is critically important. She challenges her audience to take action and initiate changes that will create a world we desire and deserve. I am so grateful that she found her voice and has given us the gift of her activism and of this book. Her message is a gift of hope and inspiration that helps countless others on their own journey of healing and self-realization."

— Lynn W. Murphy
Bestselling Author of Women Who Push the Limits Presents - 50 Life Lessons from Inspiring Women.

***

"As a Licensed Clinical Social Worker, I had years of experience advocating for the rights of others before meeting Victoria Valentino. I never anticipated our chance courthouse encounter would forever change my life, and our relationship would evolve into the influential activist allegiance we hold today. My involvement with the Cosby Survivors began as a solo endeavor during the first trial with Andrea Constand. I was determined to infiltrate the media's narrative and show the rest of the world that our community believed the 60+ Women, not Bill Cosby. My antics outside the courthouse created a stir and rumors regarding my motives. Then, a brief conversation with Victoria Valentino changed everything.

Victoria offered me appreciation and validation for my activism. She recognized that my efforts were not just on behalf of the Cosby Survivors, but also for the countless other Sexual Assault Survivors whose voices remain stifled. Victoria welcomed me into her inner circle and educated me about how her personal trauma led her to working on changing the laws to benefit other Survivors. Thus, Victoria became my SHero, a living example of how one person can make a difference, and the power behind such individuals when they work together toward a greater good. My hope is that Victoria's story will enlighten and empower others in the way she has inspired me. Join us! Rise up! Let's work together to change the laws that enable rape culture. Reading this book will show you how it's done."

—**Bird Milliken**
Licensed Clinical Social Worker
Badass Activist & Administrator of 'We Support the Survivors of Bill Cosby Facebook' page

***

"Victoria Valentino is a pioneer in the fight against gender-based violence. She is so brave, yet so loving! She is never afraid to roll up her sleeves and work hard for what she believes in. In this world, we need more people like her to break the silence, to be the voice for the voiceless, and to be the change. I am honored to be in her circle of powerful warriors, and I am excited to fight together with her to end abuse."

—**Eileen Dong**
Presidential Lifetime Achievement Award Winner
Ms. Texas
Human Trafficking Survivor Council Leader
TEDx Speaker
Author

***

"Victoria and I met in 2008 at a salon for women writers. We had seen each other there several times before but this was the first time we sat next to each other and introduced ourselves. We knew nothing about each other. Our immediate connection was that she is an RN and I am a respiratory therapist by profession. We quickly became engaged in a depth of conversation that only medical professionals who are closer to their own death can usually get to inside of two minutes. I instantly found her to be intelligent, measured, and keen on doing a deep dive on the questions around the right to die, one of my favorite tabu subjects. She told me that she hosted a local cable interview show entitled, Under Our Skin, and would love to have me on as a guest to talk about the topic. She did just that the following month. A woman of her word.

It was during this time that I came to know her background and I realized that for all her demure class and manners she was a woman who could be counted on to fight for women's rights tooth and nail. The lady has tenacity and spine.

Two years earlier I had been appointed by Governor Arnold Schwarzenegger to the California Commission on the Status of Women where, in 2007, I organized and chaired the first ever televised public hearings in our state's Capitol on, "The Status of Lesbians in California," then co-created and co-organized the first ever statewide, California Women Veterans Conference, now in its fifteenth year. I had previously been a D-Girl at Columbia Studios developing new scripts and co-produced, The Arcata Promise, written, directed, and starring Anthony Hopkins. My story, The Good Girl, was published in the book, Women of Spirit.

I am well acquainted with being a foot soldier for women's issues in a man's world that only finds the topic of women's rights annoying. Where to challenge the silent pact that men have with each other to look the other way is to court swift, vicious, and unrelenting attacks on your character. And that's just at home or at the office. Multiply that a thousand times when you challenge a beloved icon.

In 2014 Victoria went public about being raped by Bill Cosby, the darling of American comedy and fatherhood. She joined the growing collective of women who had, by telling their secret, caused the nation to collectively gasp in denial. Delusions are anchored deep. The pushback was immediate. Nonetheless, women telling this truth to power was about to unfurl itself in a way the world had yet to experience.

Victoria Valentino tells her riveting story on these pages in a way that will open the eyes of every reader to the perversions of fame and sentimentality of both the celebrity and of the public, who often want to believe the lie rather than the truth."

— Elaine Suranie,
Former Chairperson - California Commission on the
Status of Women
Licensed Respiratory Therapist

***

Dirty Diamonds

The Repurposed Life of a Playboy Icon and Cosby Survivor

By: Victoria Valentino

DEDICATION

For my precious son Tony in the beyond, my beloved
daughters, Erinbrooke and Meaganlark, my treasured
grandchildren Max, Ben, Brixton, Oona, Julian and Declan
and for those who have yet to find their voices.

TABLE OF
CONTENTS

Prologue
My Life Ended… My Life Began…
January 1970

I hit the 101 heading west to Topanga Canyon in my dusty, '64, green Chevy Biscayne that Mom and Dad had given me. I threw in my guitar, my big dog, Sheesh, and whatever else I could fit. I stored what little furniture I had in Mom's garage and left L.A. without much of a plan, and even less money. I headed out blasting loud music and smoking a joint.

When I heard the siren and looked in the rearview mirror, I saw the sheriff's car motioning me over. I panicked, then resigned myself to getting busted. "What more could happen to drag me to the bottom?" I thought. I had nothing left to lose anyway. Pot was a felony in those days. I had crank windows and could only open one and was pretty sure I reeked of weed. The smoke was going to hit the cop full in his face. Nothing to do.

The Sheriff was an older man, portly with a gray mustache like my Sicilian step-grandpa. He peered at me from under his beige Sheriff hat and said, "Miss? Where are you going?"

I just looked at him and said, "I really don't know, Officer. My little boy just died. I really don't know."

There was a long beat. Silence. His eyes glistened suddenly. He cleared his throat and said, "Your tags are

expired, young lady. Get 'em fixed as soon as you can…
and… good luck."

I sat stunned, almost dizzy, heat waves shimmering
and radiating off the asphalt in the hot, dry,
claustrophobically stifling, smoggy San Fernando Valley
air. I watched him in my rearview mirror as I pulled away
and thought about what I hadn't told him, that I had, also,
just been raped by Bill Cosby.

Chapter 1
Trial
April 2018

I was sitting in Courtroom A in Montgomery County Courthouse, Norristown, Pennsylvania. Bill Cosby, the former, "Most powerful man in show biz," who was on the verge of purchasing NBC after his long career as a comedian, and at the time, supposedly worth about $500 million, walked by me in the aisle. I was not the only one of several survivors of his heinous crimes present. He acted frail, blind and old, but was only five years older than me.

I witnessed Cosby being prosecuted at long last for his decades of sexual abuse against women. This was the second trial. The first one ended in a mistrial after six days of excruciating deliberation; Devastating for us all but those six days forced us to be more intent on seeing the truth exposed and justice served.

Those trials were the first time I actually saw him in the flesh since that night in 1969 when he drugged and kidnapped me and my roommate. But I was the only one who was raped that night. I distracted him from raping her, the one he really wanted. I became collateral damage. Seeing him again was surreal.

Though only one woman's case was in question, his chickens were finally coming home to roost, because as many of us as could be there to face him, were there. He was sure to know that, considering how many of us had put ourselves forward, speaking our truth in the media for nearly four years. We were asked many times why we were speaking out after so many years of silence. It was a burning question for all of us. No victim can ever predict when the moment of truth will erupt. When the bile that has been swallowed for years will come surging forth. It's anybody's guess. Everyone has a tipping point and we reached ours.

For decades I had pushed my experience with Bill Cosby to the back of my mind. I never told anyone the dirty details. I never concealed that I had met him and thought he was a schmuck, but I never told anyone what really happened until the end of 2014 when I boiled over.

The first twenty-six years of my life had been packed with more abuse than most people experience in ten lifetimes. As I struggled back to a place of hope and healing in the years after the abuse, my six-year-old son died. Within weeks after his death, I was assaulted by Cosby. He was not yet considered America's Dad, and my encounter with him was the capper that sent me off on a many-years' odyssey of transformational healing. Speaking publicly about Cosby after forty-five years felt like the final lap in my healing journey. I became one of over sixty women who were survivors of his sexual assaults. It was overwhelming to discover that I was not alone.

What I hadn't anticipated was that it would trigger all of my past traumatic memories of rape, trafficking, abuse and grief. I had to discuss and relive the trauma of my child's death in the constant retelling to the media, because the two experiences were intrinsically connected. Cosby knew I was grieving my boy's loss. He just didn't care. He simply saw it as an opportunity in which he could take sexual advantage.

Andrea Constand, was the only one of us who was still within the statute of limitations on rape and sexual assault. The newly appointed District Attorney, Kevin Steele, campaigned for tougher laws against rape and sexual assault. He focused on the fact that Cosby had not been prosecuted for his crimes against Andrea, and he had a small window of time in which to do that. She was drugged and sexually assaulted by Cosby at his Cheltenham mansion in Montgomery County, Pennsylvania - and we, Cosby's other survivors, were there in support. She became our SHEro, our modern-day Joan of Arc − a six-foot Amazon-statured woman, former basketball player and head of the Director of Operations of the Women's Basketball division at Temple University where Cosby was on the board. She spoke softly, modestly and simply without affectation; a meditator - a spiritual being.

Her mother was with her and testified in the first trial. She spoke with such force of conviction that it was unbelievable that anyone on the jury could possibly have doubted her daughter's veracity. We all wanted Mama Gianna to be our own mother.

We rose for the jury to hear the charges against Cosby read. The closing arguments made the previous day were intense. We had been driving through pelting, gushing, blinding cold rain every morning for the last three days to be on time in line by 7 a.m. in front of the courthouse to get our passes for Courtroom A. Only thirty members of the public were allowed inside and we had to compete with a number of hostile Cosby apologists to secure our places in line. They always got there first.

When I arrived for the first trial early June 2017, I had an interview with NBC in front of the courthouse and had to go straight there from the airport. As I was leaving the interview with my roommate, my Sister Survivor, Therese Serignese, and I heard loud music blasting. I looked to my left and saw a petite, wiry woman with short shaggy, silvery platinum, lavender-highlighted hair, pushing a shopping cart down the sidewalk in front of the courthouse. There was a bubble machine pumping iridescent bubbles in great profusion into the late afternoon sky. She was singing along with Helen Reddy's version of, "I Am Woman." I was blown away.

At first, I thought she was just some homeless person until the next night when I heard the same song pouring out of a U-Haul truck window as it circled the Courthouse block. There were big banners covering the sides of the panel truck and on the back of it there was a huge hand the size of the entire rear of the vehicle with the middle finger pointing straight up and "Cosby" written in big letters all the way up the central digit. I laughed in absolute delight and shouted something affirmative. That's when I saw Bird Milliken gleefully smiling at me out of the driver's side window amidst all her bubbles, giving me the thumbs up.

I didn't meet her officially until the next day when I was walking into court. She was out there on the sidewalk every single day of every trial with her signs, her boombox, bubble machine and her megaphone in support of all of us women survivors. I think we bonded immediately.

Bird became our biggest ally during the trials and a great friend in between. She was the, "Activist's Activist," and we never had a moment of doubt in whose camp she stood. She was no homeless woman pushing a shopping cart. She was a Licensed Clinical Social Worker who had conducted group therapy sessions in the prison system for male abusers. She knew her stuff and never flinched from the truth. She knew what we were dealing with.

During that first trial while we waited for the jury's six days of deliberation, the courthouse plaza became a circus ground. The protesters were out holding signs. Jane Manning's women were there representing her group, Equal Justice for Women. Protesters with signs that had all our names written on them. There were the Cosby apologists, or recruited homeless people, wearing brand new t-shirts still with the folds in them, with a "Free Bill" logo on the front and a Fat Albert look-alike leading the, "Hey! Hey! Hey!" chants. Then some black guy shouted at Sister Survivor Lili Bernard about her being a traitor to her race, because she was accusing Cosby of rape. They got into it, nose-to-nose, screaming, eyes wild, with a crowd forming around them, media crews, mics and cameras. I was afraid for her and ran up to the sheriffs and said, "We need an intervention!" But Carl, our favorite cop, smiled and said, "We asked if she wanted out, but she said, "No." so we gave her a hand signal if she felt she was in danger and we'd get her outta

there. We're watching and will step in if necessary."
Caroline Heldman, her BFF, had her back and when
it became obvious Lili needed to decompress, Caroline
whisked her out of there to a safe space.

Sister Survivor Jewel Allison took on another
apologist but with a different approach. Jewel said
with love shining from her eyes, "If I hadn't been in a
room alone with that man, I would be you now." We
had a convert.

Bird Milliken had been out in front of the
courthouse daily with her boombox blasting, "I Am
Woman," with her bubble machine, signature lavender
hair and a variety of protest signs. That day, however,
she was notably absent during this midday break. We
were all asking each other what had happened to her,
fearful that she might have been banned from the
courthouse property, or worse. No one knew exactly,
but we believed that she must be doing something
worthwhile.

When the scene couldn't have gotten more
carnival-like, and the crowd was thick on the plaza, we
heard the sound of snare drums coming from the other
block. I thought, "Oh no! Now Cosby's got a parade
going." But then as the drums approached and got
louder and louder, - rat-a-tat-tat - we saw Bird
dancing, grinning devilishly from ear to ear with light
sparkling from her blue eyes. She came around the
corner like the head cheerleader in a high school
band, wearing a protest sign around her neck. She was
followed by at least four bare-chested black guys in
formation with snare drums hanging on straps around

their necks. They were high-stepping in sync, with great precision behind her, wearing blue, metallic, full-face masks. We may have all cut loose in a wild cheer. It was grand. We were all so thrilled, laughing in sheer wonder and delight. We couldn't believe our eyes. The energy was high. The rhythm was irresistible and pretty soon everyone on the courthouse plaza was boogying down. It was a parade alright, but a Bird-fueled one and never to be forgotten. The media was having a heyday. The cops were benevolently enjoying the scene but prepared for trouble just in case!

We waited and waited. The sequestered jury was still in deliberation. Then, we were suddenly requested back to the courthouse in a rush at 10 p.m. We raced to our cars and we all dove in together, speeding down the street and through security. We sprinted up those grand marble stairs - only to discover it was just a question by the jury about some detail or another regarding Andrea's phone records.

Disappointed and fatigued, we retreated back to our respective accommodations. Deliberations were adjourned for the night and we were glad to get some rest, jet-lagged as we were. We had to be back up and alert by 7 a.m. to line up again on the courthouse steps to wait for the doors to open.

If Cosby was found guilty, he could have been sentenced to ten years in prison for each of his three charges. We all hoped he got the maximum. We certainly had our entire lives negatively impacted by his actions - and many of us have had our careers derailed as his star soared.

My Sister Survivors and I knew the truth about this serial predator, regardless of what the jury determined. While there was never any real closure for any of us, we all gained some form of resolution that allowed us to move forward in healing.

But more than anything else, we found our voices and gave others theirs. We were bold and we emboldened others. We inspired trust and empowerment in those who confided their own assaults to us in private moments. We knew we were standing in truth for them, too. The conversation about rape culture in our society was now on the table and could no longer be denied. The floodgates were opened. When the public stats indicated that women who suffered rape were in the minority, it became increasingly obvious that the stats were skewed. Once women were breaking their silence, we were learning that in a woman's life it's not IF she gets raped, it's a matter of when and how many times.

Truth and justice became our banner and we were unified and unafraid.

In June of 2017, after we suffered the terrible injustice of a mistrial, I had the rare opportunity to cross paths with Mr. McMonagle, Cosby's first trial attorney. It was right after court while he was standing in front of the Doubletree Hotel waiting for his car. I was preparing to be interviewed with one of my sister survivors for CBS Sunday Morning. The producer, Emmy Award winner Amy Wall, had snagged us both in front of the courtroom and drove us to the first sit down interview after the verdict.

We each got a chance to tell him how we really felt. While my Sister was histrionic, flailing her arms and alternately calling down demons, lightning bolts and forgiveness on his head, I felt cold as steel. I walked towards him holding my hand out and said, "Mr. McMonagle, a woman's soul was on trial here today… and the jury failed her… and you failed her. I hope you sleep very well tonight. The work will go on." He shook my hand, nodded his head - and said, "Ma'am."

I gave Sister 'The Look' as she pleaded with me not to interrupt her. She was beyond upset. She was having a breakdown, and I went into nurse-mother mode. I quietly, yet firmly took her by the arm and steered her into the lobby. The unfair verdict had triggered all of our PTSD to the max. We were both beside ourselves, but we were expressing our PTSD in our own individual ways. I tend to react like my mother when under stress. I draw myself tighter, stand taller, grit my teeth, but then, unlike my mother, I use my words like a laser beam. My vocabulary has always been my strongest, and sometimes my only weapon.

I learned early in my life that my words hit home; From my parents and a couple of early boyfriends backhanding me across my face, to a rapist strangling me at eighteen, and my first husband's karate chops across the throat leaving me voiceless. I knew my words hit the mark. Carefully chosen, precisely aimed, calmly stated, they would always find the target. Regardless of the consequences, I would never be silenced again.

We were not surprised to hear that Mr. McMonagle resigned as lead attorney for the defense relatively soon thereafter. I hope to his credit that he realized that he was not on the right side of history regardless of the big payday.

This time we were back. Refreshed and ready for another marathon trial, hoping for a more fitting verdict this time. The judge, the Honorable Steven O'Neill, gave his endless instructions to the jury. He droned on. We heard it all before. Last June during the mistrial we were all so downcast, feeling the legal system had failed Andrea Constand… and subsequently us.

Could she still go ahead with her quest for justice, and we, who could not find our justice in court due to our expired statute of limitations, could we? Could we at least find vindication through her victory? We held our collective breath. Everything rested on whether the prosecution had made their case effectively and if the jury heard them clearly this time. Hopefully they would respond with a guilty verdict.

It could go either way. The prosecution was strong, and the defense was aggressively scattershot, attempting to poke little holes and create reasonable doubt. The female defense attorney, Kathleen Bliss, had done nothing to endear herself to women survivors in her stereotypical attacks on Andrea's character and motives for pursuing justice in this case.

This 2018 retrial brought us hope that this jury from Montgomery County, not bussed in from Allegheny County as it was the previous year, would deliver justice this time around. I sat in the back of the courtroom writing in my journal. I was jet-lagged and trying to survive the three-hour time difference between Pennsylvania and my home state, California. I was bored, fatigued, and could barely hear what any of the attorneys were saying because the acoustics were so awful in the courtroom. I confided in my journal, trying to make good use of this time before the much-anticipated closing arguments began. The defense spoke first, then the prosecutors with their burden of proof. Judge O'Neill repeated his jury instructions again before they left to begin deliberating.

There was a sense of deja vu as we the survivors, the multiple attorneys, and the activists awaited the verdict. We had become friends along with the myriad of journalists, media correspondents and producers who camped out with us day after day sharing plug-ins and take-out pizzas as we formed bomb shelter type intimacies, sharing our personal stories with each other, creating friendships that carried over into this year. The retrial is what all our hopes for justice and unvarnished truth about Cosby were pinned on. There, in those hallowed marble halls, our hopes and beliefs in American justice were still alive.

We were closing in on what we hoped was the end of this journey. We from the West Coast, were struggling to stay awake after getting up at 5 a.m. EST, (2 a.m. California time,) just to be in line to get into court by 7 a.m. It felt eerily similar to the first trial.

As I wrote, my words began to dance off the page until suddenly, I heard a thud. I jolted awake as I began to keel over sideways – not for the first time. Luckily, this time I caught myself, then scrambled to collect my fallen notebook and pen. Embarrassed, I looked around to see if anyone had noticed.

I said later, when we left on break to Carl, who was stationed on a chair in the back corner of the courtroom behind me and was the gentle, tough guy Sheriff who was always seen in photos walking into court just behind Cosby - "Did you see me fall asleep?" He smiled and chuckled, "No, but I heard your book fall."

Carl had chosen not to taser Nicole Rochelle, a former child actress on the Cosby Show, who jumped onto the walkway topless in front of Cosby and his entourage, with all our names written on her skin (mine was in an arc across her chest just below her collar bone.) Once back on my bench, pen in hand, I began writing again. The drone of the monotone defense attorney was like white noise.   gave up straining to hear it. I already knew they were spewing bullshit. Question was, would the jury see through it? The evisceration, the stereotypical shaming and blaming of the witnesses; The five women who had chosen to testify – my sisters on this journey of truth and justice, whom I knew to be truthful and authentic baring their vulnerability and gobs of pain in front of the whole courtroom and beyond.

Will the jury buy it? Will they remember the clarity of the first witness, the forty-something forensic psychiatrist, Dr. Barbara Ziv, who outlined with great clarity, clinical neutrality and objectivity, the post-rape behavior of victims? She carefully dispelled the myriad rape myths that drip so easily off the tongues of those who have never been there, and who are so quick to blame, shame, judge and revictimize.

"What were you wearing? Why did you call him again? Why did you go over to his house? You knew he was a married man! Why did you take the pill? Why did you wait so long to report?" Always revictimizing the victim.

I watched Cosby sitting next to his attorneys, rolling his eyes, chuckling at times, rubbing his bald head, then from time to time appearing as if he were falling asleep from boredom. I thought how harmless he looks now in comparison to that night forty-eight years ago, when his face contorted with anger as he moved towards me. I had distracted him from his intended victim who remained unconscious. I never saw him as an attractive man and now he looked truly ugly. Perhaps, that is what depravity does to a person... turns them ugly.

It was not by accident that I was writing in my journal about that night when he drugged and raped me in 1969.

It was in Montgomery County, Pennsylvania where he lives in the Cheltenham mansion that the former District Attorney, Bruce Castor's realtor father had assisted him to buy, where his assault on Andrea Constand occurred. I looked at him as he was sitting at the front of the courtroom next to his attorneys, acting as if the stories of our suffering were nothing to him but a pointless exercise, a waste of his time, a board game that he would win.

My journaling about my Sister Survivors' and my collective journey navigating through the tangles of our abuse, felt all the more important.

Chapter 2
Takin' a Break on a Fast Train

It was April - Sexual Assault Awareness Month. I had spoken the year before at UMD, but this year's symposium fell right dead in the middle of the retrial. I had committed to speak at their event before the retrial date had been set. I had to choose.

I knew I'd miss some critical testimony. I anguished about what to do, but in the end, I knew how important my voice might be at a college campus consciousness-raising event to help the students understand more about rape culture. I understood how necessary it was that we overcome this sexist history by speaking to the next generations, for the future of society and women's essential place in it. I knew my Sisters would be holding down the fort and would give me a full report on my return. I didn't want to let the students I knew at University of Maryland down, so I took the train from Philly to D.C. There was so much time to reflect while on the train. As the scenery streaked by, I wondered how I'd arrived at this place of speaking out. I thought back to the years of silence when my thoughts were screaming insanely inside my head. Facing my past was painful. Deprogramming doesn't come easy, but the truth is worth it.

Sitting on the train, seeing the world I was passing through made me contemplate my life. The many rapes, the variety of rapes (not all physical) that I had experienced since I was a young child leading me through despair, suicidal ideation, detours from my youthful dreams and idealistic aspirations all the way to Cosby in 1969. What a journey then - what a journey now.

Chapter 3
1944 - West Hollywood, California
1940s Hollywood-1961

People used to ask me where I got my big blue eyes. I was taught to say, "From my Daddy who is away fighting in the war." I had no idea what that meant, of course. I was thirteen days old when he was drafted, ten months old when he was shipped out and sixteen and a half months old when he became a casualty of WWII. In January 1944 he was on a merchant ship convoy being smuggled into Italy from Algeria with shiploads filled with munitions and troops to fight Fascists and Nazis. The Germans got wind of it and their torpedo sunk his ship in thirty seconds, the only one in the convoy that sank - the S.S. Paul Hamilton. He had just made Sergeant in the Army Airforce.

In the back bedroom of my Grandma's West Hollywood bungalow where we lived from the time my mother became pregnant, I remember watching her through the bars of my crib. Every night before bed she brushed her beautiful, long, chestnut brown hair with her bristle brush making it glossy - one hundred strokes every night, religiously. She stood looking at herself in her mirror on top of the chiffonier. She'd put a dot of sandalwood oil perfume behind her ears and on her inner wrists before she retired for the night. They were her gifts from my Uncle Bill, her baby brother away in the Navy.

I remember smelling the heady fragrances of blossoms wafting in on the billowing, cumulus-flutters of the sheer, white curtains. I remember my mommy telling me it was just Mr. Proctor, the friendly ghost. It was a story she had read in the Ladies Home Journal about a woman who had taken a small furnished apartment when her husband was drafted and shipped out to the war. Mr. Proctor, who previously lived there, had died. He was known to have been a bit cantankerous. She noticed sometimes that his old rocking chair would appear to move, but thought it might have been her imagination. When her cat decided to sleep on it, however, she knew better. He was abruptly tossed out. In her loneliness Mr. Proctor gave her a modicum of comfort. She often talked to him whether she believed in him or not.

One day while ironing, she was listening to the radio. Victory was declared and there was a cheering hubbub out in the street. She ran outside to join the celebrating crowd of neighbors, but forgot to sit her iron up and turn it off. When she remembered, she rushed back in. To her surprise, her iron was set up and turned off. She was convinced that Mr. Proctor was benevolently watching over her. So, throughout my childhood, my mother always attributed any lovely, but unexplained occurrences to Mr. Proctor. I passed him on to my children, too.

As a baby, barely able to walk, I managed to climb up and balance myself on the railing of my crib in that back bedroom. I joyfully threw myself across the gap on top of Mommy's double bed. Weirdly, I still remember thinking about it, calculating the distance - and then doing it! I still even remember that feeling of accomplishment while balancing myself on the railing. Flinging myself across the space between my crib and her bed was a sensation I still recall - freedom of free flight - and the elation when I landed safely. What a commotion! Mom hollered, and Grandma and Auntie Te came rushing in to see my act of derring-do! I think they were equally delighted by my achievement and terrified for my safety at the same time - and their future ability to contain my acrobatic feats!

Chapter 4
North Genesee
1946

Those early days when Mommy and my new potential "Daddy" Nino were first in love were quite intoxicating. I was only three and a half, yet I remember the feeling in the air; it was palpable. Every time he came to visit it became a special occasion. Grandma, Auntie Te and Mommy bustled around the house straightening up to make a good impression. It all began so innocently.

We were emerging from the end of WWII and there was an air of jubilation and positivity. We won the War and anything was possible. Post WWII Hollywood was friendly, clean, fragrant and full of good will. The "All for one and one for all" spirit permeated the general atmosphere. People dressed up to go shopping on Hollywood Boulevard wearing matching ensembles, hats and gloves. Everyone was polite, cheerful and greeted everyone by name. We were a close-knit community. It was a wholesome time to be in Hollywood.

We had been living up in the high desert mountains north of L.A. where my father worked as a Forestry Ranger, but it made sense when Mommy became pregnant to relocate to Grandma and Auntie's. West Hollywood was much closer to Queen of Angels Hospital. He was drafted in the Army Airforce when I was thirteen days old and was gone a lot in basic training until he was shipped overseas. My mother's mother, Grandma Refa and Grandma's sister, Ethel, who was dubbed Auntie "Te Te" because I couldn't pronounce Ethel, lived there. My 96-year-old Great-Great Aunt Una, also lived with them. She was the remaining child of the thirteen children of my third great grandparents, Samuel and Sarah Chapman, who first emigrated from England on that side of the family during Queen Victoria's reign. It was her sister, Victoria Chapman, for whom I was named - and, of course, the Queen! I can still hear Aunt Una's old lady voice screeching at me when I jumped on Grandma's bed. "Vicky! You're gonna fall! You're gonna fall!"

The house was a traditional California bungalow built by Aunt Una's brother, my Great-Great Uncle Alph. It was the only house below Sunset Boulevard in the middle of a meadow connected to the trolley by a footpath. It was always considered our family home. *1338 North Genesee, Hollywood 46* - my mother's lifelong mantra for home. When Uncle Bill came home from the Navy wearing his "summer whites" with his white sailor cap nested on the back of his head amidst his shiny blonde curls, we were jubilant. The whole block came out to welcome him home. He had that big Hollywood 1940s movie star smile - like my mother. The joy was impossible to contain.

Mommy and her younger sister, Aunt Emmy, the blonde-haired, blue-eyed girl with the family smile who I was supposed to take after, were jumping up and down as he came sauntering down the street from the trolley, carrying his duffle bag. Grandma was clutching her crippled right hand with her strong left one to keep it from curling up behind her, which it always did when she became emotional. Auntie Te was standing next to her on the porch looking expectantly in his direction. Auntie Nor Nor, our neighbor from across the street who was more like family than family, came out to the curb barefoot wearing her usual uniform - Uncle Martin's boxers and his loose short-sleeved shirt over one of his undershirts. The war was over and everyone celebrated the return of every mother's son.

Uncle Bill dropped his duffle bag and picked up each of his sisters and swung them around in full throated, open-hearted laughter. The whole neighborhood cheered and Auntie Nor Nor wept with joy. It was a moment etched in my memory for all time.

Grandma's Japanese gardener, Alfred, soon came home from fighting at the Battle of the Bulge in the Japanese-American Unit. He brought his brother, "Sat" back with him. I overheard him telling Grandma this was his brother, and so throughout my childhood I thought that was his name and called him Brother. It was much later that I learned it wasn't his actual name. Alfred finally retired and Sat took over as the regular gardener for the whole block. In those days, the gardeners became practically family. They were all Japanese and there weren't any, "mow and blowers" back then. They knew every garden like an intimate friend. Bushes were pruned and fertilized on a schedule. Things were tended to with affection and great personal pride.

Ben, the Jewish vegetable man, would come by in his truck to deliver Grandma's weekly groceries. While he was preoccupied delivering big boxes of fresh vegetables and fruits to her kitchen counter, Auntie Nor Nor would steal pea pods off the back of his truck. She'd sit me down on the curb and show me how to open them by sliding my thumb up the pod, tipping my head back and running all those fresh peas directly into my open mouth. To this day the only way I can tolerate peas is raw. Cooked ones still always make me gag. Naturally those were the ones that Mom routinely boiled for dinner after we moved back east and fresh quality produce was a winter scarcity.

Auntie Nor Nor was quite the maverick. When the Ice Man came around in his truck, she loved to steal ice chips off the back of the truck and give me slivers to suck on. While he was carrying big blocks of ice on his shoulder up the driveway to put in Grandma's ice box on her back porch, we'd sit on the curb like little rascals sucking ice chips. It was a time of simple pleasures.

Auntie Nor Nor, short for Eleanor, was the neighborhood character. Grandma and Auntie Te didn't particularly approve of her, but I loved her. She was unconventional - a lot like a big kid herself. She was my grown-up playmate and every child's savior. She rode on the backs of the other kids' tricycles and dug worms for injured birds. She was the one on the block that every kid took their injured pets to for care.

Mom had joined the chorus at the Hollywood Canteen on Hollywood Boulevard before she met my birth father. Our family always loved music and broke into song at the least provocation. It was there that she met both of my fathers. My birth father's mother, Grandma Grace who became known as G.G. when Grandma Refa and she were carving out their turf after I was born, also sang there. Mom continued on in the chorus after my father, Jim, was killed. The camaraderie kept everyone uplifted and some of those friends remained family friends throughout the rest of their lives.

One night singing at the Canteen an olive-skinned older man with gray hair and soulful brown eyes arrived. His name was Nino. Mom said from the first moment she saw him she knew he was "*The One*"- her own true love. Grandma and Auntie weren't quite so pleased. He was an "*I-talian!*" Auntie Te, a lifelong spinster schoolteacher, fretted, "We're all going to get knifed in our sleep!" But he became their favorite son when he gave them all his extra toilet paper rations.

As it turned out he was more than respectable. He was a hard-working, Walt Disney Studio background artist who owned his own home in Burbank, a home he had built himself with his estranged much older Dutch wife.

Mom's chorus friends loved to gather at our house to sing in between their regular chorus meetings, and Nino became a regular. They all arrived at my grandma's house and they'd surround her at the piano. I always sat next to her on the piano bench. Crippled as she was, she mastered playing both parts on the piano with only her left hand. It was the side that hadn't been paralyzed when she'd been afflicted with polio at four years old.

They were great times, except when Mom wanted me to perform. She would wait until everyone was seated around in the living room, then she'd smile her big self-satisfied sadistic smile and point her long red fingernail at me. "Sit!" she'd order. That meant, "Get on your knees and hold your paws up like a little puppy dog. " When I obeyed, she'd say, "Now! Bark!" She seemed to be the only one enjoying herself. No one said anything but I remember as my eyes slid to see their reactions through my flushed embarrassment, that they did not look at ease.

On Mommy and Nino's first official date, he arrived in a brand-new gray suit looking very dapper. It was clear that he wanted to make a very good impression on Grandma and Auntie Te. He was very sweet to me and swung me up onto his hip. He said that he'd have Mommy home before I could say *Jiminy Cricket*! Suddenly I felt all this warm liquid flowing out of me right onto his new suit jacket. Everyone was horrified. Auntie grabbed me and whisked me off to the bathroom, while Mom profusely apologized and rushed to find towels to sop up my pee on his nice new suit.

It didn't deter him apparently, because from then on, they took me everywhere with them. I guess I'd made my point. They'd wrap me up in my blue "*bankie*" and put me in the backseat of his tan Studebaker coupe. They'd drive the neighborhoods of Hollywood up into the beautiful Los Feliz area to the very large dramatic Mulholland Fountain where they'd park the car. At night the fountain would send forceful spouts shooting up into the night air in pulsing plumes of constantly changing rainbow colors. It was truly magical. They'd leave me in the backseat supposedly asleep and walk over to the fountain. I'd kneel in the back window and watch them stand face to face, embracing, murmuring softly as lovers do and kissing. It was quite romantic seeing them newly in love silhouetted against the magnificent molten hues of the surging water. It was symphonic.

Chapter 5
Sojourn, Nevada
1946

Nevada was the place for quick divorces in those days so Daddy Nino took a break from the Disney Studios and took up residence in Henderson, working as a freelance illustrator. The plan was to get the divorce, marry Mom and return to Disney's. His wife had wanted the divorce until she found out that he was in love with someone else and became vindictive, threatening Mom's reputation and Daddy wasn't having any of it.

While he waited for his divorce Mommy and I remained with Grandma and Auntie. They wrote passionate letters to each other but finally Mommy couldn't stand being separated from him for another minute, so she packed me up and we joined him. Mommy was always astounded that Grandma and Auntie never tried to stop her.

We moved into a small, one bedroom apartment in a strip apartment compound out in the desert near cattle ranches. Daddy Nino worked in a little studio within walking distance and Mom would walk me over every day and hand me up to him through the open window for a kiss. At night they would drive out into the desert in his old tan coupe as I laid in a bedroll by the back window under a night sky filled with stars so bright and close, they seemed pluckable.

It was incredibly romantic. They'd sing love songs to each other as they drove out onto the desert byways under the moon. Their favorite song was Sigmund Romberg's, *One*

Alone. "One alone to be my own. One alone to feel her caresses…"

They harmonized and looked dreamily into each other's eyes. I still get misty-eyed when I think about those nights. It was an experience not many children get to have, being caught in the sphere of their parents' new love. For all of my parents' failings and frailties, for all the things they did unwisely, these moments have been caught in time, golden memories suspended in amber; Memories that still bring me to tears and enrich my soul.

We'd often drive out into the desert with Daddy's friend, the jewelry craftsman looking for semi-precious stones to create his pieces. We'd find - obsidian, *Apache Teardrop* it was called- jasper, chrysocolla and translucent *Desert Rose*. He had an old station wagon with wooden panels on the side and running boards - a *Woody*. We'd wade in the Colorado River, make bonfires in the desert at night near big stone wells covered with wooden lids. Daddy would always catch me a horny toad to play with and when I had to pee, Mom would sit me on the running board of the *Woody* and hold my legs out. Those were carefree days of absolute untethered contentment.

The apartment that we lived in was one of three apartments per strip and they were heated with coal oil, which saturated the sand surrounding the tanks. It was a smell that I always associate with big sky freedoms that go on forever.

There were huge cattle watering tanks nearby that we children were never allowed to go near, which made it all the more tempting. Being told that if the cattle came in unexpectedly, we'd be trampled had no impact. One of the older wiser boys who must have been all of six took us out there one day to throw pebbles in the water. We, littler girls, all looked up to him but one day we got caught and punished. I was rambunctious and full of energy not really understanding the danger, but I knew we were in trouble by the looks on the adults' faces. When I was called into the house, I was totally unprepared for what happened next; It occurred so quickly and without warning. Daddy Nino had me face down on my tummy. He tied my wrists backwards to my ankles like he was roping a steer. I struggled, squirmed and sweated to get free. Red-faced, crying out in anger, I writhed on my belly on the asphalt tile floor. When I looked up to my mother for help, I saw her malicious, gleeful smile; her bright red painted lips stretched back over her very white teeth. Daddy Nino was laughing with a devilish gleam in his eyes. They were both clearly entertained by my angry tears, and my struggle against the restraints. Their excitement was fed by my powerlessness. Shortly thereafter, I developed my invisible playmate named Allie. She always held my hand and no one was ever again allowed to hold the hand that I reserved for her.

Chapter 6
Heading East
1947

We left Nevada about nine months later and moved on to New York City where Daddy Nino's family lived. His wife, Holly, wasn't cooperating and Daddy thought it was best to get away for a while until she calmed down. We drove cross-country with someone Daddy knew. The men sat in the front seats and Mommy and I sat in the back. I don't remember much of the drive except for endless miles of cornfields that lulled me to sleep.

After days on the highway, I woke up on my mother's lap to that late afternoon light that glazes everything tangerine in streaks of dying sunshine. The towering skyscrapers disappeared upward into an infinity of glistening lines and small gilded squares. It was alien and disorienting, but it filled me with wonderment - New York City.

We arrived in Brooklyn at my new step-grandpa Carbé's two room apartment in a tall dingy brick walk-up with fire escapes scaffolding the exterior. It had a wooden tank toilet with a pull chain out in the hallway - no bathtub - no shower. The main room was the kitchen, unlike anything I'd seen before. Four open burners were supported by long metal legs for cooking next to a large porcelain sink, where Mommy would bathe me. It was a far cry from bubble baths in Grandma Refa's clawfoot tub. Two chairs faced each other at a wooden table between two windows opening onto a fire escape with terracotta flower pots planted with *oregano* and *basilico*. The wooden radio on the table was tuned to an opera broadcast, and I stood looking at the wooden framed photograph of the Italian military band. I was shown which one was Grandpa proudly holding his Italian horn. I was fascinated by the calendar on the wall with a coy, deeply *decolletaged,* wartime, 1940s glamor girl with her red polka dot bandanna tied over her escaping golden curls with the little thermometer inset next to her bottom.

Within a year, we had gone from warm post World War II West Hollywood with its night blooming jasmine, citrus blossoms and gardenia-scented air, to the stark desert with sagebrush, mesquite, creosote bush fragrances and heart-stopping sunsets - then to the exhaust fumes of the dirty concrete city. The aroma of Sicilian tomato sauces liberally spiced with fresh garlic, *oregano* and *basilico* filled the room. Daddy Nino and Grandpa Carbé, bantered in Sicilian and took turns stirring the pot with a long handled wooden spoon, enjoying their reunion.

At five I became accustomed to opera Saturdays. While a pot of spaghetti sauce simmered on the stove, Daddy Nino and Grandpa Carbé sat opposite each other at the little wooden table drinking from their water glasses filled with Chianti from raffia-encased bottles. They sang along with the opera broadcast from the Metropolitan Opera House. Mom in her rich mezzo soprano, Daddy with his operatic tenor and Grandpa in harmony. *Aida, La Boheme* and *Tosca* became our soundtrack. When the opera was over, Grandpa would take me to Prospect Park. I couldn't wait to get anywhere that had something green growing. I drove him crazy, "Hurry up, Grandpa! Let's go!". "*Aspetta*! *Aspetta*!"

"Wait!" When we got there, he stood in a circle and played an old Italian hand game called *Morla* with the other old Italian men. They'd throw their fingers into the middle of the circle and call out - "*Uno, Due, Tre!*" The winner was the one who guessed the sum total of fingers in the center. They never seemed to tire of it, but I was impatient wanting to run and play.

Daddy was busy looking for freelance illustration work and an apartment of our own, since living in such close quarters was not the easiest. Mommy was getting antsy.

Chapter 7
Brooklyn to Off Broadway
1947

Mom's old girlfriend, Paula, from the Hollywood Canteen Chorus, had moved to Manhattan just before we did to sing in the chorus of a Broadway show called *Call Me Mister*. She had a studio apartment on the ground floor of an old brownstone at 70th off Broadway. The apartment behind hers suddenly became available and we gratefully moved in. It had a Pullman kitchen, which was nothing more than a sink, a tiny gas stove and a fridge tucked into an alcove in the living room wall. There was one narrow bedroom filled up with our cardboard boxes and an Army cot nestled amongst them where I slept. They slept on a pull-out studio couch in the living room. Daddy Nino had set up his drawing board in the window at the end of my bedroom so he'd have natural light to work. He drew all day trying to make our big $75 a month rent.

Mommy and Daddy Nino set about decorating our new nest with great enthusiasm. They hunted through antique shops and second-hand stores finding all kinds of projects for themselves to work on in the evenings. They found an old lampshade frame that they wove new raffia onto for a *new* second-hand lamp. There was the three paneled room divider screen they found and covered with red-lacquered Chinese patterned wallpaper that separated our miniscule kitchen from the main room. And, we found the most beautiful red-orange Chinese wool rug with cobalt blue patterns for the floor, which I have to this day. We started out with three bowls, three big spoons and we ate a lot of lentil soup that Daddy called *"pasta fazool"* even though it wasn't! Margarine was new and white in those days with a yellow color pellet in the cellophane bag that Daddy had to massage until it looked like butter. So many things we now take for granted hadn't even been developed when I was little, but life was simple. Even though money was tight, we were filled with the joy of building and discovering a new life with all the new experiences that Daddy showed us - like snow in Central Park.

Paula became *Auntie* Paula from then on. She was 5'2" with carefully coiffed, bleached blonde hair. She had twinkly blue eyes that seemed to smile all the time, especially when she looked at me. She had a high tinkly soprano voice and taught voice lessons at her upright piano in between her performances. I was utterly in love with her. She was also, unlike my mom, very permissive and catered to all of my whims. She didn't have any children of her own and doted on me. I trailed after her asking endless questions, which she delighted in answering. She always had a string of Jewish boyfriends who would sit at her little table in the center of her studio eating, drinking wine and being regaled with her stories from the Broadway stage. There was *Uncle* Henry Ruben who always brought me *halvah*, a sesame seed candy addiction I still have, then *Uncle* Manning Solon, the photographer with the pencil-thin gray mustache whose studio was on the mezzanine level at the Vanderbilt Hotel - very chic - who always took me to the ballet. Then, *Uncle* Al, whom she would later marry, became my favorite.

Auntie Paula's apartment had a bay window that protruded into a sunken well area below the level of the sidewalk. She complained that drunks always fell over the railing and she had to call the cops to remove them. But, tucked into that bay window was a big trunk filled with all of her opera costumes, which I was allowed to try on as long as I entertained them. Her opera costumes hung off my shoulders and puddled in thick folds of velvet and taffeta around my feet. I loved mimicking her operatic vocal style, standing on the top of her costume trunk - my stage - with West 70th Street as my backdrop. I wanted to be just like Auntie Paula. I adored her.

When Auntie Paula was at a matinee I was allowed to go over to her apartment and play the piano. She had a rotund cleaning lady who I'm not allowed to say was the color of milk chocolate, if I'm going to come off these days as WOKE. But she would keep an eye on me while I slid up and down the piano bench banging on the ivories. I'd imitate Auntie Paula's high tinkly voice and sing at the top of my lungs, "I'm Auntie Paula! I'm Auntie Paula!"

Auntie Paula would on occasion with my parents, open up their apartment doors and have magical theater parties populated with all of her fascinating friends from the theater. There were people with foreign accents wearing caftans; Older goateed men in black turtleneck sweaters and berets; Sleek aloof women in evening gowns, others in leotards and stage makeup having just come from a performance, some wearing flamboyant headgear and others with more conservative turbans; Older seductive actresses with too much eye makeup, deeply wrinkled *decolletage* and headache-inducing *parfum*. It was a Toulouse Lautrec painting in never-ending motion. There was always red wine and opera. People would spontaneously break into song, and I was in the exhilarating thick of the *funiculis* and the *funiculas*. I loved it all.

Being the only little child in the mix, I became the mascot. Everyone spoke to me as if I was an adult - and I responded in kind. I would nod soberly as if I understood. They praised me effusively. They would say I was a prodigy, that I was beautiful, and I was brilliant and talented. They would tell each other in loud stage whispers that I was an unusually precocious little girl way beyond my years. I had no idea what many of those words meant, but I loved being showered with attention and soaked up every word of praise.

I became adept at standing in the midst of men telling dirty jokes that I didn't understand. I knew they got a laugh, however, so I memorized them and moved to the next huddle and retold them. It was all about getting the laugh.

"So, there was a guy standing on the street facing a wall taking a piss. Another guy who was passing by, stopped and asked him, "Excuse me. Are you Drew Pearson?" The guy facing the wall said, "No, but I will be in a minute."

I had no idea why that was funny, but I laughed as if I did and totally loved everyone's reaction. I learned later that it was a play on words and that Drew Pearson was a well-known journalist in the 40s with a radio show on NBC. But everyone loved my innocent, straight-faced, cherub-cheeked telling of it and broke into outrageous laughter. They said they were sure that I would become a star, everyone said so. So much so that Auntie Paula got me an audition for a children's radio show. The producer was a friend of Auntie Paula's and came to the apartment. Mommy had spent all morning curling my hair with her old, wooden-handled curling iron that was heated in the gas flame on the stove. She put me in my prettiest dress, white ankle socks neatly turned down and black patent leather Mary Janes with the little buckled strap. It was all very exciting.

Mommy walked me down the hallway to Auntie Paula's apartment and we waited for the arrival of the producer. He was very tweedy with horn rimmed glasses. The grown-ups all spoke to each other as if I wasn't there. Then he turned towards me and I was introduced. He spoke to me in a very patronizing tone and I was told to stand over by the big trunk in the bay window. I stood up straight as Mommy had instructed me to do, folding my hands properly in front of me and waited. Then he handed me the script to read. I just stood there looking at it. My face got red and hot. I felt so humiliated because I couldn't decipher the printed words. I hadn't learned to read yet - and I was already seven years old.

That year the Manhattan schools were so overcrowded, and because I was December-born, I got put off to the next year. Even the Parochial schools didn't have room for a Protestant kid. I was utterly mortified. Auntie Paula and Mommy were terribly embarrassed and that was the end of that. The man patted me on the head with an arched eyebrow, looked at Auntie Paula, looked at my mom and left abruptly. He made it clear he was a very busy man with no time to waste on this nonsense. Mommy steered me out the door, down the hallway and back into our apartment. No one ever said another word. I felt so ashamed, as if my inability to read was my fault. It was never brought up again, but my parents made sure I started school that year. Daddy Nino could be very persuasive.

Auntie Paula was quite a character and she didn't take anything off of anybody. Her gutsiness was an inspiration to me as a small child since my mother was a very restrained person and overly polite. One time we were sitting on the bus - me in the middle between Mommy and Auntie Paula. There was some guy standing in front of us hanging on to a hand strap, holding an umbrella under his arm. It kept waving right in front of Auntie Paula's nose with every movement of the bus. Politely, she would move it to the side. It kept waving back in front of her, hovering and hitting her in the nose again and again. Finally, she said something choice and grabbed it out from under his arm and whacked him with it. While my mother acted shocked, I have no doubt that she wished she had the *chutzpah* that Auntie Paula had. Auntie Paula was always defending the underdog and would yell at bus drivers if they didn't wait for old folks who were trying to get to the bus as fast as their slow old legs could carry them. She was purported to have helped organize Chorus Equity, the Actor's Equity equivalent union formed to protect the chorus entertainers. I overheard Mommy whispering to Daddy in deliciously conspiratorial tones, "Well, you know she's a Communist…"

Once when I was playing in the backyard, they were standing around the radio and called me in to hear a radio broadcast about the cowboy film idol of the Forties, Roy Rogers. He was my childhood heart throb. He had crinkly smiling blue eyes and always saved the damsel in distress. I was in love. The grown-ups always told me that he would 'wait for me.' The radio news blurb turned out to be an announcement of his marriage to Dale Evans. I was devastated, as only a little girl can be who trusted everything her grown-ups said. I threw myself backwards on the studio couch and wailed. I was inconsolable. They all thought it was quite funny. From then on whenever we played Cowboys and Indians, I never played Dale Evans, instead I always played Roy Rogers. I never in my young life forgave her. It was my first romantic betrayal. While that may sound amusing it really absolutely devastated me. It is a cautionary tale for parents to understand how literally things that adults say to children are received - and how deeply impactful they are to innocent little hearts.

During the day Daddy was always hunched over the drawing board and Mommy was always cleaning or cooking. Auntie Paula was either performing, teaching or she and Mommy would saunter off gaily to go window shopping on Fifth Avenue.

When Auntie Paula's father, *Uncle* Charley, came to stay with her, he relieved them from having a little kid to entertain all the time. She had regaled us with stories of his grand exploits fighting for coal miner's rights back in his day, so his arrival was met with great joy. He carried me on his shoulders to Central Park after lunch, so I could roller skate with the other kids, while he sat on the benches with the other old men feeding pigeons. Uncle Charley was tall, lanky, taciturn and always wore a gray suit and brimmed gray felt hat. I remember one day a pigeon flying overhead dropped a big white sloppy poop on the brim of his hat. He was not amused. I tried to suppress my enjoyment of the moment even though I was dying laughing, but more so because he looked so pissed trying to maintain his dignity.

One day after arriving back from roller skating with Uncle Charley, he said we needed to stop off at the apartment before he took me back to mine. Auntie Paula wasn't home because it was matinee day. He went into the bathroom while I stood waiting with my back against the front door. He called me into the bathroom saying he needed some help. I, being an obedient child, went in. He sat me on the toilet seat lid and suddenly dropped his gray trousers. I was eye level with this big brownish wrinkly worm-like thing laid over wrinkled sacks of hanging flesh covered with sparse gray hairs. I'd never seen anything like it before in my life. As much as I was repulsed and horrified, I was scared stiff.

He handed me a soapy warm wet washcloth and told me he needed me to wash him down there. I felt disgusted and intuitively knew it was wrong. Always afraid to disobey my elders, I held the washcloth in my hand and extended it as far as the end of his limp 'thing' but didn't touch it. I dropped the washcloth and ran as fast as I could out the front door. I still don't know how I got the door open. I ran down the hallway into our apartment and said nothing to my parents. I ran straight to the bedroom to lie down on my cot. Mommy said, "Vicky, get your shoes off the bed!"

I had never seen a man's private parts before. While I was in shock, I was also curious. Daddy Nino was a very modest man. He never walked around without his trousers and in those days, trousers were baggy and double-pleated in front. Daddy also had a silver pocket watch with a silver chain that draped down from his beltline into his trouser pocket. I had no idea if Daddy had the same equipment as Uncle Charley. I hoped not, but I wanted to find out.

The next time Daddy Nino took a shower, I started trying to peek through the keyhole to see. I kept peeking, running away and nervously giggling. Daddy Nino, who had his own issues with sex, being Sicilian and steeped in the Madonna versus whore conflict, angrily ordered me to, "Open the goddam door!" I really didn't want to, but Mommy was standing by the kitchen looking very dismayed twisting a dish towel in her hands. She said, "Do what Daddy says." Even though I didn't want to see anymore, I reluctantly obeyed. Slowly I turned the door knob and opened the bathroom door. I looked at the floor. Daddy angrily threw back the shower curtain and stood there in front of me stark naked. He said, "Now, look!" My eyes glazed over and I still wish that what I saw was only a blur. I turned around and ran away to the backyard.

The next day, I told Auntie Paula that Uncle Charley had 'dropped his drawers' and wanted me to wash him down there. I don't remember if she said anything or not, but she was suddenly tickling me almost hysterically and giggling with a weird intensity. She put a pillow over my face and held it down so hard I couldn't breathe. I flailed around with my arms and legs trying to get free. Then, just as suddenly, she took the pillow off my face and looked at me sternly. "Go home! You're a bad girl!"

I couldn't understand what I'd done. I worshiped her. I wanted to be with her. I wanted to be just like her! But I was banned for what seemed a very long time. I remember standing in the dark hallway outside her apartment door imploring her, "Auntie Paula, please let me in. I'm sorry. I'll be good."

By the time I was allowed back in her apartment Uncle Charley was gone. Auntie Paula, Mommy and I went to visit him 'in the hospital.' He was lying amongst tangled sheets in a large olive gray green crib with thick round metal bars on it. I shrank back behind my Mommy's skirts and I was eye level with his bed. He locked eyes with me and stared straight at me. I couldn't unglue my eyes from him. I didn't know if I had been responsible for him being there, but I felt petrified. No one ever talked to me about it, or anything else. Those were the days when children were expected to be seen and not heard so I suppose that wasn't unusual. It was the last time I ever saw him. Some time later, I heard Mommy say that he died.

A little boy from down the block, older, maybe ten years old, came over to play with me in the backyard. There was one scrawny little tree in the back corner by the fence and after we'd been playing for a while, he walked over to the tree unselfconsciously, unzipped his corduroy pants and began to take a whiz against its slender trunk. It triggered everything that was unresolved inside my head. I felt my heart pounding in my chest and I started sweating. I ran into the living room, threw myself face down on the studio couch and told Mommy I had a headache and they needed to make him go home. He was confused and honestly didn't know what he'd done wrong. I refused to look at him as he passed the couch on his way out and I never played with him again. Poor kid, he never understood why what he did upset me so much. I knew why I was upset but never revealed it to my parents.

I loved that backyard. It was the only swath of green outside of Central Park that I was able to enjoy in New York.

I ached for green plants and flowers. I ached for my grandma's backyard. There were lots of fuzzy white caterpillars in our white clover bedecked yard that first Spring we spent in the city. I loved them so much that I let them crawl all over the front of my dress. I wanted more.

Someone had told me that if you cut worms in half they would become two worms. So, I experimented by cutting a caterpillar in half to make two. It oozed green goo, squirmed in what appeared to be agony and died. I was horrified to think that I had been the cause of it. I put it on a concrete block that lined our little garden walkway, and piled white clover flowers on top, then I got on my knees, wept and prayed, begging God and the little caterpillar for forgiveness. I was discovering life, death, and consequences.

In those early years of my young life, I had already experienced men's bodies only in terms of anger, fear, repugnance, shame and claustrophobia. The loss of trust in my own mother, my only touchstone - the only person I could look to for my safety and security, who had, by then, failed me multiple times, was destabilizing at best. She had repeatedly fallen short. In fact, she had participated. I understood early on that I had no one but myself on whom to rely, only with myself to keep counsel. I learned to be silent because when I spoke out I was punished - or worse, ignored. I endured numerous instances of these kinds of soul rape and sexual assault as a small child. I believe it set me up for those more physically invasive rapes that came later - rapes from which I never truly recovered. I experienced conflict between people I adored who betrayed me on every core level. I discovered that I could cause death and it was irreversible. But I never understood how it all connected until I grew into a woman. As a grandmother, finding my voice speaking out about Bill Cosby's assault, and connecting with fellow survivors, a more complete tapestry of my past traumatic experiences and their fall-out in my life was woven. Healing on an even deeper level began.

I had a recurring dream as a teenager...

I was at a cocktail party wearing a beautiful pale gold ochre-colored silk sheath with emerald green spaghetti straps - a hand-me-down from Auntie Paula. I stood inside a glass cylinder as people glided past me in chic gowns carrying their martini glasses. I spoke to them, but they didn't see me. It was as if I wasn't there at all. My presence was not acknowledged. I was not seen. I was not heard. I simply didn't exist.

Chapter 8
Through Service We Are Healed

I checked my watch again and acknowledged my three other train companions, all of us heading to D.C. We were sitting face to face, impossible not to have some brief chatter. One of the women knew me from the Cosby news that she had been following. The woman to my left side began to pick up on our conversation and hinted that she had had her share of *experiences,* too.

I felt strangely drawn to the archeologist sitting across from me on the train. Her henna designs twined decoratively around her wrist onto the back of her left hand. I began to tell her that I always wanted to become an archeologist as a child, but first I mentioned a rock that I treasure that I'd picked up years before on my Oregon farm. It fell open almost as soon as I lifted it and revealed two large overlapping scallop shells fossilized within. Before I got my story out, she snapped, "That's geology!" It seemed the conversation was closed. I hesitated as I was going to explain, but then it seemed pointless so I shut my mouth.

She said she worked on archeology digs in Panama and was on her way to be a guest speaker in Washington D.C. I would have loved to tell her about devouring books as a child written by famed archeologists Dana and Ginger Lamb. I had been moved to tell her how their explorations in the Yucatan inspired me to write them a fan letter, and that I still have the treasured letter that they wrote in response. I returned to my mind-tripping and the hypnotic train sounds and movements that lulled me into time traveling.

Chapter 9
On the Santa Fe Railway,
A Visit with Mom to Hollywood
1949

My mother took me cross-country from New York when I was six to visit Grandma and Auntie Te in Hollywood. It must have been around 1948 or '49. I know I was six because I was missing my two front teeth with everyone singing that old song to me. *"All I Want for Christmas is my Two Front Teeth."* I remember seeing the pictures of me in my cowboy shirt, my Mexican hand-tooled leather cowboy boots, happily smiling in front of Grandma's West Hollywood bungalow. I had my six shooter cap guns in a holster on my hip and I had my spurs on - and a head full of big golden curls!

We were heading out West on the train. I thought I'd get to see cowboys again and maybe some Indians - and especially Auntie Nor Nor. I knew I was too big for Grandma to rock me in her arms for a nap anymore, but I secretly yearned for that feeling of contentment and safety again. I was excited beyond words!

In those old days of the American railroad, the Atchison, Topeka and the Santa Fe railroad, all of the porters were black fellows wearing very neat black or navy blue uniforms, with white gloves and caps. Just as in Agatha Christie's stories of Hercule Poirot on the Orient Express there were dining cars with white table clothed tables and specific eating hours during the day. Everyone was traditionally courteous and fairly formal.

At bedtime, the seats were folded down by the porters while we were in the dining car. They were converted to double decker bunks with carefully made beds - crisp white linens, warm blankets and fluffy pillows. The curtains were drawn for privacy. It felt like a cozy cocoon.

I woke up very early one morning while Mommy was still sleeping. I kneeled to peer out the window. It was just before dawn and we were going through the desert and the colors in the sky were rosy golden with lavender shadows still long on the sand. There was a sense of awe and anticipation of the sun's appearance. There was a profound silence except for the chug-chug-chugging of the train, the occasional long train whistle and the hum of its wheels. All the world seemed to be asleep. I was alone in my wonder and felt entirely in tune with the magical landscape. The cacti and sagebrush whizzed past my window. I didn't want Mommy to wake up yet, because I didn't want the hustle and bustle of the day to begin. I wanted those breathtaking moments to last forever.

One afternoon I slept through lunch, but woke up hungry. I'll never forget the kindness of the porter bringing me his own Graham crackers and milk to get me through until supper time. I know this is now considered 'Uncle Tomming', but these were the historical times in which I grew up. My childhood memories of people of color, and other cultures influenced me heavily - always in positive ways.

Grandma's Japanese gardener, Sat, became a family friend until he died in his nineties. My mom's lifelong friend, June, was Japanese-American. They met singing together in the USO Chorus during the war. June was born in California and her family had the largest garden nursery in Southern California. They were packed up and shipped off to the Heart Mountain Relocation Center in Wyoming after Pearl Harbor. Her mother was killed by a hit and run driver in the street the night before they were to leave. My mother and she continued to write to each other all their lives. I met June twice, but had not yet met Lani, her daughter, who was born in the camp. Lani's father was a musician from Hawaii on tour on the mainland when he was rounded up. June and Jim were married in the camp, but he took them to his Hawaiian home as soon as they were released.

My middle name is June - but then so is my mother's and grandmother's - June nevertheless memorialized.

June's daughter, Lani and I became pen pals as soon as we learned how to write. She influenced my life greatly with Japanese culture - and she said I influenced her, with my Thespian stories from Connecticut and Manhattan. We never met until we were both 68 in NYC where she resides with her husband near Columbia University. Our mothers had both recently died within two months of each other. When I visited, Lani and I walked Riverside Park looking at the gardens and all of a sudden it would hit us. We'd stop, look at each other, burst into broad smiles and jump up and down giggling and hugging like schoolgirls. It was quite a celebration.

My Grandma Grace, my birth father's mother, stunned me when I heard her use the 'N' word liberally once

I returned to California in the Sixties. I sadly never felt safe going to visit her after I became a mother to my racially mixed son - her first great grandson. It might have been a teaching opportunity, but I wasn't willing to risk my son's feelings, or mine. There were others in my family that wore their stereotypes boldly on their sleeves and, justifiably in their closed minds. There were a few other slurs that slid loosely from their tongues, as well. Even as a child, my internal moral compass rebelled.

My mother looked down on the Irish, but it could have been because she rebelled against my birth father's mother, Grandma Grace. My father held her in high esteem and my mother was very competitive. She had frizzy, flaming "carrot-top" hair and was of Irish descent. She was freckle-faced and openly emotional. My mom was overly reserved. She always put her emotionalism down and when I was being emotional comparing me to GG was her ultimate put-down. "You're just like Grandma Grace!" "It's just cheap and low class," she asserted all through my childhood. Mom even went to the extreme of wearing bright orange on St. Patrick's Day - her own personal rebellion.

My mother's prejudices began showing themselves even more when I was in 4th grade. I had always thought we were an inclusive and open-minded family after our esoteric group of friends in Manhattan. Her comments about Jews seeped out even though so many of our friends were Jewish. I was often taken aback. It was always difficult for me as a child trying to reconcile our lives, friends and then her comments once their backs were turned. It made me think, discern and hide my own feelings about the people I liked.

It was a shock when she made me sit down and write a note to the darling little black kid across the aisle who smiled at me and sent me a love note. I smiled back and was so pleased that I made the mistake of sharing his sweet note with my mommy. She sternly dictated a note I had to sit down and write telling him that his note was inappropriate because he was colored. To this day I feel so ashamed that I didn't resist and that I gave it to him. Mommy said, "I'll know if you don't. I always know." In those days I still believed in Mommy's superhuman, all-knowing powers.

Ridgefield, Connecticut where we relocated in 1953, was not officially segregated but everyone had their places clearly defined in society, even though on the surface everyone appeared congenial. I was beginning to observe the dichotomy in grown up behavior. I felt the injustices deeply but didn't know what to do with my observations.

Paradoxically, Mom was enthralled taking me to lunch at the Stonehenge Inn in Ridgefield sometime around 1957 to see Marian Anderson sing. We were only a few yards from her at a little '*twoie*' against a stone garden wall. She was magnificent, and I didn't realize the historic importance of her presence then. I was too captivated by the raspberry floating at the bottom of Mom's champagne flute.

My experiences with non-Caucasian people were always positive and caring, and all my favorite "uncles" were Jewish. I suspect it established an early pattern of expectations that folks of color and other faiths were nicer than my own parents.

Chapter 10
Cavalcade d'Étoiles
Montréal 2004

My thoughts flew by just as fast as the streaks of colored buildings and backyards flew by on the way to D.C. I checked the time. Another hour at least before we arrived at the train station where the university had arranged for me to be picked up. The train hypnotically rattled on. God, how I love trains!

I thought back to 2004 when my author friend André Pronovost asked me to sing at his book launching in Montreal. I had earned a mention in his book, "*Que la Lumiere soit, et la Musique Fut.*" "Let there be Light, and There was Music."

He was an electric guitar player with a Sixties Rock n' Roll band called *Les Cavalcade d'Etoiles* and invited me to come to Montreal to sing at his book launching. I automatically said, "Yes!" without considering that it had been decades since I sang publicly - and never with a Rock n' Roll band.

The book launch was held in Club Soda, an old theater in downtown Montreal that was converted into a nightclub. It had a fabulous professional stage with a real old theater, backstage dressing room. I could still almost smell the greasepaint and old sweat-stained costume dust, but maybe that was just my imagination. The thespian in me was instantly enthralled.

He wanted me to sing "The Train They Call the City of New Orleans." It had been a hit song in Quebec. But what I didn't know was that the rendition they knew was rewritten in French with lyrics about divorce and sung in a pop style. I, of course, sang the Arlo Guthrie version - and we rocked it.

There were images outside that fast-moving train window on my way to D.C. in 2018 that took me right back to lines in that song and early Americana. *"Passing towns that have no name and train yards full of rusted automobiles..."* I was humming it in my head.

The night of the show at Club Soda there was a blizzard raging. The temperature hit below zero sometime that night and we still managed to have a 750-person, standing-room-only audience. It was the largest book launch celebration they had ever had in Quebec. I had only two rehearsals and a sound check.

To say I was nervous was an understatement. But once I walked out on stage, the crowd applauded, the spotlight hit me and I forgot that I hadn't done this in a while. I was home. Being on stage performing LIVE is more than an aphrodisiac, it's a blood transfusion for a kid raised in the theater. It was also a fabulous reminder that I could still sing and perform after so many years - and best of all - with a Rock n' Roll band.

All I did was say yes. Saying "Yes!" was a lesson learned.

Chapter 11
Connecting Loose Threads

Meeting other women on my travels who shared certain experiences but who had not yet found a way to speak openly about them filled me with humility. When they acknowledged their gratitude that I was speaking for them, I felt honored. To be their voice helped me recognize that my work was important, necessary - and that I really was touching lives in essential ways. I felt I'd found my path - or it had found me.

It also made me reflect on my mother whose own voice was stifled all her life. My narcissist mother whose freedom was restricted; Whose dreams of becoming a professional singer were squashed by matrimony, motherhood and a patriarchal system she couldn't buck. Her rebellions were strictly confined to wearing bright orange, lots of fabulous jewelry, multiple rings on each finger, large ear bangles, and her periodic grandiose extravagances, which she hid from Daddy in the back of the closet.

Daddy; "Where did you get that?"
Mom: "Oooh, I've had it."
Daddy: "So, does that mean I didn't pay for it?"

Then, she captivated us all with her big, glamorous, red-lipsticked, perfect, white-toothed, devil-may-care, Hollywood movie star smile as she sailed out the door to go shopping at the Galleria, dressed to the nines. That usually preceded what I now see as her depressive episodes. She would throw herself across her bed without her wig on in a state of lethargy, weeping without explanation or the ability to find the words to express herself. Or she would have a week-long migraine in which very strong unsweetened black tea and unbuttered toast were her sole forms of sustenance. It was then when Daddy isolated himself in his studio, and I was tasked with catering to her every need. Massaging her neck and head, her feet, always trying to alleviate her intractable suffering.

When Mom wasn't getting enough attention from Daddy, she'd stage a crisis, create drama, have a meltdown, which inevitably culminated in her storming upstairs to her bed in tears.

In one way or the other, this same behavior continued all the rest of her life, long after Daddy died in 1993. She'd be fun, baking, enjoying life, having company and being the gregarious person that everyone loved - the person that all my friends adored and praised - glamorous, the life of the party. Then, this other side of her would take over as soon as the positive energy flagged, or there was a perceived slight, a criticism or if her position as matriarch and Queen of the Ball was threatened. She'd instigate mean-spirited conspiratorial gossip, complaints or criticisms, pitting people against each other.

When my cousin Annie and I were kids, Mom would rile up, ordinarily mild-mannered Daddy into furious tempestuous anger. It always ended up with his bellowing loudly at us and whacking us hard on the butt with his tough craftsman's hands. When I sobbed and showed her my butt bruises, she'd say, "Oh, honey, he didn't mean it. He just has hard hands." She was Iago to his Othello - needling him behind the scenes until he exploded. She would trigger his frustrated anger and when he finally blew, she'd step back innocently and pour calming oil on the turbulent waters.

She resented any woman, including me, who had more independence than she had; Any woman who had accomplished anything on her own, or who had married well. She would accuse them behind their backs of being, "kept women;" Women who had no idea how to dress properly; women who had crude manners. Or she'd criticize their inability to sing in the correct key. "Off-pitch," she'd archly intone with a knowing nod, "nasal." Or, perhaps, they didn't wash their dishes to her specifications or set their tables properly. It was always something. No matter how her lady friends doted on her, as soon as their backs would turn, she'd have some venomous criticism. She infuriated me.

When we were both older women, I was always torn between being pissed off and calling her out on her behavior, which she resented mightily - or feeling overwhelming compassion for her. Somewhere in between, we were best friends, companions. Monday night dates at the Scottish Pub piano bar where we'd sing show tunes and opera, we shared our own community of singer friends. Our daily phone calls over morning tea about nothing much were a comfort. We were each other's' touchstones. I was the first person she'd call when she didn't feel well, because she knew I'd always be there for her.

I knew at the heart of her pathopsychology were her feelings of powerlessness. She established herself as a very unique personality over her lifetime. She was extraordinarily vain. Her colors were autumn. She wore burnt oranges. She always wrote with brown ink. Her tea had to be strong, black, unsweetened accompanied by grainy whole wheat toast with lots of butter. She hung her clothes on the line, starched and ironed them. She refused to use the clothes dryer that Annie once gave her as a gift, and gave it back. She liked her towels rough. She loved polishing her own silver, copper and brass, and her routines were rigid. Polishing the silver was every other Saturday. Cleaning house every Saturday. Bed linens changed and towels changed weekly. Supper was served at six, but she went upstairs to shower and dress for dinner at four. We ate at a proper table and we stood behind our chairs until she was seated. After they returned to California the routines were a lot more relaxed, but one could almost set one's clock by her. She was the harbinger of family traditions and old English recipes brought across the Pond by our ancestors. She held the family together.

Mom could be deep in conversation and instantly, almost in mid-sentence she'd hold her hand up for silence, to call our attention to a moment of natural wonder - a sunset, a bird call, a sun-gilded leaf. I still recall indelibly the look of awe on her face. She had wild blue jays coming in through the windows and walking on the breakfast table to take peanuts from her fingertips. She had a natural understanding of wild things.

She was stubborn and contrary, so stubborn in fact, that Grandma told me that she feared for her even when she was a child. The doctors documented that she was, "*a difficult woman*." They didn't know the half of it. When she walked, she walked quickly with determination and purpose. She was straight-backed, elegant and spry. She had a gypsy fashion flair. She'd dance with fervor with us all. She sang an old 1930s Jerome Kern and Oscar Hammerstein song,

"Why was I born? Why am I living? What do I get? What am I giving?" at her ninetieth birthday party, wearing her burnt orange caftan and all her beautiful jewelry. She powered into the high notes without any hint of an old lady warble. I was never so proud of her.

She was a remarkable woman in so many ways. She overcame the loss of all her hair from the mumps and carried on with her shoulders back and head held high. We were still living in Manhattan in 1949-ish and had gone out to visit my new step-cousins on Long Island. My new little girl cousin had the mumps. I caught it and so did Mom. I got over it but Mom was desperately ill. When Daddy took her to the hospital with a high fever, it was just Daddy and me at home. I never felt so alone. It was the strangest thing being without my mommy for the first time ever. Daddy Nino wasn't sure what to do with me and I'm sure we both had our worried thoughts circulating silently in our heads. *"What if Mommy dies? Where would I go?"*

When she finally came home after about a week, we were so relieved. Daddy catered to her every need. I was a bystander as everyday Mommy would come out of the bathroom and say, "Look, Nino, my hair is coming out in my brush." He'd say, "It'll be fine. Don't worry." One day Mommy came out of the bathroom with her shoulders all slumped over holding her cupped hand out for Daddy to see. It was filled with clumps of her beautiful brown hair. It was as if she was holding a dying baby bird. She began convulsively sobbing. Daddy draped his arm around her shoulders and guided her out into the backyard. I watched them through the window. Day after day, more hair came out until Mommy was completely bald - no eyelashes, no eyebrows, nothing.

They went to the Mayo Clinic and exhausted every medical avenue they could access in the late 1940s. They were told that once Mommy had fully recovered, her hair would surely begin to grow back. It never did.

Mommy saved chunks of her hair and placed them on her forehead and secured them with big brightly colored silk scarves that became her new style. She had two - bright orange and turquoise. When we strode briskly down Broadway with my little legs trying to catch up with her long quick strides, I would look up to see her scarves billowing in the wind. In my memory she became more than a mother to me then, she became symbolic - a figurehead on one of those old sailing ships. You know the ones. They were powerful carved wooden women surging into turbulent seas, chin thrust forward looking straight ahead without a hair ever out of place. They were unsinkable.

In the 40s there were no wig shops where you could buy a wig off the rack. They were also expensive. $250 per wig. We saw Mommy having to sit for fittings. Her head was measured, a sample of her salvaged hair obtained. It was all sent to France where her hair color was matched with real human hair, then hand tied and returned to New York. When we were called, we all went. Mommy had to sit for her new wig to be fitted and styled. We waited for her to emerge, a renewed person.

She wore her hair like a flamenco dancer until the 60s. When they relocated to Hollywood, she found a rather flamboyant hairdresser with a new softer vision of her. Until then, however, Mommy wore her hair pulled straight back with a large chignon at the nape of her neck. It had a harsh hairline which she couldn't seem to do anything about. It was always obviously a wig, but she would always ask, "You don't think anyone knows I'm wearing a wig, do you?"

She had to draw on her eyebrows. She had a heavy hand and they looked an awful lot like Joan Crawford's with her dark, bold hard edges. Without eyelashes, Mommy had to use eyeliner that made her much more exotic than she had ever looked. Initially she didn't think she could use false eyelashes without having her own to support them. A decade later she learned that she could. Her lipstick had always been bright red, so that never changed. But our lives orbited around Mom's new condition. It was the first real family trauma I was ever aware of having.

Over the years, Mom also lost all of her skin color. Vitiligo, the loss of skin pigment - was what Michael Jackson allegedly had. Mom was an anomaly that even the Mayo Clinic couldn't figure out. When she was twenty-four, she had a small white spot next to the base of her thumb on her right hand. But after the mumps and the loss of all her hair, the loss of skin pigment began to exacerbate. Every day for the rest of her life, she had to wear sunblock makeup, paint on her eyebrows, plaster on her false eyelashes and secure her wig with double-sided tape. If she thought the wind might tilt it or blow it off as it threatened to do on the deck of a Caribbean cruise we shared once, she would utterly dissolve and huddle out of the breeze in tears, clinging to her wig as if it were a fly-away sun hat. It consumed our entire family life always and forever.

One late afternoon after I was a mother myself, I was at their house helping with the ironing. Daddy, who was in his late Seventies by then, sat in the breakfast room nearby swishing a snifter of brandy slowly, thoughtfully. He always got philosophical that time of day in the late afternoon light. I heard him say to me - to the ether, perhaps - in his old man memories of youthful passions, "I used to love to wrap my hands in her hair…"

Mom was a genetic catch-all. Her parents were first cousins or first cousins once removed. I could never get it straight, maybe even second cousins! But she inherited a host of endocrine system disorders all interrelated to their genetic inbreeding. She was hypo-thyroid. Mumps is a thyroid related disease, which, of course gave her the double-whammy along with the high fever ultimately causing her to lose her hair - *alopecia universalis*. It also created a lack of libido - low to no sex drive. Mom, however, was a sucker for flattery, so when a man paid her a compliment she reacted very coyly. Daddy became irrationally paranoid and jealous, because she fended off his sexual advances at home after their earlier romantic passions for each other.

After we moved to Connecticut and he let Mom learn to drive at forty, she loved the freedom of being able to go shopping in town on her own, pick me up from summer day camp and stand and chat with other parents. If we were later than he expected, he would stand at the top of the stairs in our big old ten room home and he'd glower and bellow. He unleashed his wrath on us. He was quite intimidating. He would accuse her of being unfaithful and would hold up a tube of something that as a young girl I didn't really understand. As he aged, he mellowed or hopefully arrived at some personal insight.

During a hurricane once, we were all standing in the garage with the door up watching the wild winds whipping the trees back and forth. There was a wild electric energy in the storm. I ran in and out into the driveway dodging falling branches, then running back inside to witness their strange little dance. The storm was raging outside with all its intense static energy. I pretended not to notice the weird intensity of the gleam in Daddy's eyes as she avoided him zealously pinching her nipples. I can still hear her feigning levity, "Oh, stop, Nino!"

These kinds of interactions between my parents confused me. Sometimes I sided with Mommy and other times I sided with Daddy. But I was always caught in between trying to placate each of them, trying to fill in the obvious gaps. I always wanted them to be happy.

I remember thinking I would *never* be like Mommy pushing *my* husband away! But I always seemed to choose dominating, controlling men. I believe much of my promiscuity when I was in my early twenties was a reaction, not only to the multitude of rapes I'd experienced by then - which led me to believe that my only value was my sexuality - but also to witnessing my mother's rejections of Daddy and his deep longing for her acceptance of his physical attentions.

Later, when I was in my twenties, Daddy pinched my boobs, too, as if it was just a harmless game. I recall arriving at Grandma's for my 25th birthday lunch. The family was sitting down at the table in the dining room. The women were bringing in plates of food from the kitchen and Grandma was holding court from the head of the table. I ran late and Mom was angry with me. I had stalled as long as I could, resisting being amongst them all even for my birthday. When I arrived, I said *Hi* to everyone and gave Daddy a kiss on the cheek as he was standing in the archway talking to the uncles. He laughed, got that zealous, mischievous gleam in his eyes, the one I knew so well, and pinched my nipples right in front of everyone. It was as if it was a kid's game, like pulling my pigtails or something. I was extremely unnerved but was afraid to confront him and make a scene in front of the entire family, especially on my birthday. So, I did what Mommy had always done, I made a joke out of it. I normalized it. I dodged him. I pulled away, fell on the floor laughing and rolled sideways covering my bosom with my arms. "Oh, stop it, Daddy!"

In 2010 when my cousin Anne and I were caring for Mom the last summer of her life, we had the opportunity for the first time since we were children to really have one-on-one-heart-to-hearts. We shared our stories about the horrific sexual abuses we had both experienced in our youth. The boob-pinching story came up and she surprised me by revealing that Daddy had done the same thing to her. It was a revelation.

Talking about sex was taboo in the Fifties, so neither one of us had any actual understanding of what it was, or what was normal and healthy. There was no sex education in schools and definitely none at home.

I saw my cat have kittens a couple of times and that was it until Peter Dunning set me straight. He was a freckle-faced, tough, red-headed farm kid who lived up the road. One morning at the school bus stop, Peter told me that his *gentleman farmer* dad's English sheepdogs that he bred had *gotten stuck* that morning and that was what made him late.

He said he had to throw buckets of cold water on them. I thought about that all day. I had no idea what he was talking about. When we returned home on the bus at the end of the day, I asked him what he meant.

He said, "They were fucking!"

"Huh? What does that mean?" I'd never heard that word before.

As he was running up the hill he yelled over his shoulder, "You know, the guy puts his thing in the girl's butt!" I screeched back at him, "Nooooo! That's not true! God puts a seed in Mommy's tummy!" He laughed back at me scornfully and yelled, "No! They fuck!"

"No, they don't!" I screamed as I ran down the road to my house. Once in the front door, I ran upstairs to Mom who was in the bathroom dressing for dinner. I was determined to get things straightened out.

"Mommy what does F.U.C.K. mean? Peter Dunning says it means how to have a baby!" She was dumbstruck, turned red and stammered, "Go ask your father."

I walked purposefully down the hallway to Daddy's studio where he was hunched over his drawing board and repeated my questions. He stopped what he was doing but didn't look up. There was an uncomfortable silence before he spoke again. He began with, "You know how a farmer plows the fields, then plants his seeds, then in time a plant grows? Well, that's how babies are made."

I was more embarrassed than he was, I think. So I said, in my tough, Shirley Temple style, "Well, Farmer! Plant your seed!" Then, I ran the hell outta there with less info than I had had at the bus stop. We never spoke about it again. I did learn, however, that F. U. C. K. was not a word that nice people ever used - and furthermore if I was ever heard using it, I would be sent to my room without dinner, which wasn't such a bad thing if frozen peas were on the menu.

.

Chapter 12
Interludes

As the scenery streaked by on that two-hour train ride between Philly and D.C. my thoughts bopped back to the present. But as we were often jostled side to side, the sounds of the train's motion hypnotically returned my thoughts to my folks. I wished I could share this journey with them. We had so many misunderstandings and I wished for a chance to clarify everything before they died. But it never happened.

I felt unsettled reliving those childhood memories still feeling the same discomfort and confusion I felt when I was a child. And the irony of it all is that I was supposed to be the expert guest speaker on rape and sexual assault awareness. But, understanding, like healing, is evolutionary like peeling the proverbial onion - layer by layer until you get to the core.

The train slowed down as we pulled into D.C. and I felt the reality of saying goodbye to my train mates, acknowledging their thanks for all I was doing for women by standing up and speaking out. I thought wryly of my years of silence - so many denigrating experiences where I should have screamed it all out, but instead stuffed it inside. How many more things did I continue to hold inside? How many more times would I remain silent when I should shriek from a tree top? Where was that little blonde, rosy-cheeked toddler who stood her ground on her first train ride and told the passenger in the next row who was cooing over her cuteness, "Aw, yer fadder's mustache!" It was the 1940s equivalent of "Fuck off!" I knew she was still in there somewhere - and I was going to get her back.

I grabbed my overnight case, waited for the train to come to a screeching halt, then fended for myself in the crowded aisle. I thought how fast my entire life could zip through my thoughts in a two-hour train ride. I thought about how people say that one's entire life flashes before their eyes just before they die. I wondered if it was something like that?

I was relieved to be moving, running through the train station pulling my suitcase. I was forced into the now. Motion soothes me. It always has. Moving forward to something new, something hopefully better, a new experience, a new horizon - new understandings and with the goddesses' good grace, new levels of healing.

Had I really recovered from it all? Does anyone ever, truly recover? Must we just learn to ride the trauma like a bucking bull at a rodeo and subdue it so it's power over us is finally manageable, even if at times unpredictable? Perhaps the only way towards recovery is to transform the empathy we have gained from our pain into creative action and service to others in support and healing. It has been so for me. I think it may be that. *Through service we are healed.*

I was going to give a speech at the University of Maryland later that day and for the second year in a row. I looked forward to seeing some of the people I'd connected with the previous year and meeting new ones. I loved being on the east coast where it seemed as though everything and everybody were so much geographically closer and I could squeeze in visits with those dear to me. It always felt like going home.

"In the midst of darkness, light persists."
--Mahatma Gandhi

Chapter 13
Speaking from the Podium, Listening with the Heart

The young, black, gay male student who picked me up at the train station in D.C. and checked me into the hotel, shared his survival story with me as we drove to the College Park Marriott. He had been raped by an older boy he adored when he was only fourteen. Now twenty-two and in a positive relationship, he was still haunted by what had happened to him. I began to understand why my voice was so important as increasing numbers of rape victims felt comfortable enough to trust me with their stories. They were finding their voices, their courage to speak out and their steps towards healing

I asked myself why I now found enough self-confidence to speak out about my abuse. Over the years a pocket of infection with layers of thick fibrous emotional tissue had built up within me but had not been purged. Its toxicity leaked into everything I did, shadowing and undermining my emotional and physical health, my choices of life partners, my fearful avoidance of legal marriage. I used to quip, "I don't even wear shoes I can't get out of quickly."

Everything reaches a saturation point until there's too much to hold inside. Everyone has a tipping point when the need to flush out the soul's poison becomes greater than the fear of exposing its sick secrets. All water reaches a boiling point one day if the fire is unrelenting.

Every pot boils over.

During my more than twelve-year healing odyssey when I hit the road leaving my former life and my son's grave behind, I discovered that people liked me just as I was. I was taken at face value and respected for the work I did, the person I was - no poisoned family fables. I returned to college twice during those years, had two more, not fully healthy, domestic partnerships that gifted me with two daughters who have since given me six wonderful grandchildren, and new treasured soul families along the way. Layers of pain were stripped away allowing for new healthy heart tissue to be exposed to the light of unconditional love.

Becoming a Registered Nurse at forty-two on my second foray back into academia and graduating with honors gave me a sense of accomplishment that could not be undermined. With a track record of well over thirty-five years of commitment to the care of the ill and dying, I gained professional respect. At last, I knew who I was. I trusted my own knowledge, my own voice... at least up to that point. I still hadn't completely revealed all my secrets. As my sister, Cosby survivor and friend, Cindra Ladd was quoted as saying, *"We are only as sick as the secrets we keep."* There was more work to be done.

Once I spoke out for the first time about Bill Cosby, my hidden pain was validated by many - and major media. The other women who shared my experiences with him and those who shared the experiences of rape, sexual assault, incest, domestic abuse, sex trafficking and betrayals by the church finally had a validated platform. We had opened a hornet's nest. I suddenly wasn't alone. I found a new brand of courage. Atlas-holding-up-the-world courage. Mama Lion fighting to the death for her cub's courage.

My voice was freed from its confines. I felt like a caged bird released to flight. Like a dazzling feathered phoenix shaking off decades' worth of collective ashes, cobwebs, and dust, my life had taken on an extraordinary and unexpected flight. Soaring free, I was singing my own song at last. It was an epiphany. I had become so used to working around the purulent sac of emotional and psychological detritus, that I didn't even realize it was there - until it wasn't.

In time I felt lighter. It wasn't instantaneous, but I could breathe more deeply. I could talk about the forbidden topics - the "*No-No's*" of my generation. Wow! When some young upstart patronizingly preached to me, "Hmmmm, sounds sort of like you're playing victim," I didn't buy into it. I could think, if not yell, loudly, "Fuck off!" because I had an army of survivors behind me who *got it*.

Working around the painful secrets had become so much a part of my routine choreography I didn't even understand how much emotional weight I was carrying. Once I was no longer being silenced and invalidated, it really felt as if an abscess had finally been lanced. At first, it felt worse as I addressed some of the memories face on. I had toxic reactions to discussing things amongst the sisters initially, but then once faced and framed properly without judgment, I began being able to differentiate what they were - and who I was and what my unvarnished experiences had truly been.

As with all infection once flushed, healthy tissue slowly forms, and healing from within begins. I experienced new energy, less anxiety and I slept better - at least until I started revisiting the rest of my journey. I had to be honest about it otherwise everything that followed wouldn't make sense. Writing about my abuse dredged up a whole lot of buried feelings. I had to delve deeply into my son's death and all that led up to the moment, because Cosby had manipulated my grief as part of his grooming agenda. I began waking up in the middle of the night arguing with dead people. I found myself trying to justify my very existence to people who could no longer give a shit. I couldn't set the record straight with them any longer. Tylenol, a mug of milk and rollicking historical paperback sagas became my middle of the night friends. When morning light began filtering through the trees and the jasmine overgrowing my bedroom windows chased away the night visitors, I fell into deep blissful no-dream sleep. Speaking, writing, testifying is not the perfect balm on the raw age-old wounds, but leaving the ghosts behind in the night and embracing with gratitude the dawning of a new day's promise.

When I spoke, people listened. I found that I had something valuable and honest to offer. When I stopped speaking, people came to me entrusting me with their painful stories asking for my words. *I gave them my heart.*

Society thought that the numbers of rape victims were in the minority, until we demolished those gates of silence. It was astonishing, because it became increasingly obvious that we probably were in the majority. We had just never told anyone. Now we were not only telling it like it was, but we were rallying, protesting and lobbying in the Capitol! We were moving the needle on abolishing Rape Culture. Once we started talking, we couldn't stop. More sexual assault survivors were coming forward every day. The stats were changing - at lightning speed!

The Preventing Sexual Assault group at the University of Maryland was new. It was a student organized symposium that the university held every year in April - Sexual Assault Month. It was begun by students who had been raped on campus by another student - who was never prosecuted. It had grown in spite of the lack of financial support or enthusiasm by the administration. It was my second time here and I was looking forward to reaching out again to new students, and refreshing the relationships I built the year before when I spoke with two other Cosby Survivors, Lili Bernard and Charlotte Fox.

I stood at the podium outside in the quad before a scattered student audience of mixed genders. I told my story of being raped by Bill Cosby. I talked to them about a variety of stories from being objectified as a Playboy Playmate in the Sixties to my journey through many rapes, my son's death and my tipping point that brought me finally to speaking out about my experiences. I told them how it had changed my sense of self, my sanity and my decision to find a new way of living as I evolved gradually over the years into becoming a self-actualized person. I told them about the many layers of healing and awareness, the many incarnations it took me to arrive at the place I am now. I talked about the fact that we cannot solely continue to teach women how to protect themselves from men, or heal themselves after being assaulted. We need to educate boys, young men, how to respect and honor women - and then we must teach women to feel entitled to honor and respect, in fact, to demand it.

My half hour speech was delivered and well received. There were warm hugs with friends I made the previous year, and new friends, students who came forward to thank me for speaking out and to share their own experiences.

The next day I had lunch with my 'Back East' cousins, Paul and Jackie, whom I love to pieces and by whom I feel so nourished. They drove down from Alexandria, Virginia for the day. I loved their company. Paul is the son of my stepfather's younger brother, Joe. We had only recently reconnected after my mother's death at 92 in 2011. We had not seen each other since we were both thirteen. I always feel so comforted in his presence just hearing the old "Daddy Nino New York" accent. There is a feeling of security in that. He and Jackie have been together since they were children and she is just as loving and caring as he is.

I had dinner with Scott Higham that evening catching up, reflecting back on the long four-year journey since he and his colleagues broke my story in the Washington Post on November 22, 2014. Scott, a Pulitzer Prize and Polk Award winner, has become a friend. His friendship over these last few years has been one of the perks I've enjoyed as a result of breaking my silence. He has since co-authored a book on the opioid crisis - American Cartel.

I remember Scott warning me in 2014 that once my story came out in the Post that there would be a media frenzy and if I didn't want to be imposed upon, they would field the interview requests. After all my years of being silenced I didn't think twice. I told him, *"In for a penny. In for a pound."*

The article took on a life of its own and I, along with many of my other sister survivors, were propelled into a wild ride of media interviews and activism that consumed us as we spoke out to see justice done - and hope for accountability on Cosby's part. One of the beneficial results has been that there is a growing consciousness-raising about rape culture in today's society - a new examination of the archaic laws that support and perpetuate it.

Scott was not assigned to the courthouse proceedings during the Cosby trials, but Manuel Roig- Franzia who co-wrote my article was. I had the opportunity to get to know him, too. I am so grateful to them both - men who are proud feminists.

I spent a satisfying three days and now I was back in motion. I looked forward to the train ride back to those now familiar Halls of Pennsylvania justice - American justice. We all hoped, karmic justice, for Andrea Constand… and vicariously, for us, as well.

We stood with her. We spoke out to the press, the media, whoever asked us for a statement, we gave it. Because she and so many of our sisters were in litigation, they could not speak out publicly, therefore, for those of us who could - we did. We had to be their voice.

"Life is what leaps."
--Ralph Waldo Emerson

Chapter 14
New York! New York!
1960 - 1961

In 1960 we were living in Connecticut, an hour and a half away from the city by train. I had only been in Manhattan on my own as a teenager by then for a few hours at a time with Daddy when we would take the train to see his art agent. My ballet class and my acting coach were uptown on the West side, so we would split up when we arrived and meet back up at the agreed upon time.

I usually had an hour to kill before class so I'd go straight to the big public library's religion section. Spirituality and world religions had piqued my interest so I read all the religious texts I could find trying to sort out my Sunday School lessons that were beginning to not make sense in light of other discoveries. I compared what I'd learned from Auntie Paula's Jewish husband when I spent Hanukkah with them to what I discovered about Hinduism when I discovered Mahatma Gandhi doing my written report in Sixth grade. I was fascinated. The mysticism at Friday night Temple was spellbinding and Gandhi's life story and philosophy resonated with me. I saw so many similarities between all three religions that I began questioning everything I had ever been taught - that one was not only superior to all others, but the *only* truth.

After my visit to the library, I'd walk uptown all by myself, take my ballet and drama classes then I'd walk all the way back to Grand Central Station to meet Daddy. We'd share our day on the hour and a half train ride home and Mom would pick us up at the Branchville train station. We'd sit down to a relatively tense, silent, formal dinner with no further discussion. I had so many new ideas and questions rambling around in my head with no one who was willing to discuss serious concepts. They were always open to anything I did in theater so, of course, I focused on that.

I thought that being alone for a few hours in Manhattan on the occasional Saturday qualified me to be grown up enough to live on my own in a big city. By the time I turned seventeen, in 1959, I'd managed to coerce my folks into letting me go away to New York City to acting school the following year. I had reached my rebellious teens. I was quite disenchanted with my parents and my country life and very anxious to get away. The city was my magnet.

So, through Uncle Manning's connections I auditioned for the Musical Theater program at the American Theatre Wing. I applied to the Professional Children's School (PCS), an academic school for theater kids, so I could simultaneously accomplish my senior year of high school. I got scholarships for both. Kids at PCS could do their work on correspondence if they were on tour or in a Broadway show. There were phones on every floor so they could be reached by their agents for auditions or other professional needs.

My high school was a couple of blocks west of Columbus Circle and my senior year schedule began at 9 a.m. lasting until around 1 p.m. Once I was out of morning classes I raced uptown on the subway, or bus, to the American Theatre Wing at 93rd and Amsterdam where I was in class until almost dinner time. We were rehearsing for our end of year anthology of the shows written by our school's founder Oscar Hammerstein, who had recently died.

Quite often we'd have rehearsals at the Columbus Circle Rehearsal Studios at night rehearsing our dance routines, then often go across the street to Central Park to play in the playground. We'd swing on the swings and go down the slides laughing, even though by the end of the night our feet would be painfully imprinted with the crosshatch stitching from our fishnet hose. But we loved it anyway - dancers treasuring our suffering feet - theater kids gloriously sacrificing for our craft. Life was exhilarating for quite a while. I loved my heavy schedule and studying. I had always maintained a certain level of scholarship and relished the intensity of it all. I especially relished the lack of parental restrictions.

Chapter 15
The Cast of Characters

Uncle Manning had found me a roommate who had an apartment on the corner of 79th and Riverside Drive. She seemed very old to me then at 30, and a very business-like, unfriendly redhead. She had little patience for my cluelessness. My inexperience living without Mommy doing everything for me was very uncomfortable for us both. I had no idea how to go to the laundromat, the supermarket, the shoe repair, the dry cleaners, or how to budget my meager $110 a month. So, after a couple of months, she'd had enough of me and asked me to leave. Looking back, I can't say I blame her, but I was crushed. I'd loved the little balcony off our shared bedroom where I sat brushing my hair at night looking out over the twinkling ripples of the Hudson River. I soon found another roommate though, one of my schoolmates. She was studying to be a concert pianist.

My new roommate had very long, constantly-shedding hair. She stayed in her long, white, vintage nightgown all day while she practiced piano until eleven o'clock every night. She even ate at the piano, leaving her dirty dishes piling up on her piano bench, or making the dark closet-sized kitchen with the burnt-out lightbulb, cockroach bait.

The new apartment was on 57th Street near Broadway. It was just east of Carnegie Hall and the Russian Tea Room and directly across the street from the massive Baptist church that Van Cliburn attended when he was in town. His apartment building was catty-corner from

Carnegie. My roomie was infatuated with him. She befriended the doorman who let her know when he was in town and sometimes would turn his back so she could sneak upstairs to his floor where she hoped to catch a glimpse of him. When I broke it to her that he was gay, she was incapacitated for a week at least.

My parents' friends, Betty and Charley, old neighbors from our brief sojourn in New Jersey after we left Manhattan, dropped in unannounced one afternoon. They were on their way out to visit my folks in Connecticut and I'm sure my parents asked them to check up on me. I had stopped going home as much on the weekends and they probably didn't understand why. The contrast between their uptight home atmosphere and my new life away was stark and weekends at home made me want to leave again quickly.

Betty and Charley were lifetime Army people who hailed from San Antonio, Texas and were serious drinkers. They always regaled us with hilarious stories from their times stationed in Paris that inevitably involved lots of booze. Betty told and retold with endless enjoyment her most famous Southern Belle-accented anecdote about when she got into trouble with her lame French. She meant to call a rude Parisian waiter a pig, "*Couchon,*" but inadvertently asked him to go to bed with her, *a couché.* We never heard the end of that one.

Betty in her lavish mink coat, Charley in his military uniform and gray buzz-cut, arrived to witness what apparently shocked them. I was coming out of my bedroom doing homework just after our fellow dance students, Sarah and her skinny black gay dance partner arrived. They were still in full-on stage make-up, leotards and leg warmers sitting on the arm of our old faded velvet sofa listening to my roomie practicing as usual at the upright piano in her long Edwardian nightie. Her long, dark curls were carelessly clipped on the top of her head in *deshabille* with tendrils straggling past the nape of her neck.

The whole scene must have looked like a community of refugees from the set of La Boheme, but I suspect they thought they'd walked into a Toulouse Lautrec Moulin Rouge style brothel by the priceless expressions on their faces. They canceled their offer of lunch and rushed off to visit my folks. I'm sure Mom and Daddy got an earful on their arrival.

Many years later my almost year-old daughter and I stayed with them for a week in San Antonio on my way from Louisiana to visit my folks in L.A. We were talking about the rift my folks and I had with each other when I was in New York and Charley said, "Well, remember what you were doing in New York." I grinned and said, "Yeah." thinking he was referring to my ditching school. But I thought about it again after my mom died and realized he had a different impression, which he'd conveyed to my folks, which became my mother's story about me to the family furthermore. I can't straighten them out now though because they're all dead!

Another one of my classmates was a kid named "Ronnie" Walken. It was decades before I realized that Ronnie was actually the actor Christopher Walken. Ronnie was seventeen years old then, a little younger than I, pink, soft and a bit pudgy with almost white blond hair. His dog had puppies and he gave me one for my baby sister. Carrying him through all my classes that day in a big, square, lidded basket, then the hour and a half train ride home to Connecticut, was quite an adventure. The basket was put against the wall on the slightly slanted floor of our rehearsal hall while we prepared for class. The poor thing hadn't eaten or been out of the basket all day and suddenly someone yelled, "Oh my god there's pee streaming across the dance floor!" I frantically rushed to swab it all up before the teacher arrived.

My one best friend, Jenny Hecht, was the daughter of Oscar award-winning screenwriter, Ben Hecht. They lived in Bayonne, New Jersey, so Jenny lived at the legendary *Algonquin Hotel* during the week while she was performing in *Chalk Garden* on Broadway. Her folks would come to pick her up on Friday after school and include me for Friday night dinner at the hotel. They'd drive me home to my apartment and come upstairs to make sure I was safely tucked in. Mr. Hecht loved the architecture and decor of my apartment and said it made him think of a Chagall painting. I had to go look up Chagall. I'd always loved Lautrec and had a big poster of his work over my bed, and so he inspired me to learn more about the French Impressionists.

One time Jenny and I ditched school to go look at the mummies at the Metropolitan Museum of Art. We got lost on the subway trying to get back home and wound up at the Grand Concourse scared shitless. We spent the rest of our day trying to get home and finally the rest of our allowances on a taxi. She always mercilessly chewed her nails and cuticles and while we were in the back of the taxi, she showed me how bloody and infected her fingers were. When I saw the red streak going up her arm, I recognized immediately that it was blood poisoning. She got it from the lead-based grease paint - *Clown White* - that had gotten into her bloodstream while she was performing. I made her get hold of her parents and she was immediately hospitalized. She never came back to school and I never saw her again. I was at a loss for a real friend. I thought of her often over the years - her frenetic energy, her frizzy blondish hair and big, dark, haunted eyes.

A couple of years ago I googled her to see if maybe we could reconnect after all this time. When I discovered that she had overdosed and died at 27. I cried for hours and wrote her a poem with my tears nearly obliterating my written words. The Hechts were long gone and Jenny was their only child. I grieved.

Chapter 16
Something Wonderful

When we toured around New York performing in our various hospital shows, I got to play Anna in *The King and I*. We traveled by school bus and in between shows I'd mend my fishnets and my dance partner's collar buttons. We always tore them when he brought me down from a high lift during our finale. We had no dressing rooms so my big hoop skirt was held in front of me while I changed and then thrown over my head and zipped up right in front of our enthusiastic audiences. I loved playing Anna because the show held important memories for me. When I was about twelve, I spent time with one of my *Courtesy Aunties*, Terry Saunders, while she was performing as the Head Wife, Lady Thiang, on Broadway at the St. James Theater - and in the film. Her signature song was *"Something Wonderful."* Those self-sacrificing lyrics would, along with my own upbringing, reinforce the programming that groomed me in so many ways to accept misogynistic dominance from men. It reinforced women's passive tolerance, and silent, patient, long-suffering. Women tolerating their intolerable men and never demanding they suffer the consequences of their own behavior. - However, as a 1950's pre-teen I was addicted to its music and the romanticized self-destructive message.

*"He will not always say what you would have
him say, but now and then he'll say something
wonderful. You'll always go along, defend him when*

he's wrong and tell him when he's strong - he is
wonderful..."
-- Oscar Hammerstein

I loved going with Aunt Terry to the theater and watching her transform herself into the Siamese head wife. The magic of the costumes, the pounding on the dressing room door as we got closer to curtain time - "5 minutes, Miss Saunders!" Then the thundering footsteps of all the cast running down the metal steps onto the stage and getting into position. The orchestra warming up and then the overture began. My heart was in my throat and shivers ran up my spine while I stood in the wings watching and waiting. In my head, I played every part and sang every song. One day, I told myself, it would be me out there on the stage.

Sal Mineo, who played the Crown Prince was about sixteen then. He and his stand-in shared the same dressing room and had a TV. It was pretty impressive in those days since we were still listening to the radio at home. They used to tease me and make me guess which one of them was the real Crown Prince. In makeup they both looked almost identical. Sal would put his arm around my shoulder and paternally escort me around backstage to show me the ropes. I was hooked.

Yul Brynner had just left the show and Alfred Drake had taken over the part of the King. One day I was wandering around backstage alone when Alfred Drake came into the wings swearing angrily in Italian about something. He never saw me because I hid behind a big thick dusty velvet curtain. I knew certain Sicilian swear words from Daddy and Grandpa - "*Manag America!*" "*Manag a Dio!*" But

"*Shkivooz*" and "*Bafangool*" were new ones. I was much older before I learned what they actually meant and I still can't spell them. I used them liberally anyway when I was out of earshot from my father!

On Wednesdays and Saturdays, the matinee days, the whole cast would go around the corner to a deli for lunch in full-on stage makeup and street clothes. Alfred Drake wore blue jeans with a tight T-shirt that had broad red and white horizontal stripes hugging every muscle of his torso. His gray sideburns and black, exotic, eyelined, *King* face emerged from it. I wanted this world.

Mary Martin played *Peter Pan in* the same theater. As Tinkerbell's light was feebly flickering out in the most dramatic moment in the play, Mary Martin got down on her knees imploring each one of us children in the audience to save Tinkerbell's life. "Do you believe in fairies?" With tears streaming down our cheeks, we all cried out! "Yes!!!!" And to our vast relief, Tinkerbell's light pulsed brighter and brighter, and she lived! And we the children had made it so. It was the first group magic I had ever shared.

Following *The King and I*, there would be *The Flower Drum Song* with its beautiful signature songs, "*A Hundred Million Miracles*" and "*I Enjoy Being a Girl.*" that I later performed in our Glee Club recital. And, then, in that same theater, there was *West Side Story*. The St. James Theater held all my young dreams vibrantly alive in song and dance. One day, I told myself, I would be there, belting out those marvelous songs to the back rows. From being Kipling's "Mowgli" with all my wild animals sleeping around me in pastoral serenity on my bed, to archeology digs, to feeding starving children in Africa, to Broadway!

Those were the aspirations on which I built my young life - and somehow, I was going to do it all!

"Encode memory with light".
--Mary Pipher

Chapter 17
Brother of the Universe

The director of our high school held Sunday afternoon teas at her posh, graystone on Sutton Place. She invited the diplomats from the United Nations who were in session that winter - and all the Senior girls from class. We were instructed to review the guest list - the international who's who - and we were expected to perfect our international etiquette. It was an eclectic selection of men. I do not recall seeing any women diplomats there - or male classmates, for that matter. It has since made me wonder. We were a lovely bunch of young girls.

We clustered around the guest list in the kitchen before anyone arrived and learned each man's country of origin and anything special about them we should know. A Nepalese diplomat was mentioned as someone to watch out for because he was a flirt. When we were finally introduced, I found him to be rather sweet, round-faced and awfully cuddly looking. He hardly looked dangerous. Of course, being an impetuous girl, I was intrigued - and his name, Vishwa Bandhu translated into English, meant "Brother of the Universe." What could go wrong?

He invited me to dinner at his favorite place, *The Russian Tea Room* with members of his delegation. Conveniently, it was right next door to my new apartment on 57th Street. He suggested *blinis*, Russian pancakes, the size of the entire plate. They were sandwiched with succulent red caviar, sour cream and saturated with drawn butter. There was fuchsia-colored, cold, beet borscht topped with dollops of sour cream. It was utter heaven. He invited me to the U.N. the following day to see international politics in action. I was thrilled and ditched school.

Chapter 18
Learning the Ropes

My fellow students used to joke and say that being taken out to dinner was the only way to survive as a student. If their dates tried to put their foot inside the door and insist on more, they'd say, "Whaaat? You want your dinner back?" then slam the door and laugh uproariously. I was learning from kids who were more city savvy than I.

My monthly allowance was only $110 a month. My rent was $75, not including utilities, and there were the bus and subway tokens to my two schools. I'm sure my parents were clueless about the cost of living in Manhattan, and they certainly never sat down and budgeted my allowance with me. I always overheard my dad worrying to my mother about money. I was afraid to ask for more because he always looked stressed, complaining about every penny Mom spent and making the monthly mortgage as a freelance illustrator. I didn't realize the money they were giving me was coming out of the war savings bonds my biological father had left me. Since I didn't want to stress Daddy any more than he already was, I scrimped.

Like a lot of my fellow classmates, I was a struggling student living on black coffee, doughnuts and whatever I could scrounge together, diet, so being treated to dinner was a delight. From some of the starving actors I met, I learned to make free lemonade at the Automat, with a glass of water, sugar packets on the tables and free lemon wedges. Also, the advice I got from my folks was in stark contrast to the advice my other classmates received.

My mom: "Now, honey, always carry a dime in your pocket for a phone call, wear clean underwear in case you have to go to the hospital and if you need a quick pick-me-up get a chocolate malt."

Daddy: "Kid, I'm going to tell you something that's going to stand you in good stead when you leave home." He paused as if to impart some profound advice. I looked at him expectantly with big eyes.

Me: "Yes, Daddy?"
Daddy: "There is no God."
Me: "Oh..."

One of my classmates' mothers was a French actress who lived half the year in Paris and the other half in New York and imparted this: "Always carry your book bag in one hand, a lit cigarette in the other, and if a guy attacks you, jab him in the face with your cigarette, hit him hard with your book bag, and run like hell. Don't walk too close to the buildings or the parked cars. Don't ever ask a New York cop to escort you down a dark street, because they're worse than the crooks - and if you get raped let them. It's easier to get an abortion than it is to come back from the dead."

Chapter 19
"And, Ye'll Never be a Maiden Anymore"

I became mesmerized by international goings on and I was ditching school frequently to join my new Nepalese gentleman friend in the Fourth Committee at the United Nations. It was quite fascinating. Mrs. H, the school's Director, got wind of it and had me paged. *"Miss Carbe' in the Fourth Committee."* Stupidly, I answered the page and was caught. I can't remember what my cover story was, but it got back to my parents, I'm sure.

One day my beau invited me to join him at the Mayflower Hotel for dinner. I accepted, thinking there was a restaurant there, but that was not the case as it turned out. The desk clerk directed me upstairs to his suite. It was very small, uninteresting and my gentleman friend was boiling chicken in a saucepan on a hot plate. I was looking forward to white table cloths and solicitous waiters again. I was quite disappointed, but polite.

He invited me to sit down on a small sofa and while the chicken was simmering, he began regaling me with stories of his life in Nepal. He had been a governor of a province before he became a U.N. delegate. He told me about his arranged marriage, how he and his wife were traveling by train when she went into labor with one of their five children and how he delivered his baby by the roadside. I was utterly captivated by the incredibly exotic male version of *Scheherazade's, Thousand and One Nights*. I was hanging onto every word as he fed me pieces of utterly tasteless chicken by hand. I didn't know that was a lover's custom in his country. I was more concerned that he was going to get my suit stained. Once the tasteless chicken was consumed directly out of the saucepan, he continued to share his incredibly fascinating stories well into the night. The tales went on and I soon learned that when his eldest son was a toddler, he fell out of an upstairs window, landing on his head. Though the child lived, he was brain damaged. While his wife took care of him, and the other four children as well, she was overworked and very tired.

I forgot the time. He gently suggested that since it was so late, I should stay overnight and he would escort me home in the morning on his way to the U.N. He assured me that I was safe. I hesitated. I said I really needed to be in school in the morning after being recently reprimanded for playing hooky one too many times. He assured me that he would have the embassy limousine deliver me home in time to get ready for school and that he would sleep on the sofa in the living room. I could have the bedroom all to myself. I was very tired and also on my period so I figured I was safe enough. He had always been a perfect gentleman and, of course, he was married, so I naively believed him.

I closed the bedroom door, undressed down to my undies and petticoat, tucked myself into bed and turned out the light. As I began to doze off, I felt someone lifting the covers and sliding in beside me - naked. At first, I was indignant but as he crooned softly in my ear, I found myself yearning to be held. As a seventeen-year-old virgin I had only fantasized about being intimate with a man. As soon as he touched me, I slid into the hottest molten moments of my young life and all of my restraint dissolved. That night he introduced me to the delights of womanhood.

While it hurt it was also fascinating to discover what all the hoopla was about. Once he had moved me into possibly every position in the Kama Sutra, he took me into the bathroom and ran a tub bath in which we both lay together as he whispered sweet and tender words into my ear. He realized I had been a virgin and dried me off tenderly before tucking me back into bed. He followed our embraces with his yoga routine at around 4 in the morning. I laid in bed and watched him perform the Peacock Posture. It was incredible. Yoga was not new to me as I had a book at home on Christian Yoga and had tried meditation. What an exotic initiation. I was timidly, cautiously thrilled. I was so thrilled, in fact, that I called Greg, a young fellow in the ROTC who was a friend of a Connecticut classmate. He and I occasionally dated, but he lived in New Jersey, always wore his ROTC uniform, wore a buzz cut and had slightly fanatical blue-gray eyes, was a bit of a prude and never wanted to 'neck.' So, I never took our relationship more seriously than that. I was focused on becoming an actress and was sure he understood that.

Since I'd always been told by the older "Uncles" associated with Auntie Paula, that to become a truly great actress one had to experience a tragic love *affaire*. While losing my virginity hadn't been tragic, I somehow felt that as a new initiate, I was now worthy of potential theatrical greatness. I couldn't wait to share. I had to let him know that I had become a woman!

What I hadn't anticipated was that Greg was planning on asking me to marry him. He let me know coldly that we were both supposed to be virgins on our wedding night. I felt like shit. My enthusiasm was in the toilet.

When my Nepalese diplomat called to invite me out to dinner again, I decided to tell him that I would not be continuing our relationship. I understood after my conversation with Greg that I was supposed to feel ashamed instead of thrilled and by then, I really did feel ashamed. My enthusiasm was successfully dampened.

I showed up at Vishwa Bandhu's hotel room once again, but this time he was in his bathrobe and clearly had other plans. I stood just inside his hotel room door and made my announcement. I would not be seeing him anymore. He was astonished. He said he wanted to marry me and bring me home with him to Kathmandu to become Number Two Wife to help Number One Wife with their children. He assured me that I would be revered because of his position. And then he laid on the blame, the guilt. "How as a virgin could you have allowed me to take your innocence if you didn't plan on marrying me?" I was getting it from both sides. I really had no answers. I just said *no* and turned around to leave. When I looked back, he was weeping face down on his bed. It seemed overly melodramatic and manipulative. Even at seventeen, I got that. I walked and wept all the way up 7th Avenue pondering what had just happened to my life.

I called Greg from a pay booth on my way home to tell him I'd ended it. His mother answered and said he never wanted to speak to me again.

Chapter 20
All That Jazz

During my Fourth Committee visits, I had met many interesting people. An older French diplomat, Monsieur Max, had slipped me his card, so rebounding, I called him. He couldn't understand why I refused to sleep with him, but he turned me onto jazz, for which I will be forever grateful. He took me to the Apollo Theater in Harlem for the first time, a Daddy Grace Revival, Count Basie's, Small's Paradise and Birdland. I was hooked.

He was a handsome forty-year-old man, slender with aquiline features; a bit pompous he would stand arrogantly on the subway without holding onto the poles or hand straps. He folded his hands behind his back standing akimbo trying to act cool, but when the subway lurched, so did he. I was subtly amused, but tried not to react as he regained his balance and composure. He also wanted to marry me and take me back to Paris to care for his elderly mother. I wonder what maternal qualities I was exuding on those dates that made men want me to care for their family members - even as I tried to be sophisticated, glamorous and blasé.

When I was invited to a party at his condo on 72nd and Park Avenue by Saalem, a rather jolly, gregarious Libyan diplomat who I kept bumping into in the U.N. hallways when I was visiting, I, of course, accepted. I was enjoying this new intriguing international crowd of fun-loving people.

At the party I was enjoying a conversation about the upcoming vote in the Security Council over Red China's desire to become a U.N. member with a very neatly coiffed, gray-haired, reserved gentleman, over a Scotch and water. He politely invited me to dinner. He said he looked forward to continuing our discussion. I did, too.

Chapter 21
Rude Awakenings

Mr. Frank was wearing a nice gray suit and tie, when he met me in the lobby of my building. He suggested we go to a lovely restaurant he knew in Uptown Manhattan on the West side, but first he wanted me to meet a couple of his friends who would join us for dinner. We got off the subway and entered the lobby of a tall apartment building. We waited for the elevator and chatted casually about where we were going. Once we were in the elevator I was startled when he hit the button and it took us down a floor. It opened into a wide area that didn't seem like an apartment at all. There were pieces of furniture set about with a young couple standing there looking a bit awkward as we were introduced. As they chatted, I asked if I could use the bathroom.

I tried locking the door but discovered that the keyhole on the old-fashioned door was painted over with thick white paint. I couldn't turn the lock so I just struggled pulling down my panty girdle with the garters on my stockings and sat down on the toilet just inside the door next to the wash basin.

Without warning the door smashed open and Mr. Frank yanked me off the toilet so fast that my high heels came off and I was practically standing on my ankles with my feet half in my shoes and half on the floor. He slammed me up against the wall, put his hand over my mouth and wordlessly raped me standing up. My panty girdle had slipped down and was twisted below my knees and I couldn't find my footing. He zipped up and quickly walked out without looking at me and without a word. I was in so much shock that I just stood there with my mouth agape.

I was terrified to walk out of the bathroom, but I had no choice. I had no idea how to extricate myself from this basement in a building with a big old rickety elevator and metal accordion pull gate. I was afraid to try to run. My mind was speeding through my options. I didn't think I'd be able to get away fast enough on my own. If I tried and got caught, what then? I had this fear that I might be killed down there and no one would ever find my body.

I pulled myself together, untwisted my girdle, straightened my stockings, pulled my skirt back down, put my heels on, walked out with as much cautious dignity as I could muster. I had no idea what I was walking into. I must have looked disheveled, in shock, and stood there blank-faced and silent. I didn't look at anyone. The young couple stood next to him solemnly, chatting in an abbreviated manner. They were clearly not dinner companions. I wondered if he owned the building and allowed them free rent so he could bring his rape prospects there. I was sure they must have known. I sensed that I couldn't ask them for help and if I said anything they wouldn't come to my defense. I got the feeling they were afraid of him too. So I just stood there rigidly, on alert. We walked to the subway, got on and when we got to my stop, I bolted off and ran as fast as I could back to my building. I never saw him again and I never told anyone.

I was so ashamed and in so much shock when I got home that I wasn't sure what to do. I locked myself in the bathroom and got into a hot shower and let the water pound down on my neck and shoulders until I could barely stand up for another minute. I scrubbed myself until my skin felt raw and scrubbed my underwear to get his stink off of it and then went to bed. I got up and was even on time for school in the morning. I wanted to be around people, people my own age. I needed to be somewhere structured and predictable. I didn't go anywhere except school for quite some time.

Chapter 22
Ya Habibi

Saalem called one evening to invite me out to go out clubbing with him and his Algerian friend. I needed something lighthearted to put between me and what had happened. I needed to feel clean. Saalem had been such a fun sort of fellow that I didn't stress. We clicked and totally fell for each other. We laughed so much that I was able to put what had happened behind me. He was the perfect medicine. After our first evening together, we became a couple and did almost everything together. I felt protected. While I kept my apartment on 57th Street, I stayed overnight at his place most of the time. His maid Josephine was very solicitous of me when I arrived back from my long days in class. My bath would be drawn, my evening clothes would be laid out with my matching jewelry for our evenings out. On occasion we'd stay home and Saalem would teach me how to cook his favorite Libyan dishes or I'd sit and do my homework. Friends would drop by and I was getting used to being very pampered.

I was often ditching school to go with him to work at the U.N. I found the meetings on international politics utterly fascinating. There were Security Council meetings in the evening. And we'd take our strong *demitasse* of sweet, thick, black coffee and honeyed *baklava* in the Delegates Lounge schmoozing with his diplomat friends, who took delight in teaching me the proper way to cut the layered pastry without smashing it. The Secretary General Dag Hammarskjold with whom I was in awe joined us for lunch once. There was a very tall Tusi king with his delegation that glided more than walked as if they were moving in slow-motion, through the hallways in their European tailored suits. Everyone stopped to watch them in awe. I sat near Krishna Menon who appeared to be ill sitting like a weary lion king on his throne throughout the day in the South Delegates Lounge with his minions fussing over him. Saalem whispered in my ear that he had an important speech to give later and was feigning illness to throw his adversaries off guard. It was quite dramatic. After the General Assembly was well in session, the doors at the back of that grand room burst open. Everyone's head turned and all attention was on Menon as he strode with his back straight looking stronger than ever down the central aisle and took command of the podium. He spoke with such great force, his gray-streaked wavy black mane, his prominent nose and dark, eagle-fierce eyes belied every sign of weakness we had previously thought we had witnessed. There were so many different cultures there. I smelled the sandalwood scents of the throngs of delegates from the Far East and North Africa. The multi-colored silk saris of gray-haired, Indian lady delegates with diamonds studding their noses. I could feel the high focused energy in the bustling hallways and the importance of the work in the committee meetings. I was in love with everything about it. I absorbed everything I could.

My new high school's curriculum was so far behind my Connecticut school that I lost interest. I wasn't feeling intellectually challenged there at all. But international politics was a different story. It was pertinent and never ending in relevance. I was hooked. I thought seriously about changing my career. I began playing with the idea of possibly redirecting my goals and applying to George Washington University, American U or Columbia to study Political Science. I knew I'd have to step up my attendance and knuckle down on my studies, even though somehow, I always made it to my afternoon Theatre Wing classes. Meanwhile I was enjoying being chauffeured in embassy limousines and rubbing shoulders with a fascinating international crowd who had important work to do for the world's tumultuous conditions.

In the evenings Saalem and I would go out clubbing with his dear Algerian friend, Mohammed Benyahia who later became the Minister of Foreign Affairs. Mohammed was an incredible dancer. He had long legs and knew all the latest Latin dances. Being a dancer myself, I loved having him join us. Saalem did not dance. So, I had the pleasure of being whirled around the dance floor in some of the most fabulous night spots in Manhattan that year, while Saalem sat benevolently watching us, happily drinking his Scotch and water, and smoking his Kent filters.

Mohammed became my confidante and mediator when Saalem had his little temper tantrums over other guys giving me the eye when we were out. Mohammed was like the big brother I never had, always kind and a perfect gentleman. Shortly before my eighteenth birthday, Saalem proposed marriage. I enthusiastically said, "Yes!" Mohammed was to be his Best Man and we could be married at the mosque in D.C. when he returned from his meetings in Geneva and Rome. I was elated. I felt I had found the life I wanted to live and forgot all about my schooling and career for the moment.

Saalem hosted my eighteenth birthday party at his condo and it was fabulous. I invited a couple of my teachers from the Theatre Wing, all my school friends including Ronnie Walken who got super drunk and had a very unsettling encounter with a tribal-scarred African embassy worker who also attended. One of my teachers was the incredibly handsome, black actor, Ramon San Jacques who had the most deeply resonant, Shakespearean voice, and always looked very bohemian wearing his black turtleneck sweaters. He taught fencing and dramatic acting and was later known in films as Raymond St. Jacques. It was a lovely party.

We often flew down to D.C. for the weekends to party with his D.C. embassy friends and go to the mosque. There were three couples who we routinely hung out with in D.C. when we visited and we'd all get together and cook. There was Abdul, the financial manager of the embassy, and his Scottish fiancée, Maggie. She was an embassy secretary. There was Omar and his German girlfriend, Krystal. I wasn't close to them so much, but we spent a lot of time with Maggie and Abdul.

When the U.N. session was over, everyone went either back to their own countries, or off to other countries for meetings. I never saw any of them again, though Maggie and I wrote letters to each other for years. I often wondered about Mohammed Benyahiya.

In 2016 I took a road trip with an old buddy to New Orleans. We grabbed a taxi to take us to the French Quarter and the driver mentioned that he was Algerian. I told him that I had once had a dear friend,

*a diplomat from Algeria named Mohammed
Benyahiya. He gave me a look and then slowly and
sadly told me Mohammed's fate. In 1982 while
Mohammed who had become the Algerian Minister of
Foreign Affairs was mediating a peace agreement
during the Iran-Iraq War his plane was shot down and
he was assassinated. No one accepted responsibility,
but the driver told me it was well known amongst the
Middle Eastern community that Saddam Hussein had
ordered it. My heart dropped. I remembered when that
plane had been shot down but I never for one moment
imagined that my dear old friend was on it. How
curious it is that the past sometimes comes back at the
least expected moments to hit us in the face - and tug
at our heart.*

Saalem left for European conferences in Geneva,
Moscow, London and Rome at the end of the U.N. session
that year of 1960-61. He wrote me love letters regularly and
sent me gorgeous clothing, jewelry and encouragement from
the cities wherever he was having his meetings. He kept
telling me to be patient until his return. I was so depressed
without him that when Abdul called and wanted me to be
Maggie's Maid of Honor at their wedding, I was over the
moon. He said he wanted it to be a surprise gift for Maggie
and treated me to the airfare.

I felt I was still being included and respected as
Saalem's fiancée and was grateful to still be part of our
circle, our diplomatic family. I felt less lonely. I had begun
studying the Quran and had already spoken to the local Imam
about converting in preparation for our own wedding. I was

trying to learn Arabic by singing along with the Arabic pop songs on the lps I played on my little pink portable record player that Saalem had given me for my birthday. I packed my head scarf to enter the mosque for the wedding ceremony, and had my gray silk linen suit ready to wear for the wedding. I'd tucked in the filigree seed pearl bracelet and string of pearls Saalem had given me as an engagement gift. I wished he was with us and I couldn't wait to write to him to tell him all about it.

Abdul picked me up at the airport and said Maggie was getting things ready for the wedding the next day but we would see her later. We hugged and I was so delighted to see him and be back in the company of friends. He said everyone was meeting over at Omar's studio apartment for a midday meal and we'd go there first to give Maggie time to be on her own. Abdul mentioned casually that Krystal and Omar had broken up. I commented that I thought that was too bad because they seemed to be good together. Everyone was cheerful and celebratory with the next day's wedding vibe in the air. We sat around the long table scooping the *shakshuka* up by hand with our pita bread. I loved *shakshuka*. Saalem had taught me how to prepare it and I felt very accomplished. It was a very spicy hot Libyan tomato-based dish with eggs poached directly in the sauce. We chatted and everyone was very lively.

All of a sudden, I became so sleepy I couldn't hold my head up or keep my eyes open. I thought it must have been because I was staying up too late studying and carrying such a heavy schedule. I had been trying to catch up after missing so many classes when I was preoccupied with Saalem. I couldn't seem to shake the drowsiness. I was literally falling asleep sitting up and couldn't stop it. I felt so embarrassed. Abdul very kindly assisted me the few short steps to Omar's bed so I could lie down for a bit. It was the last thing I remembered until I woke up with a start much later to discover that everyone had gone and I was all alone - with Omar.

At first, I didn't realize that my being at Omar's was pre-planned. It was a stunning revelation. Apparently, they thought that because Saalem was in Europe that they could just plug me in to the empty slot Krystal had left when she and Omar broke up.

I drowsily got up and asked how I was going to get over to Maggie and Abdul's since I thought I was staying with them. Omar explained they had all gone to Abdul's but we would meet up later. Since it would be their wedding night the next night, I was expected to stay with him. I quickly explained that that was not my expectation. I would be staying with Abdul and Maggie. At first, he was very polite and solicitous, trying to put a comforting arm around my shoulder but then became insistently amorous. I kept telling him that I was Saalem's faithful and loving fiancée, but he got pushier and pushier as I resisted. He became increasingly aggravated by my continued assertions that I was engaged to Saalem and faithful. I was beginning to panic. I stood up to get some distance from him as he lunged and swooped me roughly up into his arms and threw me on the bed. He dove on top of me, pinning me to the bed with his full body weight while ripping off my panties.

I kicked and screamed trying to push him away. He clamped his right arm across my throat and pressed down on my windpipe as he jammed himself inside me. He cut off my air as I struggled. I fought to get just a little breath, then he snarled menacingly, "If you make another sound, I will kill you." His tone was so sinister that I didn't doubt for a minute that he would do it. I had a feeling it wouldn't have been the first time.

I turned my head to the side away from his pungent, foul breath. I closed my eyes with tears pouring down my cheeks. I can still smell the sour sweat emanating off his damp hairy skin. I can still hear his barnyard grunts. When he was done, he released his arm from across my throat, got up and ordered me to the bathroom. I grabbed my torn panties, ran in and locked the door. I didn't know what to expect next. I was frantic about what to do. There was no way out of the apartment except the way I'd come in, so I had to cross the whole room to get to the front door.

Maggie and Abdul's apartment was the only place I had to go, so when I finally opened the bathroom door, I told him that's where I was going. My overnight case and purse were by the chair near the front door. Someone had apparently brought everything in. I grabbed my things, walked quickly to the front door and discovered that the door had three locked deadbolts. I couldn't get out. He was instantly beside me breathing down on me, smirking, dangling the keys in his hairy hand. I wasn't sure if he was going to let me leave. "That wasn't so bad, was it?" I didn't answer. I looked at my shoes. He refused to unlock the deadbolts. "If you want out you must smile at me. Look me in the eyes and smile." I wasn't sure if I was capable of accomplishing that. I hated him. I feared him, but I forced myself to turn up the corners of my mouth. He unlocked the door and I ran out onto the street and hailed a passing cab.

There was a moment in which I thought I would tell the taxi driver to take me straight to the police, but in the end, I gave him Maggie and Abdul's address instead. I wanted the support, comfort and advice of my friends. I knew they'd be horrified.

Once there, I raced up the stairs to their apartment hysterically weeping and banged on their apartment door. Maggie opened it and was in shock at my disheveled hair and mascara streaming down my cheeks from my swollen reddened eyes. I burst in and blurted out in hysterical tears what had happened. Abdul was casually sitting on an ottoman talking on the phone. He looked up and said, "This is Omar on the line. He says don't believe anything you say." I hysterically told him everything again, but he just looked at me and said, "Saalem can't marry you. Don't you know that? You are a foreigner. He is a diplomat. He has two Muslim wives already. One lives in Beirut and the other, the mother of his two-year-old daughter, lives in Tripoli. Forget him." I dissolved sobbing. My knees buckled. I wavered as I tried to remain upright. I couldn't believe what I was hearing.

Maggie finally took me by the arm and like a robot I let her steer me into the bathroom off of her bedroom. She closed the door, helped me get out of my clothes and turned on the hot water in the shower. She assisted me into the shower. I was unable to communicate. She said she had to go to the store to get a few things for the wedding tomorrow but when she came back, we would both go to the hairdresser. She had made an appointment for us both. I stood under the hot water sobbing quietly. I heard her slip out and close the door softly. I couldn't absorb everything that had happened. I was in so much shock.

Then the shower curtain was pulled back and Abdul stepped naked into the shower. I felt completely defeated, trapped without a will of my own. I understood then that Abdul was going to take what he wanted, too. He needed to cover up what Omar had done by having sex with me so that if I tried to report it to the police, he and Omar could say I was just a girl who 'got around.' This was protection against an international incident.

Maggie came home later busily preparing for her wedding and the reception afterwards. I wanted to tell her what happened but then I was conflicted between telling the truth, ruining her wedding or letting her marry a guy like Abdul who had conspired with Omar to set me up. I remained silent - trauma-induced silence. She took me to the hairdresser.

The next morning, we dressed in preparation to go to the mosque for the wedding. I never looked once at Abdul. Maggie and I sat in the back of the car together. Abdul was behind the wheel. When he stopped in front of Omar's building, my guts turned to water.

Omar got in the car very cheerfully, solicitously greeting me as if nothing had ever happened. He unrolled his wedding gift - a scroll in beautiful Arabic calligraphy - an Islamic prayer that he had written by hand. I remained mute and expressionless as Abdul praised him highly. Maggie slid her eyes in my direction, reached over and squeezed my hand.

As I write this, I realize that adopting a flat expression became a posture I would adopt for years to come. It became my armor through all the years of struggle so no one could guess what I was really thinking or feeling while I bluffed and brailed my way along. Later on, I would add biting sarcasm and a cynical one-sided smile - for which I am now paying with the resultant wrinkles on my left cheek.

I had to return to New York on Monday morning after the Sunday night reception. I had decided that I would not stay with Maggie and Abdul. I couldn't look at him another minute, so by the end of the party when they came to gather me up to leave, I had already asked the host if I could stay overnight and hitch a ride to the airport in the morning. I never wanted to see Abdul again and I couldn't face Maggie. I looked down and shook my head 'no.' Of course, my host took his pound of flesh, too. By the end of that weekend, I had lost all faith and my will to live.

Chapter 23
Flirting with Razor Blades

I arrived back at my apartment and became so despondent that I couldn't get out of bed. I just let everything go. I'd wait till my roommate left for school then I'd slip out of my room, fix coffee, light candles and lie on the sofa. I'd progress to glasses of red wine not knowing how I could ever face anyone I knew again.

I wrote Saalem a letter at his address through the Ministry of Foreign Affairs in Tripoli. I told him what had happened. I confronted him. His return letter was less than comforting. He acknowledged that he couldn't marry me. He admitted that he had two wives and a little daughter - but he hoped to see me again next year in our little "love nest" when the U.N. was in session again. He said he was sorry to hear about Omar and Abdul but don't worry about it, "You'll be ok."

I raged. I wrote him a blistering letter. I threw things. I broke things. I stood in front of the medicine cabinet. I flirted with razor blades, but the razor blades were double-edged. I didn't want to cut my fingers while I was slicing my wrists.

Eventually, after my absences from class became increasingly chronic and my grades tanked, the school called my parents. Daddy called and yelled at me. "You get home on the next goddam train or I'm coming in with the cops and dragging you home!"

I was just two weeks shy of finals. Mom said that there was no way I could pass. I knew I could. I had been talking myself into rallying. Generally, I was a very good student and I was pretty sure I could pull it off, maybe not at the top of my class but I knew I could pass. I had to graduate.

I called the Theater Wing and dropped out so I could focus on studying for my finals. They tried to talk me out of it, because I was the lead in the final show for the season, Anna, of course, in the *King and I*. I wanted so badly to do it but I felt my priority was to graduate high school. My pleas fell on Daddy's deaf ears and I was still totally intimidated by him. I talked to a few friends trying to come up with alternatives, but everyone advised me to go home because it wouldn't be wise to alienate them. I even refused a marriage proposal by a classical trumpet player friend named Walter who wanted to save me from having to go home.

Walter had gifted me with an LP of Laurindo Almeida's Spanish guitar that I played endlessly. *Concierto de Aranjuez* with its emotional *crescendos* that spoke to my soul. I stopped playing my favorite Arabic pop song with its familiar refrain… *Ya Habibi.. Ahaibak.* "My *dear, I love you…*" Sometimes I think I should have just married Walter.

Chapter 24
Tail Between My Legs

It hadn't occurred to either Daddy or me that I was of legal age and I didn't have to obey him anymore - and I lived in a different state where he had no authority. It's hard for me to understand that I didn't just go get a job and stay where I was. But I still feared my parents' wrath, so I obeyed and went home.

They sent me back to my public high school in Connecticut to humiliate me. Humiliation was always their mode of punishment. They even advised me to use it when I became a parent myself. I continued to dress the way we all dressed in school in NYC - high heels, my nice knit suits and dresses that Saalem had sent me from Rome. I wore my pearls and the gold wedding band my mother had given me that had been hers from my father, Jim. I wanted to pretend I was above it all and connected to someone, because I simply didn't fit in and wanted to be anywhere else but there.

I felt so disconnected and tissue paper translucent that I thought I might float off into space. The humiliation I felt in front of my former classmates was, I'm sure, all in my head. They undoubtedly had no idea - and furthermore probably couldn't have given a rat's ass.

After a couple of weeks, the principal called me into the office and questioned why I was wearing a wedding ring. "Are you married?" he questioned. I had to admit that I was not. I told him I was engaged and my fiancé was in Europe. He admonished me for pretending and reminded me that married girls were not allowed to attend high school.

I fell desperately, deathly ill almost immediately. I was too sick to get out of bed and had a high fever. I was hallucinating and had muscle spasms in my back. I wasn't sure what was happening to me, but looking back I'm sure I was having a nervous breakdown. I was malnourished after not really eating regularly after Saalem left. I've always lost my appetite when I was upset anyway. I wanted the world to disappear - and me with it.

I was bedfast for over two weeks, so weak that Daddy had to practically carry me to the toilet. Mom brought me hot strong unsweetened chamomile tea with aspirin to break my fever. Poached eggs floating in butter on toast, with endless bowls of soup. They were always good at taking care of me when I was sick. I had to give them that. Oddly, my youngest daughter recently told me the same thing about my mothering.

Mr. S, my dashing tweedy, leather elbow-patched, mustachioed, Speech and Theater Arts teacher with "rust-colored-curl-carefully-placed-on-forehead-to-look-casual," came and brought me books to read. He sat by my bedside and introduced me to Ibsen's "Doll House," Chekhov's play, "The Cherry Orchard," and his collection of short stories, Tolstoy, Dostoyevsky - and Sagan's "Bonjour Tristesse." He was very solicitous of me. I looked forward to his visits and the books. I devoured what he brought as I lay listlessly in my bed. My parents weren't comfortable with his visits and eavesdropped. They may have overheard him asking me to come stay with him after I got well, for the ten days that his wife and five kids were in France. I hoped they also heard me say, "NO!"

Decades later at a high school reunion I sadly heard that he had died - and that he had had a penchant for his pretty young students.

He had meant so much to me when I was in 7th Grade. My desk was in the front row closest to his. He gave us writing assignments and I poured my heart out in my compositions. He invited me to join the Ridgefield Players, the town's local theater group where he was the director. I was cast as the Native Girl in Somerset Maugham's play, *Rain*. When I played George Bernard Shaw's Saint Joan, I had a moment when I *became* St. Joan as she was pleading with the Inquisitors not to imprison her for the rest of her life, not to keep her from riding free through the fields on her great charger and take her away from her *angel voices*. In her impassioned pleas, she unwittingly consigned herself to the flames. When I came back to myself, I was on my knees center stage in the single spotlight. I felt dazed and confused. I looked into the wings and saw Mr. S's face underlit by the lightboard. Tears streamed down his cheeks and I found myself walking towards him and collapsing in his arms. He was my mentor, my inspiration and it seemed to my young misunderstood soul that he was the only person who saw me, heard me - and cared...

When the doctor visited for the last time, he said that if my fever didn't come down by morning I needed to be hospitalized. I overheard him discussing the possibility that I might have mononucleosis, the *Kissing Disease*. They had apparently whispered something to him about their suspicions of my extracurricular activities while I was away at school. I heard them and shuddered. I thought of the cost to Daddy if I had to be hospitalized and, just like that, my temperature was normal by morning.

My parents had been misinformed by the school in Manhattan and the fact that I was missing too much school was misinterpreted in unsavory ways. They were never people who asked concerned questions, nor had pragmatic discussions. They simply leapt to conclusions, assuming the worst and responding in kind. Listening with open, concerned and loving hearts was not part of their playbook.

My birth father's sister, Aunt Pat, had cautioned them that I was too young to be allowed to live away from home. Of course, I bridled at that. I didn't care what anyone said, I was just impatient to be out on my own. At sixteen going on seventeen no one could tell me anything. I had no idea how to survive without my family's support, but that thought never occurred to me. My growing rebelliousness was creating constant arguments. I bridled against their restrictions and I resented their hypocrisy. I questioned everything they taught me. My obvious fervor for New York theater was my escape, but it overrode my good sense - and theirs. I think they were only too happy to simplify their day to day lives and were not equipped to deal with a confrontational teenager.

Chapter 25
Death of a Dream
1955

My view of my parents had begun to radically shift when I was thirteen and my cousin Anne came to live with us. She was four years younger than I. She had pretty much just been born as we were leaving Hollywood. Aunt Emmy was so beautiful that Mom said men threw themselves at her feet but she never noticed. She could have had anyone she chose, but, according to Mom, the men she chose were never up to family standards.

One evening my folks were going out to dinner and I was dropped off at my mother's friend Carmen's house for the evening. Carmen was an interesting woman, rather petite with frizzy gray hair who owned her own boutique in town. I was looking forward to spending time alone with her in her silver and pale lavender, frothy decor. We were just settling in when Mom and Daddy abruptly returned. I could tell by the look on Mom's face that something was terribly wrong, but hard for me to decipher. Daddy walked in slowly, ponderously as if he was walking to the gallows. He sank down heavily on the sofa hanging his head low. My mother just stood there as if she was in a trance staring off into space.

Carmen pressed for an explanation, "Betty! What's wrong?" Mom stood and stared ahead and said flatly to the air, "My sister is dead." "What sister?" I chanted knowing full well there was only one. Seeing my mother so stricken was almost impossible to fathom. Imagining my beautiful precious Aunt Emmy dead was utterly incomprehensible. I became hysterical, threw myself into Daddy's lap and wept uncontrollably in his arms.

The story I overheard Mom tell Carmen was this: Aunt Emmy had separated from her second husband. We didn't know why, but the family was relieved. They had never liked him and made no bones about it. She and her two kids, Anne and Johnny moved in with Grandma and Auntie Te at the ancestral home in Hollywood. Aunt Emmy was returning from evening out singing with her chorus. She had gotten off the trolley at the corner of Sunset and Genesee and was walking the block and a half home. Her estranged husband was sitting in his car in front of the house and motioned for her to get in the car to discuss their issues. We'll never know what was said, but he shot her four times with a revolver he happened to have along for the ride. The defensive wounds in her hands told a story of surprise, terror and desperate pleading for her life. He drove around and around with her hemorrhaging body until he finally drove to the police station and turned himself in. She was rushed to the hospital in a coma, but the blood loss was too profound. She never recovered consciousness.

Mom was immediately on a flight to Los Angeles to help Grandma and Auntie Te arrange the funeral - and to bring Annie home to live with us in Connecticut. I was left to care for Daddy. Uncle Bill who was living in Kansas City with his first wife took Johnny. But he was a traumatized toddler, unceremoniously whisked away from his mother, familiar relatives and home, and they were unable to handle his behavior. A family in their church fell in love with him, fostered and eventually adopted him. He grew up never knowing the truth and was told that both his parents died in a car crash.

His father was sentenced to five to twenty years in San Quentin State Prison, but got out in eight. We never heard from him again and everyone was greatly relieved.

Anne was nine and I was thirteen when she came to live with us. She moved awkwardly and was a bit slow in her speech patterns. She was chunky, a little pigeon toed and seemed a bit developmentally delayed. She had long *banana* curls, straight-cut, dirty-blonde bangs and she tagged around after me like a lost puppy. She copied everything I did. If I ate one peanut or three, she had to do the exact same thing. From then on out we did everything together. When we played together alone out in the cow pasture, she'd share tidbits of what had happened to her.

She told me that after Johnny was born while her mom was at work, her stepfather kept her locked out in the backyard until just before her mom arrived home. She showed me the scars where he had burnt her with cigarette butts. At thirteen, I had no way of processing what she told me, but I was horrified. She said it in such a matter-of-fact way without emotion, almost as if she was talking about someone else or an inanimate object - or reciting her one plus ones. I felt a kind of sickness in my soul that I'd never experienced before. Of course, I told Mom. I had no idea what she did with that information, but typical of Mom, her way of dealing with unseemly things was to never speak of it again - ignore it and hope it would go away. It didn't.

The summer of 2010 when we were both taking care of Mom in her last summer of life, Anne and I had heart to hearts that we hadn't been able to have since we were children - and in ways children never could have had. She revealed the things she couldn't find words to express when she was nine. She told me that he had sexually abused her - raped and routinely sodomized her. She shared details that I can't repeat. I was sick to my stomach, and worse - sick in my heart. It explained so many of her behaviors after she came to live with us - behaviors that my parents were unable to address. It also explains, perhaps, why Aunt Emmy took the children and left.

Chapter 26
Built-in Babysitter

My mother, who had never been able to become pregnant since she gave birth to me, suddenly was pregnant within the next few months after Anne came to live with us. Daddy was overjoyed. I was thrilled at the prospect of a baby sister or brother. Annie, however, became increasingly anxious. After the baby was born, she began spacing-out in school. It was as if she was regressing into an almost toddler-like behavior pattern. She'd sit and stare off into space. Mom was called into the principal's office with regular reports. Daddy became increasingly short tempered. Their behavior was overly critical, highly judgmental and relentlessly unkind. Daddy was riled up by Mom's needling complaints. Dealing with Annie's behaviors exasperated her, but rather than seeking professional help, she complained to us both, trying to get us to align ourselves with her against Anne. She and Daddy became routinely abusive each in their own distinctive ways, while Annie and I were caught in the crossfire of Daddy's explosive wrath.

Mom's abusiveness was expressed indirectly in a behind-the-scenes nagging way. She would tell Daddy and me, "She puts her dirty underwear back in her drawer." "She shoves her clothes under the bed." "She looks sloppy. She can't keep her shirt tucked in." Daddy whacked Annie's knuckles at the dinner table for not holding her fork properly. I observed everything and all the while felt their unjust treatment of her deep in my soul. As a result, Annie and I bonded more closely.

We found our solace playing out in the woods on the neighbor's farm up Mopus Bridge Road. We always tried to climb up on the big old, dapple-gray, plow horse that grazed in the field with the herd of cattle and sometimes tried to ride the elusive burros. One time I assisted Annie up on the back of one of them, then I whacked it on the butt as hard as I could and started laughing as it took off running downhill into the deep lush green grasses. It terrified her, even though it stopped abruptly to graze and she hadn't fallen off. I had laughed uncontrollably while she and her curls bounced up and down as she hung onto its mane for dear life. Every time her bottom hit the burro's back with a thud, a yelp would come out of her mouth. Guiltily, I tried to make amends and attempted to whittle a flute for her from a tree branch with my pocket knife. But I sliced right through my jeans leaving a tidy little scar on my left thigh as a lifelong reminder of instant karma. I think she finally forgave me by the time I was forty.

One Saturday morning, the only day I was allowed to sleep in, I was awakened by loud yelling on the stair landing outside my bedroom door. "I'm gonna kill her! I'm gonna kill her!" Daddy was backing Annie down the stairs hitting her and bellowing. Annie's arms were up trying to protect her head and face while Mom backed down the stairs behind her pleading. "No! Nino! No! Stop!" I pulled the covers over my head and peeked out trying to become invisible.

Apparently, Mom left Annie to watch the baby in the bathtub while she went into the bedroom to get a diaper and for some unknown reason Annie bit the baby. Mom as usual immediately told Daddy and the insanity exploded. I never saw my parents in the same light ever again. I began hating them and lashing out. I confronted them on every infraction I observed. It was soon after that, that Annie was sent off to *see Grandma for the summer.* She never returned and I retreated into my thoughts more and more, resentment building and burning.

I had already been in charge of the younger kids when the folks went out to the Couples Club at church, but once Annie was gone Mom relinquished all the care of the baby to me. The baby had uncontrollable temper tantrums that my mother never seemed to be able to handle. So, when I was at home her care was turned over to me. I was the only one to whom she seemed to respond. One day after school, Mom, finding it impossible to control the baby who was running and screaming out of control, handed me a length of clothesline and told me to tie her to the newel post so she wouldn't hurt herself. I did as I was told, but decades later that toddler, all grown up, accused me of tying her up. I had forgotten, but then I remembered and thought back to when Daddy had tied me up. It made me wonder if Mom hadn't been behind that, too. Or had she gotten the idea from Daddy? I realized that their own abusiveness had fueled each other's. While Mom instigated the dramas, she inevitably blamed things on everyone else, so she came out of it looking like the beleaguered victim.

I put my toddler half-sister to bed every night, sang her lullabies and rocked her in the ancestral cradle. When she experienced her first anaphylactic reaction to a wasp sting, it was I who took her to the doctor driven by a neighbor. Daddy was off running errands in town and he was driving our only car. Mom couldn't cope. As I schemed to get away from them, I fretted about abandoning my toddler sister, but I also knew she was ultimately their responsibility. I knew I had to go.

I was receiving a lot of positive reinforcement from acting, singing and dancing in the Glee Club and Thespian Society at school. I began adopting a black-turtlenecked, bohemian persona and wearing exotic black eyeliner, acting blasé and adopting an existential philosophy. I read Kerouac, Ginsberg and Sartre. My new style was purely a facade, but I needed to act as though nothing affected me, although everything had - deeply. I was adding another layer of protection.

Underneath it all I was still that little girl who tracked deer spoor up the trails in the deep woods with my trusty black cat Bagheera. I was still that girl who ice skated alone for hours to the music in my head on the solid frozen marsh behind the hills across our dirt road. I was still that little girl who wrote *haiku*, dreaming on my big *thinking rock* on the edge of our sapling grove that burst into riotous bloom every Spring. That was the patch that Mom called *The Park* because it was so magical. In the early whispers of Spring, it was carpeted with crocus, daffodils, bloodroot and snowbells amongst the white birch and sugar maples. The loamy soil smelled primal - rich and fecund. Despite every superficial modification, I remained that child who laid on her back amongst the wild lilacs casting her dreams onto the fluffy-white drifting clouds. I still was that child who communed with the cardinals and the red-winged blackbirds nestling in the white blossomed apple trees. I just adopted a *masque* that belied who I was within. In no way was I prepared to live independently in the city.

Chapter 27
The Family Spin

I never told my folks about the rapes I'd experienced while I was at school in NYC and on my weekend in D.C. Sex was, of course, a topic never discussed. Talking to them about rape was unimaginable and beyond my purview. I thought they were furious with me because I was playing hooky from school and letting my grades tank - along with disapproving of my eclectic mixture of friends. I suspected they knew I had had sex but we never talked about it. I was ashamed that they knew that I had lost my virginity at all. But later I understood that there were only unclarified assumptions based on what the Corley's had misinterpreted and reported from their brief ten-minute visit - and coupled, of course, with the reports of my absences from school.

Once I had my strength back, I wanted to say goodbye to my friends in New York before leaving for Grandma's for the summer. My pal, Bugsy, told me that the newly popular Nigerian drummer, Olatunji, was playing at *Birdland* that Saturday night with Maynard Ferguson on the bill and I wanted to go see them perform one more time before I left for my summer at Grandma's in Hollywood.

Bugsy offered to treat me as a going away present. He worked at the Columbus Circle Rehearsal Studios and sometimes got free passes. He used to let me know if there was an audition coming up that I might be interested in and sometimes he'd rehearse scenes with me. He was a sweet, skinny kid, pallid looking with freckles and a big gap between his front teeth. Mom told Daddy that Bugsy was 'colored.' Daddy freaked out and the fires were stoked. Daddy started yelling at me! "You're going into New York to see a black monkey with a nigger? " I totally lost my cool. Utterly unhinged, I screamed back, "You always raised me to think that people who used that word were ignorant!!!" The next thing I knew I was backhanded across my face with so much force that I flew backwards into the hall closet. I honestly don't remember anything after that. I always wondered if he ever regretted that moment. He knew I was right. I knew I was right!

The whole weekend was bookended by angry outbursts. Mom rifled through my drawers accusingly, found and stole my brand-new diaphragm that I had been advised to get by a wiser person than she. Mom seemed to think that if she took my diaphragm, it would prevent me from having sex. It didn't - just not that weekend. I returned home from my last New York weekend excited to be off on a new adventure and away from them.

On Monday I was put on a plane to Los Angeles. My mother walked me to my seat and hugged me tightly. Those were the days when you could be escorted to your seat and assisted with your luggage by a friend. This mother of mine - the woman who rarely cried - was suddenly in tears. It was bewildering to see this woman who had been such a livid witch two days before, sad to see me go. I was only going on summer vacation, for heaven's sakes, and she had certainly seemed glad to be rid of me.

My personal diaspora began the summer of 1961. I was sent off to see Grandma and Auntie Te for the summer - just as they had done with my cousin Anne the previous summer of 1959. I wasn't as enthralled with Hollywood as I'd thought I would be. As they proudly drove me down the lauded Sunset Strip from the airport all I saw was dingy insignificant ticky-tack buildings, nothing compared to Manhattan skyscrapers and historic architecture. Once I got to the house, there was nothing to do. Grandma and Auntie Te watched Lawrence Welk, read the Sears Roebuck catalog and went to church. Aside from going next door to sit in the Bleiweiss's kitchen to sit and complain, I had little to occupy my time. I was bored stiff.

Annie was devoting most of her time to riding horses on the trails up at the Griffith Park Stables and took me along. But I wasn't really into it, although she seemed to be thriving. She'd grown taller, thinned out and seemed to have a new sense of confidence. She was at a private school for kid actors, similar to the one I had gone to in New York. But I could see that we were both experiencing unaddressed severe post-traumatic stress symptoms from what we had suffered. We just didn't have the terminology then to interpret what it was. Our whole lives had been upturned and we were just kids reacting. Our symptoms were ignored or judged instead of treated. The family was unable to handle what they didn't understand and what we, ourselves, didn't understand. We didn't even know what we needed. We couldn't even articulate our need for help and just muddled along. Psychological counseling? Someone to hold us, comfort us, tell us that it wasn't our fault, and tell us that we'd be ok? It is no wonder that Annie and I shared such a deep bond, albeit unspoken most of our adult lives.

I'm glad Annie and I were finally able to open up and share our experiences before she died of cancer in 2015. We were a great comfort to each other in the end. But I still weep when I remember how she looked up at me after receiving her terminal diagnosis in that little girl vulnerability I knew so well. "So, when do I get to enjoy life?" I had no answer.

We talked endlessly in the days before she died about the baby girl Grandma had made her give up for adoption when she was sixteen. She said she put my name on the papers at the Salvation Home for Unwed Mothers in case her baby ever came looking for her. Three years after Annie's passing, she did. I received a message on Messenger. She said, "I don't know if you know about me..." The baby has become a grandmother to a new baby girl named Emmy... and her name is Lori... Seasons come around and bring blessings - wistful, but blessings nonetheless.

Chapter 28
Only The Shadow Knows

I never realized how sensitive Daddy was to the idea of me calling him out on what he had said to me as being ignorant. Though he was a legendary Disney artist, he had not finished high school. I had no idea that bothered him so deeply. He was extraordinarily well read and knew fine art, literature and classical music and played classical violin when he was young. He had the most beautiful operatic tenor and when he sang opera and solos in church the beauty of his voice made me weep. He was an autodidact of the highest order and had taught himself anything and everything he ever wanted to do.

Daddy had to drop out of school in 9th Grade becoming the breadwinner of his family after he kicked his mother out for having an affaire. He was sick of his parents chasing each other around the house with meat cleavers, he said. But, in my mind, it established where his mistrust of women's faithfulness began. He went to the Cooper Union to study art and apprenticed with the great fantasy artist, Willy Pogany, whose watercolors were on the covers of the New York Times Magazine in the Forties. I remember Willy and his wife Elaine. They had the most spectacular apartment in a vintage Manhattan building. The ceilings were two stories high with a staircase along one wall leading to their bedroom. Elaine's dressing room overlooked the living room from a balustraded balcony. There was an easel with a partially finished nude painting of his wife in the

Great Room. It was so tall that it almost reached the balcony. Elaine took me up to her dressing table to show me her beautiful jewelry box and drew out a long strand of pearl sized turquoise beads which she ceremoniously placed around my neck.

Daddy created the pen and ink drawings for the first illustrated, published copy of Mary Shelley's _Frankenstein_ in the United States in 1932, and painted the backgrounds for Disney's early classics, _Fantasia_ with the Sugar Plum Fairies and Night on Bald Mountain segments. He did backgrounds for the original Pinocchio, Bambi, Dumbo and many more. He was an old master and became legendary in the annals of Disney history because of his backgrounds.

Towards the end of Daddy's career, he was the senior artist for Animated Filmmakers that produced Flipper. He loved being sent to Manila for three months to teach the Filipino artists how to paint fast Hollywood backgrounds. I think he enjoyed the peace away from Mom. He said he loved having a quiet apartment at the end of the day with a maid to cook and clean, then leave. Mom complained that he was so grumpy when she arrived and made him go shopping all over Singapore and Hong Kong that she had difficulty motivating him at all.

Daddy was a background artist for Woody Woodpecker in the last ten years of its existence. He was a member of the Academy of Motion Pictures and was really quite remarkable, never needing to feel _less than_. But, "_Who knows what lurks in the hearts of men... only The Shadow knows._" He taught me to _Paint and Ink_ by hand in the old-fashioned way, before coloring cells became computerized. And I didn't realize how much I'd absorbed from him watching him draw all my childhood in his home studio until I began publishing my own fan magazine in the Nineties. It was before computer editing programs and I did everything the way I saw Daddy do it on his drawing board - old fashioned lay-outs and paste-ups - such a satisfying organic process. I wish he'd lived long enough to see it.

Chapter 29
Hollywood 46

My summer with Grandma became an eight year "summer" that expanded far wider than Grandma's sphere, with many challenges and adventures along the way - more traumas, many disappointments, new awareness's, and important lessons learned - many lessons I could have lived without.

I was never allowed to return home even though I begged in the beginning. Mom told me it was because they were planning on relocating to L.A. in a couple of years anyway, but it didn't make me feel any less abandoned. By the time they arrived the damage was done.

My earliest memories of warmth, safety, security and good kitchen smells were in Grandma's home, our family home. My last memory of being rocked in anyone's arms was in Grandma's arms for my afternoon nap in the ancestral rocking chair in the dining room. I remember that feeling of contentment against her soft, warm apron-covered bosom that always smelled like warm flour and carnation-scented talcum powder. The filtered afternoon light wafted softly through the gentle movement of the palm tree fronds outside the window. Grandma's rocking and humming fell into sync with its rhythm. I was deeply content, safe and secure - until my mother's voice jarred me awake as she stepped through the door from the kitchen. "Mom! You're going to spoil her. Put her down!"

After I returned to North Genesee in 1961, I yearned for those precious moments with my grandma, those moments suspended in my memory, but they were never recaptured.

As a result, I learned that I had to create the idea of "Home" for myself. For a long time, it was a fantasy place in my heart and soul, the castle in the clouds; The log cabin with the roaring fire nestled in the woods where all the wild animals would feel at home - safe harbor - sanctuary. In time I created nests for myself and my kids wherever we perched - an oasis wherever I found myself. I used to joke that I could make a cozy home under a bush if I needed one. My obsession with the concept of home was a little elusive, always somehow just out of my grasp. I still yearn for a piece of land that is all mine that no one can take away from me where everything I own is safe. I have learned that creating a home within myself wherever I am, however, is much the same as having to become my own mother - as we all must. I had to become the mother I never had - and create the home within myself that I dreamed.

Mother and Home are sacred spaces we create within our own souls that we must nourish and nurture for our own wellbeing. I think we must create little shrines to ourselves, to honor those benevolent spirits with whom we speak in the candlelight of our souls.

Chapter 30
Dumped in L.A.
Summer 1961

I utterly lost sight of myself after my parents sent me off from Connecticut that summer of 1961, nearly 3,000 miles away from everything I knew. My poor crippled grandma in Hollywood was ill-equipped to deal with one more trauma. Another screwed up girl on the heels of Cousin Annie. Both of us dumped on her, as if a crippled woman and her spinster school teacher sister on pensions were better able to handle troubled teens. Annie and I were both carrying so much baggage, rebounding from so much trauma, yet so was Grandma. She never truly recovered from the murder of her own child, Aunt Emmy - Annie's mom, any more than Annie and I had. We were traumatized and grieving each in our own way.

Auntie Te seemed to be the only person who just kept going. I can still see her purposeful, determined walking - one foot in front of the other. Sometimes I catch myself walking just like Auntie. It makes me smile. She wore her sensible black lace-up oxfords with the thick heels, her cotton print dresses or slacks with a tailored blouse and a cardigan sweater. Her hair was short and gray. She wore silver wire-rimmed spectacles and always had her nose in a book. She'd write poetry, short stories or was found managing the house finances with a pencil gripped between her teeth. She managed the business side of running the house and recorded books for the blind in her spare time. Her life was always purposeful. She retired after forty-nine years of elementary school teaching and quit before her fiftieth year. "I don't want anyone to make a fuss," she firmly stated leaving no room for argument.

In the weeks that followed my arrival back at Grandma's in '61, I'd go horseback riding with Annie up on the trails in Griffith Park. After dinner we'd walk up to get a chocolate malt at Thrifty's, which was next to the old famous Schwab's Pharmacy where Lana Turner was purported to have been discovered. We'd pass by the house of Alan Hale, Jr. the actor who played the Captain on Gilligan's Island. At that time of day, he was always out on his porch watering his hanging plants and he'd always wave at us. We helped Auntie Nor Nor across the street dig worms for her injured birds that she always seemed to have in cages rehabbing. I was having a lovely summer reconnecting with my earliest childhood memories. Sat, our old gardener, was happy to have me back all grown up. It was like old times, for a while.

But when my footlocker arrived filled with everything I'd ever owned and a check for $100 made out to Grandma, the bottom dropped out of my world. I realized I'd been thrown away without any concern for my own wishes, just as they'd done to Annie. The money was undoubtedly out of my own small inheritance from my birth dad, although I didn't realize it then. Finally, it dawned on me why my mother was in tears as she walked me onto the plane. She already knew. The betrayal cut me like a knife. It was a conspiracy the whole family had been in on and I was the only one who was in the dark. Mom in her old age, vehemently denied it. "Of course, we told you!" she said indignantly. No one acknowledged responsibility.

I fell into a deep state of despondency, deeper than I'd experienced since the three rapes. It was the first time I'd been away from home when I wasn't wanted back. Abandoned and betrayed, I was swallowed up in the blackest mood I'd ever experienced. The hurt was so deep, that it turned to rage. I could barely get out of the chair at Grandma's. I just sat for days staring at nothing, hating them all and wondering what in hell I was going to do.

Auntie Te tried to have me write about it. She told me I could still get my high school diploma if I just wrote a simple composition about my year away at school in New York. She had a teacher friend who could arrange it. I thought, "Really? You have no idea!" There was no way I could tell anyone what had happened to me in New York - or D.C. I certainly couldn't imagine telling her or her nice friend about it! There was no cleaned-up version that I could construct.

Grandma then handed me the L.A. Times Classified section and highlighted a couple of salesgirl positions. She said I needed to go get a job. Never having had a job, my stomach cramped as I went off for an interview to the Broadway-Hollywood Department Store on the verge of diarrhea. I got a part time sales position and made little more money than my bus fare. To make matters worse, the store manager called me into his office to take a phone call. It was June's daughter, Lani, my childhood pen pal. We had always talked about going to Columbia University together and becoming roommates when we grew up. Lani was calling from Los Angeles International Airport on her layover from Honolulu. She was on her way to New York City to attend

Columbia University. There are no words to describe how left behind I felt.

Auntie Nor Nor was the only person to whom I confided anything at all. She knew how depressed I was and how stifled I felt after a more sophisticated lifestyle. I loved jazz and so did her son, Ralph, so she suggested that he take me to a jazz club in Hermosa Beach for the evening. Grandma was trying to push me to date the pimply-faced Church Youth Group Leader who was my age, because he was so nice to her. I preferred his crazy Argentinian roommate with the Vespa, laughing and zipping wildly around the streets of Hollywood.

When I told Grandma that Ralph was taking me out for the evening to hear some jazz, she got totally hysterical and started screaming at me. "You're going to turn out just like Aunt Emmy! You're going to wind up just like Aunt Emmy!!!" I guessed she meant dead. I felt as though I'd just been cursed and it pushed me over the edge.

I had a girlfriend or two I'd met at the department store where I worked so it gave me a good cover story whenever I wanted to go out in the evening. There was a local jazz club a few blocks from Grandma's house on Sunset Boulevard we went to and I'd become acquainted with the emcee and decided to move in with him. I can't recall if he asked me to or I just did it. I packed a suitcase and spun a story that I was overnighting with a girlfriend from work and left. I'm sure they didn't believe my story, but they felt powerless to stop me. I didn't return. I moved in with Larry the emcee, but didn't stay long after he started quoting Jehovah's Witness literature and reading Bible scripture to me in bed.

I found my own little studio apartment tagged onto the back of an old wood-framed house on a hill in Echo Park for $30 a month on Manzanita Street. My landlady was an elderly Jewish woman, who dressed a lot like Golda Meir, lived with her mustachioed spinster daughter. My apartment had one room, a kitchen, a very small bathroom and a screened porch. There was a walkway down the side of the house and the whole place was nestled amongst the trees and bushes. The strains of Rhapsody in Blue played by a neighbor boy on his alto sax filtered through the foliage in the evenings and suited my mood. The best part was during Hanukkah when they invited me upstairs for Seders.

I got fired from my sales girl job because I called in sick all the time. I started hanging out at a local coffee house called the Xanadu on Melrose Avenue. I hoped I could figure something else out from there. The Xanadu reminded me of Greenwich Village in New York, and I was homesick. The walls were lined with floor to ceiling bookcases. There were old stained sofas, easy chairs and scratched up coffee tables with chess sets in constant use. Bookish tweedy guys hunched over their next chess move and engaged in political and literary discussions. Jazz, classical music and Dylan were played on a record player on the back shelf near the coffee urn and coffee was a dime a cup on the honor system. I'd found my milieu at last.

Chapter 31
Manzanita, Xanadu and the Balladeer

Living in Los Angeles was a culture shock. I had no idea how to make a living. My training was in live theater but the so-called professional theaters in L.A. seemed more amateur than our little acting group in Connecticut, plus they weren't paying. I knew nothing about the film industry and didn't know where to begin learning. I was still rebounding from being thrown out by my folks and as I understand it now, I was experiencing a lot of post-trauma behavior.

Even though I was deeply depressed, once I began hanging out at the Xanadu, I began feeling a lot more content about life on my own. I was making friends at the coffee house and was finding other distractions. I put up big travel posters on my kitchen walls, painted my kitchen table and chairs a matte black. The guys from the Xanadu were looking for a place to gather and play poker so I opened my kitchen to them one night a week. I'd cook big pots of chili or spaghetti and they'd bring a big jug of red house wine since I was still too young to buy it myself in California. At the end of the night, they'd cut the pot for me. I made enough to pay my rent without a whole lot left over, but enough to get along.

In the Seventies the Xanadu was profiled in the L.A. Times Magazine in an article about the cool coffee house scene in L.A. during the Sixties. They talked about the notorious faux chess game that some of the guys had rigged to get even with a haughty young chess player who fancied himself quite the champion. It was well publicized. I was there behind the scenes with the organizers who were the same guys who played poker at my apartment. One of the guys actually was a chess champion, but not Monty, the tweedy guy who posed as the challenger. It was a major farce. There was a dais set up in the midst of the Xanadu with a table, two chairs, chess board, a boom mic and lights. Monty sat facing the kid who had his back to the serving area in the kitchen. There was a duplicate chess board set up there with the real chess master matching each move. The moves were announced loudly and Monty would take exaggerated amounts of time, chin in hand dramatically pondering his next move until the real chess master held up a huge sign with the next strategic move clearly printed out. Everyone was in on it, except the kid, of course. Monty won and the joke was revealed. For the most part it was taken in good nature. We, certainly, all had a good laugh.

It also mentioned a young folk singer named Hoyt Axton whose mother, Mae, co-wrote Heartbreak Hotel with Elvis Presley, and who had his eye on a young girl, Victoria Valentino, who would later become a Playboy Playmate. My mother sent me the article while I was on my walkabout in the Seventies. Reading about it all sitting under an apple tree in an Oregon orchard was surreal. It was like reading about characters in a play from someone else's life.

The Xanadu was the place where I crossed paths with the men who would change the course of my young life forever. A professional photographer named Harry Drinkwater was one. But it was folk singer Hoyt Axton, who invited me on another trip that gave me a very different perspective.

I became his *old lady* for a short while as we toured the various coffee houses throughout the northwest in 1962. We drove from The Drinking Gourd in San Francisco, to the Green Spider in Denver, Colorado, to Grogan's Saloon in Salt Lake City. I learned my first basic chords on the guitar from Hoyt and began putting my poetry to music. Hoyt began scribbling lyrics to his song *Greenback Dollar* on a torn piece of envelope on the back of the blue and white '53 Plymouth he was driving when we pulled to the side of the road for a break. Hoyt's first LP was recorded by then and he was waiting for its release. It was, and he was, *The Balladeer*.

For days we drove through the Rockies and all through the night with little or no sleep just to get to the next gig. Another folk singer had tagged along and rode with us in the backseat. We had little to no money and were living on one peanut and honey sandwich on white bread and a mug of milk a day. Sometimes he'd barter with a roadside diner owner for a mug of coffee for each of us and a bowl of hot chili in exchange for a song or two. In between times he'd be popping pills into his mouth and mine, drinking his Cherry Kijafa that he carried in his leather wine bota slung on the rearview mirror. He said the pills were so we wouldn't be hungry and we could stay awake all night driving. He said they were like the NoDoz that I used to take in high school when I had to stay up all night studying for exams.

I remember sitting up so wide awake one whole night behind the steering wheel while Hoyt snored. His massively heavy head weighed down on my lap cutting off the blood supply to my legs, but I couldn't make him move. The other folksinger was passed out in the back seat. It was so bloody lonely in the very dark, high Rocky Mountain peaks, and I was buzzed. I sat there and waited till I'd begin to see the headlights of a semi coming up over the ridge getting brighter and closer. Once they were adjacent to our car I'd wave like crazy. I couldn't tell if anyone ever waved back, but it made me feel less alone. Eventually dawn came and we'd get moving again.

When we arrived in Salt Lake City too early, we went on to Denver because Hoyt had heard of a coffee house there called The Green Spider that had a stage. Once we arrived the owner let us stay in a big old rambling house where the other performers stayed on their way through town. We got in so late at night that it was locked up and no one answered our knocks on the door. We slept at the top of a flight of stairs that were out of sight but barely protected from the bitter cold night winds. We used his big old guitar case as a pillow and covered ourselves with newspapers.

Next morning, we were let into a big attic room with lots of other wayfarers who all shared the one dirty clawfoot tub in the bathroom. The owner of the coffee house was so impressed by Hoyt that we were invited to his and his wife's house for dinner that night. Hoyt was invited to perform the next couple of nights while I passed the hat. He sang *One Grain of Sand*, *Whisky in the Jar*, *Black Girl*, *Swananoah Tunnel*, *Midnight Special* and *500 Miles*. I seriously related to *500 Miles*, *"Not a shirt on my back, not a penny to my name, Lord I can't go home, well - this - a- way..."* He always captivated his audience with his commanding presence and down-dirty, gritty delivery. We made just enough change to get to Salt Lake City and I stashed it in my zipped-up change purse in my backpack.

The next day we hung out at the guitar shop next door so he and the guitar maker could talk about instruments. Hoyt told me to go in the back and make a couple of sandwiches with what we had left of our peanut butter, so I did and brought his to him and I had mine in hand. He looked at me and asked, "Where's the one for John?" the owner of the shop. I was taken aback. I hadn't made one for him because we didn't have another slice of bread. I hadn't eaten all day and the shop owner didn't look as if he'd ever missed a meal. It didn't occur to me that I was expected to make a sandwich for him, too.

Hoyt whacked me across the face right in front of the guy. I handed the shop owner my sandwich but he refused it. I lost my appetite and went into the back room. That really caught my attention. That was when things shifted for me. That was the third time I'd ever been slapped in the face. The first time was my mother, the second my father. I wasn't having it. I put on my *mask*. I stopped talking and stopped showing a reaction.

The folk singer who had traveled with us to Denver decided to go his own way when we left, so for the first time, we drove off down the highway alone. Hoyt stopped at a gas station to get a fill up so we could make it to Aspen before we headed to Salt Lake. When I reached into my case for our money, it was gone. Hoyt accused me of not hiding it well enough. It was obvious that the folksinger we'd been riding with had split with our cash. Hoyt told me to hand over my 35 mm camera that Bugsy had given me as a going away present when I left New York and he traded it for the gas.

We drove on to Aspen, Colorado on our way to Salt Lake City. Hoyt had heard that Travis Edmonson of the folk duo, *Bud and Travis*, was performing there and he wanted to connect. When we got there, he and Travis went skiing, leaving me in the lodge with his wife, Carmen, and no money to buy even a cup of coffee. I was so pissed at him over my camera that I didn't speak to him all the way to Salt Lake. Once there at Grogan's, he and the pretty, red haired head waitress started vibing off one another. When he told me they hadn't provided enough accommodations for more than the performers, I figured he had that waitress on his mind. He bought me a ticket on the next Greyhound back to L.A. I rode that bus all the way back feeling pretty bleak.

I learned a few things from Hoyt on that trip, but the positive ones were the few basic guitar chords that I learned to play. I acquired a guitar and began to set my poetry to music. In spite of everything, I started writing and singing my own songs. I found an outlet for my thoughts, feelings and observations.

Once I returned to my Manzanita Street apartment, Judy the dulcimer player who had been staying at my pad while she was playing at the Troubadour asked if she could stay a while longer until she got another gig. I said, "Sure."

Chapter 32
Louie! Louie!

Judy came home one night with a blind black folk singer named Don Galloway. He was led by another black guy who said he was from Cuba by way of New York. His name was Louie. He had a New York accent spiced with a Spanish phrase or two. He had deep dark chiseled mahogany features and he moved like a big cat. He was thin and wiry and said he had once danced with a black modern dance troupe, the Katherine Dunham Dance Company, when he lived in New York. He had on a tweed jacket with a narrow-brimmed tweed hat that he wore on a slight angle. He had a gray textured button-down collared shirt. He was rather dashing, sophisticated and we shared memories of my favorite city.

They camped out for a couple of days and everyone was in the zone smoking a lot of weed, talking about our lives and life in general. Louie cooked Cuban food and regaled us with stories about recipes from his childhood. We played music, danced and confided in each other. Judy and Don moved on but Louie kept coming back. We'd go for drives and talk and seemed to have a lot in common. And the attention was nice.

Louie showed up at my door one morning after our days-long marathon jamming sessions. He said, "Give me your Italian knit suits. Your hemlines are too long for this season. Let me take them to the tailor for you." I was a bit surprised yet oddly comforted, because that's what my parents did with all my hemlines every Fall in preparation for the new school year.

I was used to having my hemlines altered every Autumn. That's the way it was in the Fifties. The hemlines and styles changed every Fall. My parents, holding their yardstick with pins between their teeth, would stand me on a stool in the middle of the living room while I turned slowly as they carefully adjusted my hemlines on each skirt that came out of the attic trunk for the winter. Mom would hem my skirts by hand while she sat in her usual place on the sofa in front of the fireplace after dinner. It seemed like the most natural thing in the world for me to hand over my clothes to Louie to have them taken to the tailor. I was actually touched. That simple action that bespoke of home, endeared him to me. He took over my life in no time.

Hoyt came back expecting me to be waiting for him with bated breath. I wasn't. I had moved on. He had sealed our fate with that slap across my face and taking my camera. I was not having him back. He was furious going around my back doors and windows in the middle of the night banging on them and demanding to be let in. I went outside finally amid all his shouting. We argued loudly on the front walk and I told him to get lost, but he never forgave me. He wasn't used to being blown off.

Louie showed up one day and said, "Go brush your teeth. You have morning mouth. Meet me in the car." He was driving a white sedan of some kind. He let me drive and directed me up the winding roads into Griffith Park towards the Observatory. It was a gray wintery day. He said, "Pull over here." It was a turn-out in the road surrounded by shrubs, deciduous trees growing amid the occasional palm and very tall, wild grasses. It was beautiful. We sat and looked at the nature around us listening to music on the car radio, idly chatting. It seemed that he had something on his mind though. He was not someone who spent too much time in casual conversation outside of our occasional socializing with friends from the Xanadu. He always seemed to be on a mission, taking care of business, New York-style vibe, quick-moving energy. I liked that about him.

He looked at me intently and said, "I love you." It caught me totally off guard. I wasn't sure what to say. I stared at him and dared to whisper, "Do you mean marriage - children?" "What did I say?" he said. I took that as a *yes*.

Just then, the winds picked up, the sky darkened, the tree tops began waving wildly back and forth. The tall grasses were being whipped violently by sudden high winds. The clouds turned black and they were moving fast all of a sudden. There was ear-splitting thunder and quick flashes of lightning. I saw it as an omen of some sort, even then. "Danger! Danger! This is a warning." The synchronicity of the weather picking up almost on cue had a dark energy about it, but instead of paying attention and running the opposite direction, I felt a sudden passionate karmic intensity about it all. It called up images of Wuthering Heights and Heathcliff on the moors. I was desperate for someone to love and need me in their lives. My parents obviously didn't and I was at sixes and sevens about where to go next. Louie was giving me direction. He seemed to care - and I needed someone to care.

As a result of the commotion at my apartment, I was evicted from my little studio on Manzanita Street. The guys playing poker in my kitchen every Wednesday night, Hoyt bellowing, Louie *"The Shvartze,"* as my elderly landlady called him, being a frequent visitor upset her. Additionally, my mother had assigned her old Belgian sculptor boyfriend from her early wartime USO days to be my guide and protector upon my arrival in L.A. Since he used to bounce me on his knees when I was little and bring me dolls, he was one of my *uncles*. Once I was grown up, he made unwelcome advances and became infuriated when I pushed him away. He broke into my kitchen window, stepped from the outside stairs into my kitchen sink and yelled at me. He called me a whore and demanded I give him back a sweet little dress he had given me when I first arrived. He said he was going to give it to a virgin. I guess not wanting his tongue forced down my throat offended him. I was in utter shock. It was all too much for my landlady and her gray-haired mustachioed spinster daughter upstairs. It was all too much for me, too.

Louie packed up my belongings and I found myself back at Grandma's for a while. Neither she nor Auntie Te were at ease with Louie's visits. The terse, snippy, side-swiping remarks became intolerable. I made our friend Harry move me into Louie's house down on Wilshire near MacArthur Park. He resisted and I think he knew what I was walking into but wouldn't actually come out and say it. I thought he just had his designs set on me. He had made that fairly obvious, but he was my mother's age. I loved him as a friend, loved being his photographic model, but I never felt romantically towards him. I probably would have overwritten his concerns anyway. I was going to be with someone who said they loved me, and that was all I cared about. I wanted to be free of the insults, personal attacks and hurtfulness inflicted on me by my family.

I was stubbornly bouncing off of everything and everyone. All the signs were there with Louie but I was a nineteen-year-old rebel with braces on my teeth and a lot of pain in my heart. I had lots of screaming going on in my head and my decisions were purely reactionary.

Chapter 33
Into the Breach
1963

When I first moved in with Louie, I saw the shock on his face, but he didn't turn me away, so I just established myself in his life feeling quite entitled. After all, he'd said he loved me and to my young mind that meant marriage and children. Thinking back, I'm appalled at what I did and I wonder where I got the gumption. Harry Drinkwater visited regularly and Louie had become infatuated with the idea of becoming a photographer and with Harry's encouragement he began building a dark room on the screened back porch of the house and studying every photography magazine he could get his hands on. Louie turned out to be a highly skilled carpenter and the dark room was incredible. Stacks of photography magazines were piling up and Louie walked around with his reading glasses on his nose poring over all the articles. Harry and he became inseparable and discussed photography constantly. I became their model. It was a lot of fun trying on different costumes, different poses, moods and shooting at different locations. Harry had friends whose homes had wonderful contemporary architecture and many of my most famous shots were taken by Harry at those locations. Their partnership grew daily. They began putting their heads together, muttering to each other, looking at me, then back to conferring with each other. We were taken to exhibits of Harry's photographer friends, poetry readings of

Langston Hughes' work. We were living a wonderful artistic life and I was completely happy.

His friends, the Varones, came over frequently and I began babysitting every day for their little 4 year old girl, Mandy Sue. Louie played his conga drums when he could get them out of hock. But, when he didn't have them, he'd get all the pots and pans out of the kitchen cupboards and C-clamp them to a tall metal stool and we'd all immerse ourselves in the beat. He was an incredible drummer. I'd never heard such complex rhythms and counter rhythms. I still hold every drummer I hear to the very high bar he set, and I'm always disappointed. He was brilliant at so many things.

He told everyone that he learned from his uncle the famous Cuban drummer, Mongo Santa Maria, with whom he lived in Spanish Harlem as a young man when he jumped ship from Cuba. I later discovered he told so many lies that I am still not sure about the truth in anything he ever said. But at the time it was fun and I believed it all.

Louie cooked Cuban style *frijole negros*, deep fried *pompano* and baked *platanos fritos*. We'd smoke weed, eat and dance. Because weed was a felony then, Louie had us all play a game standing in front of the bathroom mirror convincing the person in the mirror that we weren't high. Harry was always there photographing us all dancing and enjoying life. It was a good time in our lives. It never occurred to me to ask how he was paying the bills.

We met Moe McEndree, who became like a brother to me for the rest of his life, at a cocktail party of some small-time film producer named Hal Marshall. Moe was the producer of John Casavettes' black and white landmark film,

Shadows, when it first came out. I had seen it on Times Square before I left NYC and it had left quite an impression. Blues singers Sonny Terry and Brownie McGhee were there, smoking and picking guitar, playing mouth harp. Lightnin' Hopkins was jamming with Brownie and Sonny. Being immersed in the Blues was a new high.

My first image of Moe is forever burned in my memory. He was sitting on the floor cross legged in a dark corner centered in an inverted cone of light. He was wearing black slacks and a black turtleneck. His short strawberry blonde crew cut and Kansas farm boy face somehow didn't fit the surroundings, but he and Louie began talking and Moe was soon a constant pal. In time we'd meet all of his Cassavetes troupe, including John who smoked a lot of weed with us. Moe loved dancing free-form as much as I did, so we'd dance together while Louie played drums. Those early Sixties impromptu Beatnik happenings were filled with a unique energy that I've never experienced since.

Meanwhile Louie constantly studied his photography books and magazines. There were constant discussions with Harry about f-stops, lighting, the best 35 mm, Hasselblad and 'still' cameras. I heard the word *Playboy* begin to crop up in their conversations. It was supposed to be a magazine that would put them on the map as photographers. I would be their model. At this point the focus of our modeling sessions changed. We were now shooting semi-nudes, then nudes. I didn't really think anything was wrong with it. After all, Willy Pogani's wife was his model - and my dad's nudes always had breasts that looked suspiciously like my mother's. This was art and we were artists living the creative life.

Louie took me to a dentist who removed my braces and for the first time since my grown-up teeth grew in, I had perfect teeth. I smiled at myself in the mirror every time I went into the bathroom and I could finally begin smiling in the photographs Harry was taking of me.

After Louie and Harry were satisfied with the selection of photos they submitted them to *Playboy Magazine* - the magazine I'd never heard of - the magazine I didn't know was such a big deal. They were sure it would secure their status as photographers. Very soon after that I was informed by Louie that I had been accepted as a Centerfold and things moved very rapidly. The studio shoot date was set for a couple of weeks from then and everyone was excited. I kept thinking, "I hope my dad doesn't find out about this because he'll kill me." The big disappointment though was that Harry, nor Louie, would be the photographer. My shoot was turned over to Mario Casilli, Playboy's West Coast staff photographer. Harry seemed to disappear from the scene and I didn't see him again for quite some time.

I found out years later when we reconnected that Louie had absconded with the finder's fee and insult to injury, Harry never got credit for the iconic photos that Playboy published. They were credited to Mario. Harry never got over it.

We went to Baja for a long weekend to celebrate with the Varone's and I saw utterly shocking things that first night in Tijuana night clubs that I never in my wildest imagination could have conceived. On the second day I became a tequila shot aficionada and we got married with the Varones at our side. On the third day we all came down with paratyphoid. I'd never been so sick. It took me months before I could eat anything with oil in it again, but we were married and life seemed to be on an upswing as we anticipated my first photo shoot with Mario.

We even returned to Baja with Moe for another tequila-wild weekend trying to find and secure a location for the next Cassavetes film. We wound up being nearly arrested and Moe, who didn't speak Spanish, slammed his Screen Actors Guild card down on the desk of the Chief of Police, grandly demanding our release in pigeon-lingo. It worked and we were allowed to leave. We jumped in our car and sped towards the border so fast looking back every minute till we got into San Diego! We had lots of stories to tell about that trip - stories that were a lot more fun in retrospect.

Chapter 34
A Reality Check

One day Louie told me to pack an overnight bag, because we were going away for the weekend. He said we'd be spending time with a business associate of his, a metal sculptor and his wife, Bob and Arlene, out *in the Valley*. Louie said they were planning an art exhibit through his personal connections with an art gallery owned by a famous actor. At the time, I had no reason to doubt him.

I packed a few things for the weekend, locked up the house and we left. The sculptor lived in Canoga Park. It might have been Outer Mongolia as far as I knew. I had no idea where we were. His wife, Arlene, had short dark hair and doted on her two black and white, long-haired cats. Her husband was busy talking business all the time with Louie, in the midst of his many abstract metal sculptures. Arlene and I just hung out drinking coffee, playing with the cats and Louie would sometimes photograph us with the sculptures.

My first hint of Louie's temper was when we were watching television that weekend and there was a documentary showing Queen Elizabeth's wedding to Prince Philip. I, who had been raised by a mother of English descent, who taught me to revere the Queen and our British heritage, choked up at the pageantry of it all. I was telling Arlene that as a nine-year-old girl, I had written to the Queen on the occasion of her coronation and had been enthralled when I received a thank you note from her, written, of course, by her Lady-in-Waiting.

To my surprise, Louie became utterly enraged. He began tirading about the Imperialist British and touting Fidel Castro's revolution. He ranted on until his eyes became reddened slits in his darkening face, and he was becoming quite wicked looking. I burst into tears and locked myself in the bathroom.

The next day I was told that we would be staying another week as he had more business to accomplish setting up the exhibit. I overheard Louie telling Bob, our sculptor host, that he managed actor Raymond Burr's art gallery. I was puzzled because I'd never heard anything about it before. As the next two days ensued, I overheard endless streams of stories that Louie was spinning that I knew to be obvious lies. Suddenly I realized that he was scamming them out of all of their savings. I was indignant and morally outraged. I really liked these people who were easygoing, regular folks with high hopes just trying to make ends meet. Arlene and I had bonded immediately, probably over her cats, and I knew that they were putting up all their cash on this potential art exhibit. I felt compelled to warn them.

I took the sculptor aside and told him of my suspicions. When Louie's con went sour after the sculptor confronted him, Louie took me outside to have a few words. I knew he was furious but I knew I had done the right thing. He began lecturing me and I felt smaller and smaller as if I had done a terrible thing by telling the truth. Louie's voice began escalating in volume and intensity until all of a sudden, I found myself face down in the dirt looking up at Louie in disbelief. It happened so fast that I hadn't seen his hand strike out. The impact took the air out of me. He grabbed me by the hair and yanked me to my feet - and told me to keep my mouth shut.

Had I known how to leave him right then and there, I would have, married or not. But with no money, no car and no guarantee that Grandma and Auntie would even take me back, I hatched a plan instead.

I was booked to shoot the Centerfold with Mario Casilli in his Playboy studio on Highland Avenue in Hollywood within a day or two. It was the perfect excuse to go back to our house to get a change of clothes for the photo shoot. I decided to ask Arlene to drive me to our house to help me do that. My idea was that once I got there, I would have her help me pack up all my belongings in her car and drive me to Grandma's. Once I was safely at Grandma's I would call Playboy and cancel. I wasn't sure what I'd do next but I knew I wasn't going back to Louie.

Casually, Arlene and I left for the Wilshire house. I was using all my composure not to create suspicion. I decided that I wouldn't reveal my plan to her until after we got to the house. We arrived and parked, but when we walked up on the porch, we saw a big padlock on the front door. There was a huge eviction sign in the window. My heart dropped into my shoes. I couldn't believe it. I peered through the windows and peeked into my bedroom. Instead of seeing my belongings inside as I had left them, there were rows of washing machines, stoves and refrigerators. I had no idea what to say or think. I was so humiliated in front of Arlene, and didn't know how to explain what we were seeing.

Where had my closet full of beautiful clothes gone? Where were my Shetland wool sweaters and my mother's tweed skirts that, I'd inherited from her college days. It crossed my mind that my three-piece Italian knit suits that Saalem sent me from Rome were never returned from the tailor as Louie promised. I was beginning to *get it*. My Evan-Picone silk blouse that my mother bought me for my seventeenth birthday, my beautiful black silk peau de soie gown that I wore to a dance at Cherry Lawn Prep; my first pair of high heels, my Capezio flats, scarves, lingerie - my most precious books, all my record albums, my portable record player all gone. And my very good jewelry; my string of pearls, my gold filigree seed pearl bracelet, all gone - and the string of turquoise beads from Willy Pogani's wife.

It all started sinking in; my gold and blue topaz ring from Grandma Grace, a small aqua cloisonné pendant with a pink rose in the center on a sterling silver chain, a natural pearl necklace that looked a bit like a fang on a gold chain both that my birth father, Jim, had given me before he left for the war - gone. Gone was the sterling silver charm bracelet that my parents added to each Christmas with its large cluster of charms - each one represented every Christmas morning of my childhood.

On Christmas Eve after I went to bed, Daddy would carefully pry open a walnut, remove the nut meat, pad the interior with cotton, nest my new charm inside and glue the nut back together. Then, he'd throw it into my stocking with a handful of other mixed nuts and it was my Christmas morning challenge trying to find which nut harbored my new charm.

There was a book I'd received as a gift on my seventeenth birthday that was my treasure. It was from my mother's best friend, the daughter-in-law of a very famous Shakespearean actor, Walter Hampden, who lived up the road. He had his own theater in New York. I had been gifted with his playbook of Shakespeare's *The Merchant of Venice* on my seventeenth birthday. He directed and played the character of the Duke of Venice. It had all his handwritten stage directions scribbled in the margins. The inscription read, *"T'was said that Portia was only seventeen when she flummoxed Shylock and saved Antonio. Happy 17, Sweetie!"*

I was in so much shock, I stood there bereft, gutted. All my belongings and childhood treasures - simply gone. My entire life, my childhood, my identity as I knew it, was wrapped up in everything that had been confiscated. Being stripped of everything I owned was like one more slap in the face. It was becoming a pattern.

Arlene wrote down the telephone number on the eviction notice and handed me a dime. I found a pay phone on the corner and called the landlord. It was a very hot dry dreadful day and amid the deafening traffic noise. I asked the landlord why the house was locked up and where my things were. He told me that Louie owed him $450 in back rent. I told him that I had no idea. He said, "Give me $450 and you'll get your stuff!"

I pleaded with him - instead of demanding. I didn't know what he did was illegal and it never occurred to me to call the police - or even threaten to call them. He refused to budge.

At that point I realized I had no choice but to return to Louie if I was going to get my things returned. My escape to Grandma's was thwarted. Arlene and I drove back to her house in silence.

I told Louie about the eviction notice, the padlock, what the landlord had said and done, thinking, of course, he'd be irate. I was sure that he would call him and storm over there to retrieve my things. I was wrong again. Later it hit me that he had orchestrated our whole "vacation." It was his get-away - and my things were barter. Initially it was too outlandish to imagine - but I hadn't lived with him long enough yet. I was still reeling from Hoyt exchanging my camera for a tank of gas. I had nothing left, not even my dignity.

Later that same day, my breasts were feeling a bit tender and I noticed that my waistband on my jeans was a little tight. All of a sudden it dawned on me that my period was late and my heart dropped. I was pregnant - trapped.

Chapter 35
Shooting the Centerfold

Like a lemming I allowed myself to be taken to the Playboy studio to shoot some candid shots the next day. I borrowed a dress from Arlene. It was blue and kind of a soft denim weave with a high neckline - not my style - the buttons barely stretched around my expanding body. Every time I look at the photo of me playing guitar on Playboy's *Centerfolds of the Century* trading cards, I'm wearing that dress. It is a constant reminder of deep personal loss and I still feel a painful sinking twinge in my heart.

The next day after that I was scheduled to shoot the Centerfold. My photographer, the iconic Mario Casilli, manned the only Playboy outpost on the West Coast. In those days all the shots were sent to Hefner who still lived in Chicago. Nothing could go forward without his artistic directions. His decisions were final. My original candid shots were taken on a Hasselblad and were 2 ¼" by 2 ¼" color transparencies. When the film was returned from processing it had a green tint and was unusable. There was no photoshop then, but Hef loved one pose and wanted it recreated in the studio with an 8x10 still camera and modifications that he directed.

He wanted my dark blonde, soft, wavy hair dyed black. The gentle-yellow, poofy-sleeved peignoir with the soft late afternoon sunlight filtering through the folds to become black lace. He wanted the brown Italian marble column on the grand palazzo staircase in the Hollywood Hills mansion, to be replaced by a white column. It changed the whole dreamy feminine ambience. Hef chose a classic Latin look that had every element of a modern Madonna that could easily have been an early Renaissance painting hung in the Louvre - or the Sistine Chapel. Unfortunately, it didn't create the same reverence. I hadn't met Hugh Hefner yet, but in that one photograph, he changed the entire trajectory of my life. I got typecast and to this day people think I'm Italian.

Since there was no time to have my hair properly dyed black, Louie went to the pharmacy and found black hairspray. It created the severe Flamenco hairstyle I wore that day. It also made my hair stiff. It reflected my dark mood. I felt like a statue made of stone. I was carefully posed and had to hold that position for hours with mini-breaks. It seemed to me during those hours that I had lost every last bit of control left in my life. I remember feeling like a slave standing on the auction block while others decided my life.

During my first break I wondered where Louie was. He was supposedly so interested in the photographic process, that it seemed odd for him not to be watching everything Mario did. I asked the photo crew. They told me he had gone out to his car for something, so I went to the back door and pulled back the little curtain on the window to see if the car was still there. It was nosed into the curb right in front of the door. He was sitting behind the wheel with his head tilted back with his eyes closed. At first, I thought he was napping, but then I saw the blonde head bobbing up and down over his lap. I almost vomited. It was his tall lanky blonde "photo assistant," with the crooked teeth who had recently attached herself to him. She must have arrived after I had been posed. I was filled with disgust and despair. From then on, they didn't hide their attachment and she became a regular fixture in our lives. The angrier and more resentful I became, the more she lorded it over me and the more domineering Louie became. She was assigned to guard me when he went out. I was on the verge of bolting. He saw it in the resentment filling my eyes and he was taking no chances. He wanted to make sure that when my paycheck arrived from Playboy, I signed it over to him. It soon became clear that she was his partner in crime and I wondered how long she had been part of his schemes and the entire picture - before I arrived on the scene or after? I discovered that she forged checks for him and got her more affluent friends to co-sign loans for his *photo studio*. I realized the studio was his latest scam. He used her to keep a close eye on me so I couldn't get away before he got all the money, he could out of me. I was now just his cash cow Playmate celebrity leverage for his latest scams and I had become inconvenient once I became pregnant. He was trading off my Playmate status.

"Why didn't you just leave?" I ask myself time and again. I remind myself over and over again that I was still a child pregnant with a black conman's baby before the Civil Rights Act and very alone in an unfamiliar city. I had no idea how to get around on my own. No money, no clothes of my own, no car, no friends - and a family who had made it clear that I was no longer wanted, in fact, I had heard I was disowned. I clung to the only person I knew who hung onto me - even if for all the wrong reasons. I was a multirape and childhood abuse survivor before we had ever met.

I was the proverbial sitting duck. Understanding the dynamics of Stockholm Syndrome now more than then helps somewhat. When Patty Hearst was captured and charged, I understood her completely.

I only say this time and again, not just for those of you who are reading this dark tale, perhaps judging me, asking the same questions I ask myself, but for myself. I repeat it not for you to forgive my sins of passivity or complicity, but to try to forgive myself. I still whip myself after all these years. Mea culpa - mea culpa - mea culpa. "Father forgive me for I have..." what... been an abused and abandoned child? How many Hail Marys do I get for that?

Forgiving oneself for being young, stupid and victimized is not an easy task. I think we all think we, coulda, woulda, shoulda, been able to do something to save ourselves, if only... but, if only what?

If only we had been us - now? Us with survival tools, a support system and understanding?

Chapter 36
Bun in the Oven

For Louie, my pregnancy was now the wrench in the works. I was a liability. Abortions were a felony then. Since I'd had one just before I met Hoyt, I knew how impossible it would be to do it again.

The first time I discovered I was pregnant I was on a road trip through the South and mainland Mexico with a pal in 1962. I knew it was from the jazz club emcee. There had been no one else after I broke up with him and there was no way I could complete that pregnancy. I asked my neighbor, a Registered Nurse, what I could do. She worked with a doctor in the ER at L.A. County Hospital and said he'd do it for me as a favor to her. I breathed a deep sigh of relief when he arrived in his copper-colored Mercedes convertible and took me to his zebra skin-rugged apartment to perform the procedure. He laid me on a mat on the floor and gave me an IV of what he said was sodium pentothal to relax me. It immobilized me. He climbed on me with his big rough beard pressing on my face, had sex with my inert body - and then moved me to his kitchen table and inserted a catheter into my cervix. It took four days before I began bleeding. He was at work at the hospital and called me throughout the day to have me check my own temperature and pulse. He instructed me to walk in the neighborhood as much as I could. Eventually, I began cramping until I passed a huge clump of what looked like liver in the toilet. I dug around in it trying to find something that I could identify as a fetus, but found absolutely nothing in the gory mess. When he arrived back at his apartment, he took me home without comment. No post-op instructions or post-op check-ups; no antibiotics and no conversation.

Welcome to a world without Roe v. Wade. Without a woman's right to choose her own life path, to own her own body. Women will be held hostage to nightmares like this and more. Abortions will always continue, as they always have. But they'll be under unsafe clinical conditions and women will be at the mercy of butchers, rapists and the proverbial crochet hook. I remember seeing gray-faced, blue-lipped, hemorrhaging girls back in the day who tried to do it themselves with whatever instrument they could insert; Girls on pain of imprisonment or death, who couldn't seek help to save themselves.

Louie began isolating me and starving me during my pregnancy. Perhaps, he hoped I'd miscarry. He told me I had to give the baby up for adoption - and he knew a doctor. I wondered how he so easily knew one. He dropped me off for my prenatal visits, warning me not to let the doctor know that my baby was racially mixed. He'd wait in the car then he'd drop me off in a motel somewhere in L.A. and go out for cigarettes. I wouldn't see him for days. I drank water out of the bathroom faucet. He took my few clothes and left me with the bare minimum - my scotch-taped, torn flip flops and a cotton shift with a torn shoulder strap. I was ashamed to go outside and had no idea where I was. When he finally came around, he'd bring a plate of cooked food and cigarettes, then disappear again.

One day out of sheer desperation, I asked the motel manager to use their phone. I'm not sure why I hadn't thought of it sooner. Embarrassed to be seen or admit I had a problem, I guess. They were very kind and talked to me about finding Jesus. I guess they thought I needed Him. I certainly needed something.

I called the Playboy studio office and shared an extremely limited bit of my situation with the receptionist. I had already shot the Centerfold so I was officially on their payroll, I suppose, though I hadn't gotten paid as yet. She told me to take a cab to the studio and Playboy would cover it. I wasn't sure what I would work out once I got there, but I hoped I could talk it over with them and figure out my next move. When I arrived Louie was waiting, looking annoyed. It seemed as though I was trapped again. I felt utterly out of control of the situation. I felt like I was the main character in the plot of a theatrical drama I didn't understand, yet simultaneously dismissed as a necessary nuisance. Everyone always seemed to know how to get hold of him, but me. They were dealing directly with him and I was completely kept out of the business discussion and the communication loop. I didn't even feel entitled to inquire. I just mindlessly, silently went along with it. It was like one of those horrible dreams where you try to scream and no sound comes out, like you're in a car plummeting over a cliff and you know you're going to die but you can't remove yourself from the inevitable doom. It didn't help that my belly was getting bigger daily, and I was looking more and more skeletal around it. I was feeling weak and often faint.

Chapter 37
Malibu, Tortillas and The Twist

From the Playboy office Louie silently drove me out to Malibu to a motel where he had been living while I was being held hostage in a West L.A. motel. I discovered that Louie and his 'photo assistant,' Ruella, shared a bungalow. He put me in a separate one alone and split his time between us. She was left to guard me when he was gone. It was a dawning nightmare. The motel was a cluster of one room bungalows near the entrance to Topanga Canyon with a Mexican restaurant next door. Right across the highway was the broad expanse of the Pacific Ocean. The sea air and awe-inspiring sunsets revived me for a minute. It was better than the motel in L.A. I had to find something positive in the situation that I could focus on and the ocean's open horizon and the shooshing of the waves were soothing. I was consciously trying to feel detached about the child growing within me, trying not to think about it being given away to strangers. I was trying to be optimistic about my centerfold issue being released and whatever professional success I was told would surely come of that. I was really grasping at straws.

Occasionally she'd go out to the cafe on the corner by herself and briefly leave me. I'm sure she figured I wasn't going anywhere - and she was right. I felt so entrapped mentally and was so uncomfortably pregnant, that I never felt I could get away anyway. I felt sure Louie would always find me whatever I did, wherever I'd go. I just lived in the moment-to-moment existence of my entrapment. She and I developed a strange relationship. I hated her more than I've ever hated anyone in my life, yet she was the only person I knew besides Louie and we shared him, so we had something in common. Louie was gone most of the time, so we had no choice but to try to co-exist as congenially as necessary.

I used to walk daily along the Pacific Coast Highway to maintain my sanity and one morning I passed two guys standing in the doorway of the Mexican restaurant. They looked at me and jokingly said, "Fine Playgirl you make." I laughed and threw back some silly *one-liner* not knowing what they actually meant until I opened the door to my empty bungalow. I found the new Playboy issue with my Centerfold tossed carelessly on top of the bedspread. That was how I found out that it had hit the magazine stands. Alone and deflated I laid down on the bed wondering what it all meant, and took a nap.

Ruella returned and was now staying in my room with me. Louie was gone most of the time by then doing whatever he did. Who knew? That night Ruella and I decided to go over to the Mexican restaurant. She had been crawling into the empty bungalows through the back windows facing the underbrush late at night. She broke into the coin machines that made the beds vibrate. On a good night we had enough to get breakfast at the corner cafe. At the restaurant we could get two tortillas for five cents and the guys often treated us to a beer. The bar area had a roaring fire in the fireplace where everyone sat and the camaraderie of those strangers was a distraction. That night in front of the fire I danced to Chubby Checkers singing *The Twist*.

I went straight to bed after we got back, but then I was jolted awake by a knock on the door. Ruella jumped up to open it and there was Auntie Nor Nor standing there. Uncle Martin was waiting outside in the car. She bustled in effusively hugging and kissing me and sat down on the edge of the bed all the while Ruella stood by the door eyeing us suspiciously.

Auntie Nor said she remembered my description of where I was during our last phone call and got Uncle Martin to drive her out to try to find me and bring me home. I was in shock. She pleaded with me in every way she could think of to leave with her. Completely unprepared I couldn't think what to do. Escape was at hand. Ruella was sending me threatening looks as I was being pulled more tightly into Auntie Nor Nor's arms. I wanted to just walk out with her, but I was afraid. It seemed that every time I had tried to leave in the past Louie always caught me and dragged me back into his web. The consequences of leaving Louie and having the baby across the street from Grandma and Auntie Te's were mind boggling. I stalled, torn, trying to decide what to do. I didn't want Auntie Nor to leave me, but I was too afraid to go with her. I kept imagining Louie showing up on Auntie Nor's doorstep possibly hurting someone I cared about - and then the shunning of my family across the street. So under Ruella's threatening intimidation, I looked down at my feet and mumbled, "No." Auntie Nor Nor, my life line, reluctantly left and I cried myself to sleep.

Chapter 38
A Son is Born and His Name is...

On one day I was Playboy's *Playmate of the Month, Miss September 1963* without any fanfare- and the very next morning my water broke at 6 a.m. and I went into labor. I didn't know what it was. I thought I'd wet the bed. I ran to the toilet and sat there expecting it to stop, but it didn't. Ruella was not there when I awoke, so I ran to the manager's office making mud puddles with each step. I stood there in terror, confusion and disbelief with my waters pouring down my legs.

The manager of the motel grabbed the nearest available person in her lobby to drive me to the hospital. I told the guy I was supposed to go to the UCLA Med Center, where the adoption doctor had made all my birthing arrangements. The adoptive parents would be waiting there to collect the baby. I didn't tell him all that so when I arrived at the hospital, I assumed it was UCLA. I didn't know I wasn't until I mentioned it to the nurse while she was prepping me for delivery. She snickered.

I delivered my son at 10:30 a.m. that morning on August 22nd at Los Angeles County Hospital in a crowded maternity ward. I was also the only white woman and the only woman giving birth for the first time. I was teased. The stories of my escapades in the Labor Room were told with good natured laughter by the mother of ten who was in the bed next to me having a breach birth without anesthesia. She mimicked me to all the other mothers as I was being rushed onto a gurney and raced into the Delivery Room, "Shit, Doctor! What's happening now!?"

I had dilated so rapidly, from two centimeters to ten that they were caught off guard. First time labors are historically much longer than subsequent ones, I was told. I attributed it to my childhood addiction for National Geographic Magazines with stories of Native American women and reading the Pearl Buck novels that Mom gave me. I had an idea what I needed to do. I remembered Pearl Buck telling the story of her protagonist squatting in the rice fields, giving birth, cutting the cord with a sliver of bamboo, wrapping her baby, slinging it against her bosom and going right back to work. I was going to ride that bronco. I resisted the nurses' ordering me to lie down flat on my back and I sat up cross legged just working with the muscle contractions the whole time, while the woman in the neighboring bed wailed. But they unnecessarily gave me a *saddle block* and an episiotomy while my very small 5 lb. 8 oz. baby boy's head was already emerging from my emaciated 116 lb. body.

Since it was a teaching hospital the doctor came around to examine everyone with a group of surrounding interns observing. To the doctor's chagrin and my later misery, I learned that he had stitched me up too far. As there were no secrets on that ward, everyone started chuckling when they overheard the doctor doing the '*Show and Tell*' for the interns. They had a field day with that! Hilarity broke out on the ward. "Baby! Tell 'em to stitch you ALL the way shut!"

Louie's adoption arrangements were to go into effect once I delivered the baby. The adoptive parents, a South American couple, were to pick him up as soon as he was ready to be taken home. They were paying the doctor who in turn was paying Louie to care for me during the pregnancy. While I never knew any of the arrangements at the time, I also never received care. Louie just kept the money. One more scam. He'd already had me sign over the $1,000 check for my centerfold and the several thousand that my mother sent closing out my birth father's war savings. I guess selling the baby was going to be his next big payday, but I hadn't realized that yet.

I lay there amongst all the joking veteran mothers surrounding me in two long facing rows of gray metal framed beds, disconsolately trying not to think about that little teensy thing they had brought into my line of vision as I lay on the delivery table. I thought about his huge wonder-filled eyes, his three little tufts of brown frizz that made me immediately think of Ferdie the Fox, a cartoon character from my childhood. They showed me his blue bruised-looking bottom as they turned him over, Mongolian spots, they said, then wrapped him back up and whisked him away to the Nursery. Someone told me that Mongolian spots were always on the tushies of children of color, and would eventually fade weeks after birth. It was all new to me and I was trying not to get emotionally attached. The less I knew the better.

The nurses and my wardmates urged me to go visit my baby in the Nursery. They didn't know he was to be adopted. I didn't want to see him. I didn't want to feel anything. I couldn't allow it. I felt dead inside.

It finally occurred to me that Louie was expecting his final payment once the baby was delivered. He was just keeping me around until the final installment. I was nothing more but another one of his *Cash Cows*. I was beginning to suspect by then that he had a stable of other women that he used to support him and when he was out, he was just making his rounds. I wondered how many other children he had. I didn't understand the implications of everything he did with me or Ruella for a long time, but in the end the chips all fell in place.

It took me a day of the nurse's urging before I finally walked over, moving slowly and in pain from the episiotomy stitches. My breasts were swollen, hot to the touch and hard as a rock and I smelled funky like old blood and sticky vaginal secretions. I wanted a hot shower badly. I stood looking through the window and had no idea which baby was mine. I had to wait until they pointed him out. I looked at him as if I was observing a stranger from a distance. I was engulfed in an endless gray fog of despair. I shuffled back to the ward where I was told that someone was picking me up. My clothes were handed to me and I dressed as if I was in a trance. I had no idea who would even know where I was.

I sat waiting and wondering. Ruella suddenly walked in. The nurse followed her and handed me my swaddled baby. I was confused, speechless. I didn't understand what was happening.

Ruella sneered at me and said, "Louie says you can keep him. They didn't want him. He's too dark. We've decided to name him Ramon Juan. Let's go."

I was in a daze. I hadn't allowed myself to even think of a name, but I hated that name - and the fact that she and Louie had made that choice for me was intolerable. But my brain just wasn't computing and so I passively signed discharge papers that the nurse shoved in front of me. It turned out that the birth certificate was amongst them. I slowly followed her out to the loading dock where Louie was waiting in a car I'd never seen before. I shuffled painfully in my tattered sandals. I looked down at this little alien, my newborn son, wrapped in his hospital-issue blanket, undershirt and diaper and had no idea what I was going to do with him or where I was being taken.

Louie never looked at me - or the baby. I was placed in the backseat with Ruella riding in the front and he drove without a word. He was pissed and I felt it. The baby and I were a nuisance and had thwarted his game. It was getting dark and I had the feeling that they didn't know where we were going either. Louie slowly drove down an empty street in a very shoddy looking neighborhood as if he was looking for an address. I learned that we'd been locked out of the beach bungalow in Malibu and what few belongings and baby clothes I'd accumulated were gone. I was ushered alone with the baby into a room fit for a derelict. He and Ruella took a separate room. We were in Venice Beach.

Chapter 39
Miss September ... In August

The motel Louie found was dirty, shabby and depressing. I laid there with gorged breasts, a baby who wouldn't latch on and who was crying desperately. I was crying right along with him. We were both inconsolable. Louie and Ruella's bed started banging up and down violently against the adjacent wall - and I lost it. I came unglued and started screaming. "Louie! Louie!!!" He angrily entered my room and descended on me. For a moment I thought he was going to hit me, but instead he impatiently tried to show me how to get the baby to suck. He obviously had more experience than I. I begged him to stay with us, but he turned and stalked out. The noise on the other side of the wall resumed.

Until that moment in my life, I had never had any idea how despondent I could become. I thought I had already experienced the worst I ever could. It was becoming a way of life. I was pretty sure it couldn't get any worse. After every event that stripped me of my autonomy, my self-esteem, my will, I thought, "This is my darkest moment."

He bounced me and the baby from motel to motel for over two months. He dropped us off, said he was going to get cigarettes and would then disappear for a couple of days. I was beginning to understand the code.

Sitting cross legged alone on a motel bed somewhere in South Central L.A. watching TV like a zombie with my two-month-old baby asleep in a bassinet, there was breaking news! The picture was interrupted and there was a lot of crazy turmoil, I couldn't make out. President John F. Kennedy had just been shot in his motorcade in Dallas, Texas. I watched it unfold, waiting. Jackie was climbing over the back of the car and there was chaos. No one was saying yet if the President was dead or not. I sat glued to the black and white staticky images. And then it was announced. The President was dead. I wept and wept and wept - for him, for his wife, for our country., for myself. Every unshed tear for myself and my baby poured out. I cried until I thought I couldn't cry anymore, but then I'd cry some more. I had no one with whom to share the horrible news with except a sleeping baby and a world from which I'd been cut off.

When Louie dropped off some rudimentary toiletries and diapers along with a plate of cooked food, I rushed to tell him about the President's assassination and all he could do was spout off his Fidelista rantings. I shut up. I had gotten used to being hungry by then. Lack of food hardly registered anymore but what I truly hungered for was someone I could talk to. The loneliness was unbearable. Louie frightened me, but I was dependent on him. He performed his responsibilities to me perfunctorily as if he was feeding his hunting dog in a cage. But he was still the father of my baby and he was, I thought, my husband.

I didn't know that Mexican marriages weren't legal in this country unless they were registered here. He, of course, knew but as long as I was in the dark, he was able to control all my money. It was years later that I had an "Aha!" moment and put it all together. When he could no longer collect from the adoptive parents, and there was a baby to support, he was angry. I was nursing and it was slowing down his game. He couldn't make money from my new Playboy celebrity, a celebrity that I had no idea existed. I was an actress and model and he was going to capitalize from it. He was impatient for me to wean the baby so I could go out on auditions, enjoy the Playboy celebrity life, so he could ride in on my coattails.

One day he arrived at whichever motel room he had us in and said he'd found a place on one of the Venice Beach canals, but Ruella had to rent it for us, because she was white. They wouldn't rent it to us if they saw him - or me with our dark-skinned baby. While Ruella's presence plagued me for the rest of the time I lived with Louie, this time was the one time I ever felt grateful for her presence. She secured a nice little pueblo style duplex with a backyard near the beach on the historic section of the Canals. Once we were settled in, he delivered his two toddlers from his ex-wife, Lilliana, whom I had never met. It was the first time he had ever brought Rico and Nita to me for more than a quick visit or a rare outing. This time they arrived with suitcases.

Suddenly I had three children under 4 years of age and I was barely able to care for myself. They were beautiful children who were very insecure and frightened. I wondered if he moved them from place to place as he did us, but over time I was sure he moved them from woman to woman to use them to get sympathy and leverage financial gain. He said their mother was dealing with a lot of racism where they lived and they'd become a problem for her - and her mother's young husband was fondling Nita. My heart went out to them. My energies were redirected to loving them and trying to make them feel safe and secure.

Once Louie had me and the children established, he ordered a diaper service, dropped off several *onesies*, a couple of bags of groceries and as usual *went out for cigarettes*. I was so exhausted that sometimes the baby would cry right next to me and I'd sleep through it all. When I'd be nudged awake, I'd find Ruella standing over me smirking, "Your baby's crying."

One day she was gone. Once I was alone with the children, I was much happier, but I was always in a holding pattern waiting for Louie to return with groceries. I waited and waited for him as we were usually running out of food. I had connected with this lesbian couple on the next canal, who had six kids between them and loved having Nita and Rico over to play, so they'd get the snacks while they were there. It was such a relief. We'd do laundry together and they'd give me advice about nursing my baby and how to wean him so I could go get a job.

Finally, when I ran out of what little food I had left and he still hadn't come home, I scrounged together a little change to make a phone call. The kids were with the neighbors, so I took the baby with me to the corner where there was a payphone. I had one telephone number for him, which was a miracle in itself. It was at a printing shop where he said he was working.

It was so hot when I stepped inside and closed the glass door, I thought I'd bake. I dropped in my few coins, sent off a quick prayer to the universe and dialed the number. It rang and rang as I stood waiting, holding the baby in one arm with my milk beginning to leak down the front of my blue and white checked cotton shift with the torn shoulder strap. Just when I thought no one was going to answer, a guy with a heavy Spanish accent picked up. "May I speak to Louie, please?" "Louie? Louie? Quien? Un momento," and he left the phone. I could hear him asking "Quien es Louie?" I was feeling frantic, running out of change, juggling a wet baby, oozing milk and feeling lightheaded from the heat.

As I waited, I looked out and saw a white Porsche with the top down, glide around the corner. It pulled up to the curb in front of the pay booth and parked. The driver was a serene looking guy with a long sleek white ponytail. He got out of his car and walked up to the booth while I was still waiting for the guy on the other end to return to the phone. *Porsche Guy* was dressed in white flowing Indian cotton pants and a white collarless tunic. He rapped on the door of the phone booth. The operator was asking me for more coins which I didn't have and I motioned him to wait.

Porsche Guy ignored me. I finally opened the door and pleaded with him, "Please, just give me another minute!" He looked at me with the most serene blue eyes I had ever seen. They caught the sunlight and were set like sapphires in his tanned, smile-creased face. I tried to look away, and then he said, "Victoria Valentino - You are the most beautiful woman in the world."

I was speechless and then the phone went dead. It was my first clue that being *Playboy's Miss September 1963 - Playmate of the Month* gave me a face recognizable from an isolated phone booth on a street corner in a shabby beach town. It felt out of reality... as if I existed with the baby in an alternate universe. My worlds were colliding and I had no idea what it meant, nor what to do about it. His name was Otho Pettijean and he invited me and the children to join him at his friends where he was visiting. They were just a couple of blocks from our house. We spent the day there and I felt so peaceful that I fell asleep sitting up in a chair nursing the baby. He woke me to say that it was cool running into me but he was returning to his home in Las Vegas. I watched him drive off and disappear around the next corner giving me one last wave. The kids and I walked home to an empty fridge and an empty house.

Chapter 40
On the Boardwalk

Louie finally came home with bags of groceries, but he was getting behind in the rent and he moved us to another motel. The children and I were becoming so attached. They were so small when he brought them to me that over time, they thought I was their real mother and called me Mama. I loved them as my own - it was impossible not to. They needed a lot of affection and I had a lot to give.

At the laundromat I began connecting with another racially mixed couple who had a toddler. I introduced the husband to Louie on one of his rare visits and we began talking about possibly sharing a two story Victorian white frame house that was walking distance to the beach. They were interested in renting it and if we shared the rent, it would make it doable. Louie and the husband seemed to like each other and they came to an agreement.

I loved the house when I saw it. It felt wonderful. We got together in the living room for dinner and wine on our first evening together. The bedrooms were upstairs and there was the prettiest dresser in ours that was painted soft butter yellow and the drawers were decorated with bowers of little pink hand painted roses. The room was spacious, airy and in the morning, it was filled with sunlight. I wanted to stay there forever. I hoped that we would finally be settled for a while with these lovely people. Over morning coffee Louie told them he had to go to the bank to get the remainder of our share of the rent - *and pick up some cigarettes*. My heart sank. He didn't come back.

I kept making excuses. They were getting more and more aggravated and I couldn't find the words to explain. I began hiding out in our room instead of trying to discuss the situation and come up with a potential solution. I was so fearfully ashamed that I couldn't confide in them. They kept asking when he'd be back with the rent. I kept stalling and hoping he would show up and do the right thing for a change, but as usual he didn't. I didn't even have money to buy food.

After the kids were asleep, I'd sneak out at night leaving the front door unlocked and run down to coffee houses on the boardwalk to beg them for a quart of milk. During the day I'd take the children walking along the boardwalk pushing the baby in his stroller. He was a silent child and was becoming weaker. I could see it. I mistakenly weaned him on the gay couples' advice, so I had no milk of my own to feed him and he wasn't eating real food yet. It was a big mistake.

It was the week before Christmas and it was bitter cold at the beach. The wind was whipping and it was almost dark and beginning to rain by the time I got the kids back to the house. We had been out panhandling as usual and returned shivering and wet. When we approached the front steps, I stopped short. Our belongings were bundled up in an old sheet sitting out on the porch. I knew there was no point in trying my key or knocking. They had reached their limit. Devastated and confused about what to do with very tired, hungry, cold and wet children, I walked us all back down to the boardwalk. We slept in the roofed gazebo that night. I covered them with my body trying to protect them from the cold wind. My fingers were numb and stiff trying to clutch my sweater around them through the night.

Three days before Christmas, with Baby Nito in his stroller and Rico and Nita hanging onto the handles, I tried to make a cheerful game out of it. We sang the new Beatles song, *I Want to Hold Your Hand*. It kept us together.

Back in 1963 Venice Beach was a place lined with retirement homes and lots of bundled up old folks sitting on benches along the boardwalk. Rico always had such a charming smile with his chipped little front baby tooth. The old people would call him over and hand him a quarter or a dime. We looked forward to those quarters. We could get three big day-old brownies for 25 cents to share between us. It was the only thing I could find to eat for a quarter that was enough to go around. I could get small cartons of milk to fill Nito's baby bottle with a little for us and that was it.

The night we were locked out was the coldest and rainiest ever. I was terrified about having to stay out all night in the gazebo again but I couldn't think of a solution. The gay couple with the kids had moved to another part of the city and I had no way of reaching them. By late afternoon the next day we were so cold and wet that I couldn't imagine what I was going to do. I went back to the house and knocked loudly on the door, but of course, no one answered. Our things were still there and too big to carry so I had to just bleakly walk away.

We went back down to the boardwalk. The gazebos were roofed but open to the air with built-in benches inside. At least we could sit and be protected from the rain. It was the second night we slept there. Again, I covered the children with my arms and body. It was utterly freezing. I never really slept because I was on alert all night, fearful of bad guys and the cops too. I was so chilled to the bone by dawn that my fingers barely bent and my knees and hips were painfully stiff. In the morning we just kept walking up and down the boardwalk panhandling. We got a few quarters - enough for a couple of more day-old brownies with some change left over for some milk.

As the day wore on, I sought out our familiar gazebo to sit out of the cold wet winds. I tried to figure out what to do next. I couldn't stop shivering and the children were not much better. They asked incessant questions that I couldn't answer. The baby fretted and I rocked him with his light flannel receiving-blanket tucked around him. We were not dressed to live outside in December beach weather. We sat out the worst of the wind, but we were warmer when we kept moving. The kids were tired and hungry and I had run out of ideas. I tried to make it fun for the kids, and we sang our little songs. But I was running out of games and energy. We just sat down exhausted in the gazebo again, and I was fighting tears. There was a guy who was watching us from the opposite corner of the gazebo bench and he began making small talk. I was leery at first, but our dilemma, the deep bone chill, hunger and solitude finally loosened me up and I heard myself pouring out everything I was holding inside - almost everything. There were things I still had no words for. I heard Louie's voice in my head even as I unloaded our plight, "Don't put your business on the street," he'd always warn. But I'd almost stopped caring.

"Well, I just happen to have a rental cottage not far from here that's vacant at the moment. I can let you stay there and help you sort things out."

I was floored. I didn't even question whether it was the right thing to do. I needed to get the kids out of the weather and some food into our stomachs before we passed out. He led us to his car, passed by our house and loaded our bundles into the trunk. Then he drove us up Rose Avenue a few blocks, turned into a dirt driveway and behind an apartment complex. There was a small white cozy-looking bungalow and there was even a lawn. Thinking about it brings me to tears even now.

Chapter 41
Christmas
1963

This man whose name I didn't even know, opened the front door for us, letting the rush of welcoming warmth embrace our chilled faces. The front room was so beautifully clean. He showed us the bedroom that had a double bed with clean bedding. White sheets, fluffy pillows and a big white comforter. I couldn't believe it. He dropped us off and said he'd be right back.

He returned with bags of groceries and a big pizza. Then he went back outside and carried in a great, big, aromatic Christmas tree that almost touched the ceiling. I burst into tears. The nostalgic smell of the pine from my childhood forays into the woods with Daddy to cut our perfect tree every year made me ache inside. I hadn't had a Christmas tree, or even celebrated Christmas since I'd left Connecticut.

His name was Irving and he was Jewish but he said he knew that the children had to have a Christmas tree. A Hanukkah bush from a Jewish Santa Claus - and our Christmas miracle.

I had no gifts to put under the tree and no ornaments but I had an idea. I looked through drawers in the kitchen and found a little sewing kit with scissors like the kind you find in hotels. There was white paper in the living room on a shelf even though there was no living room furniture.

The stub of an old Maybelline lipstick turned out to be perfect to color the shapes we cut out of the white paper for the tree. I found Q tips in the bathroom and dug out the dregs of the remaining lipstick to smear on the paper circles, stars, angels and trumpets that I cut. I threaded them with the needle and we tied them to the branches. There was aluminum foil in the kitchen, which made a perfect star for the top of the tree and I made a few round foil balls to hang for a little sparkle. The children were delighted. It may have been the most beautiful tree I'd ever seen - but also the very saddest.

The next day the kids and I took a walk to a thrift shop I found nearby. With a little change I had left and a little furtive sneaking I acquired a couple of small toys and clothing that I slipped under the baby's blanket in his stroller. There would be presents under the tree from Santa.

Louie showed up late on Christmas Eve. I couldn't figure out how he'd found us and he wasn't revealing his sources. Sometimes I wondered if he had spies everywhere. Was this Jewish guy someone he planted on the boardwalk? I've always wondered. Louie squeezed into the double bed with us that night - two toddlers, a baby and me. In one way it was comforting, but in another way, I wished he hadn't found us. It had felt so lovely for a few hours.

We shared a Christmas Day community cook-out in the area in front of the cottage with all the inhabitants from the front building. A motley crew playing conga drums, smoking weed, children playing freely with other kids and eating to their heart's content at the long table covered with pot luck dishes. I really wanted to stay in this new sweet little place. I was afraid that with Louie on the scene, the owner of the cottage wouldn't let us stay and things would go back to awful. I worried that we'd be back bouncing around from motel to motel without food again. I was right to worry.

He took us away the day after Christmas even though I pleaded with him. Why couldn't we rent the cottage? No answer. He plunked us into another depressing motel. This time on La Brea Avenue down in South Central L.A. *and went out for cigarettes*. We stayed for about three days alone without food. Rico was acting out from all the instability and wouldn't get into the shower to bathe and there was no tub. The force of the water coming down frightened him. I had to force him, but the kids needed to wash off the weeks of accumulated dirt. Nita clung to my legs to the point I could barely walk and began wetting her panties. But, finally, once clean, dry and tucked under the bed covers, the TV was once again our saving distraction. Louie showed back up with a couple of plates of cooked food eventually and left again.

We watched TV endlessly. Just the sounds of other adult voices and the silly cartoons that kept the kids engaged got us through. I tried to keep the kids positive about more food coming when Daddy got back *from work*. It was hard because I never knew when that might be… an hour, a day, a week?

Chapter 42
The Apartment
South Central L.A., Early 1964

When Louie finally returned, he said he had found an apartment for us. It was right across the street from the motel where we were, but on a side street facing away from the traffic. It was an upstairs furnished studio apartment with a Murphy bed behind French glass-paned doors, a kitchen and bathroom. It had a back utility room we made up for the kids with a great big bed in it that blocked the back door and we slept on the Murphy bed that pulled down at night. He ordered Altadena Dairy delivery service, a diaper service, then went out and returned with groceries. For the first time in what seemed like forever we had a fridge loaded with food. He set up his dark room on one side of the living room and began developing photos from what he said were his photo assignments. They were black and white matte finish photos of street scenes and one of a little girl in a shabby dress wearing a man's hat.

At first it seemed as though we were finally settled. He hadn't hit me since that one time just before I shot the centerfold. I was beginning to breathe easier on that score at least. Things seemed to be falling into a normal routine. It was not the life I'd grown up with, but after what we'd been through, I was grateful. We had the kids. We were cooking. And life took on a sense of normalcy. A couple of his friends I'd never met before came over with their kids and I babysat for them and made a few bucks during the day. Best of all it provided playmates for Rico and Nita. Louie was home every night. I began to relax, but there was always that lingering anxiety.

Then, as I feared, one morning he went out for cigarettes and disappeared for days. I had no idea where he was or what to do. We had no telephone, no television this time, no car, and no food again, except for the Altadena Dairy delivery. We lived on eggs, bread, butter, cheese, milk, orange juice and carrot juice until they refused to extend my credit any further. No matter how I begged and pleaded, the compassionate-eyed delivery guy apologetically said, "I'm so sorry, I just can't do it any longer. They won't let me." Then there was nothing.

I began shoplifting at the only store I could access, the Sav-On down the street. With the toddlers and pushing the stroller with the baby in it, we were fairly innocent looking so I could slip a bag of peanuts or whatever I could under the baby's blanket. I kept things going until Louie came back with either a couple of plates of cooked food or more groceries. When he finally came back, he stayed for a while, developing his photos while we sat in the dark breathing toxic fumes. He'd dry the wet prints on the tile walls in the bathtub, take pictures of us then go out for cigarettes again. The babysitting helped a little but not enough to pay any bills and it didn't last once they moved out of the neighborhood. The landlady next door offered to babysit so I could go and find a job. I got a job as a cocktail waitress in the evening and began making tips right away, but I was terrible at it. The noise and the crush of people confused me. I got fired after three days.

Then the electricity was turned off. The kids and I went to bed as soon as it got dark. I just did what I could from day to day until he showed back up with food. The gas was on, so I was at least able to open the oven door for heat when the evenings were cool.

An Afro-Cuban couple moved in downstairs. They didn't have children and loved having us come downstairs once in a while. They always had big pots of rice with some delicious spicy sauce they didn't mind sharing once in a while but I couldn't expect them to feed us forever - and I was hesitant to fill them in about our strife. Coincidentally they were from the same Cuban town that Louie said he was from - Santa Clara. I thought they would bond and maybe he'd stick around for a while. I imagined we might get back to some good times cooking Cuban food, playing drums and dancing, but he met them once and avoided them after that.

The wife had little altars to the Madonna everywhere around the house. She prayed for children of her own. Sometimes I wish I'd left the children with her and walked away. She would have loved them to eternity and back, and they would have grown up in their father's culture - if he had allowed them to stay. The weird thing that struck me was that they said they didn't understand his Spanish when he spoke - nor did I after two years of high school Spanish. I used to attribute it to my lack of understanding and not being that fluent myself, but it made me begin questioning even that part of his story.

One evening after Louie came home with groceries, he told me to get dressed up, that he was going to take me out to listen to some jazz. I was stunned, but thrilled at the idea of going out on an actual date. I hadn't been anywhere in so long and he had already arranged for the landlady to babysit. I put on my one black skirt, the white lace ruffled blouse that Louie bought me with my Playboy money, and I put my hair up in a beehive. I didn't feel very polished but I was excited to go out, listen to jazz and have a drink for a change like a normal person.

We arrived at a club on Washington Boulevard called the *It Club*. It was famous back then for its live jazz - and its Numbers racket. Louie played the Numbers. I had no idea what they were, but I was always pleased when he won and I'd learned not to question. We sat down at a little table in the very dark club. The musicians were playing and there was a steady buzz going on amongst the customers. I noticed that a lot of the people were looking at me and then I realized it was because I was the only white person in the club. The waiter came to the table to take our drink order and I went blank. I hadn't ordered an actual drink in a public venue for years. I stammered around trying to think what to ask for and then suddenly remembered Auntie Paula and Uncle Al's Bloody Mary's on Shabbat morning during Hanukkah. So, I said, "I'll have a Bloody Mary, please."

The waiter hesitated, looked at me, then at Louie. When he returned to the table, he said they didn't have any Bloody Mary mix, but they could send someone down to the liquor store on the corner to get some if I didn't mind waiting. I said, "Of course not. That's fine." I looked at Louie thinking maybe he'd suggest an alternative, but he became silent. His face darkened and his eyes narrowed. He grabbed me by the hair, jerked me out of my seat, dragged me forward, so I was unable to maintain my footing. I was tripping over my feet and I couldn't see where he was taking me. He pulled me out the back door into the alley, then out onto the street where he hailed a passing cab. He pushed me roughly into the back seat and never spoke a word the entire time. I was mortified but more than anything else, I was terrified. His silences were always lethal. When we got home, he yanked me out of the cab, up the front stairs to our apartment and pushed me inside. He began railing on me about ordering a rich, white woman drink, and embarrassing him in front of his buddies, making them go down the street to accommodate my spoiled-white-woman-whims. I tried to explain but he didn't care. He was on a roll.

He tiraded, and became more intensely sinister by the minute. He ranted in escalating incantations. His voice crescendoed and then his hand shot out from nowhere. He exploded on me. He whacked me across the face so hard I landed on the floor. Before I could get my breath, he picked me up and threw me head first through the glass window of the Murphy bed doors, then as quickly, he yanked me back out and hit me in the face again. I landed on the floor and curled up in a fetal position to protect my head and face. He kicked me over and over again in my back until his fury was exhausted. I laid there, not moving, barely breathing, waiting for the next onslaught.

I held my breath, tensed, waiting for his next assault, then I heard the front door slam. He was gone. I waited to be sure he wasn't coming back before I moved. Cautiously I dragged myself up to my knees. I could barely stand. I went into the bathroom to see if my face was cut up, but there was nothing much - a few scratches from the broken glass on my face and chest. I washed it off, smoothed down my hair, sat on the toilet to pee while I tried to compose myself, then I went next door to collect the kids.

What else could I do? Where else could I go? I had nowhere else. I had no one else - and it was after midnight. Even if it had occurred to me to call the cops, I didn't have a phone, so I stayed silent. I didn't trust the landlady and avoided her as much as possible. She always seemed to know how to contact Louie. She always put the *make* on me. I had to dodge her groping hands and insinuating eyes every time I asked her for a thing. When he came home again, he drove me to the store and when I asked him for something rather mundane that I needed, the hard side edge of his hand shot out sideways and karate chopped me across the throat. I had no voice for fifteen minutes. The next evening, he was developing photos after the children were asleep and slapped me across the face for no apparent reason. "Just to keep you in line," then he pulled me to my feet and made me stand still in profile while he photographed me. *I kept the photograph.*

Chapter 43
A Working Girl
Laurel Canyon

Louie came home one night and said he'd found a nice house up in Laurel Canyon and we'd be moving there within the week. It was a very cool place to live in one of Hollywood's many beautiful canyons. A lot of show biz people resided there and it was a hip place to be; a far cry from South Central L.A. The house was a large brick ranch style house at the top of a very long flight of red brick steps that led straight up to the house from the narrow winding street below. There were lots of windows, sliding glass doors from the dining room onto a patio surrounded by a rock garden with the tree-covered hills rising above it. The house was filled with light. The attached photo studio curved around in an L-shape with a wall of sliding glass doors leading out onto the back patio too. As soon as I walked in my heart did a little jump for joy. I knew not to get too excited, or too comfortable with Louie in the picture. It was always going to be a cautious dream that could become a nightmare in the flash of his hand. I had lost confidence that I would ever be safe or at peace. So, I kept my head down and directed my energies to the children's care as usual.

Louie never answered my questions about how the house came to be ours and what he was doing to make it so. He would just say, "Business," then he'd give me the look that I knew meant that I had better shut my mouth. He began driving a metallic bronze XKE Jaguar convertible and he gave me a white 1964 Ford Mustang with an automatic gear shift and blue interior. He hired a Mexican live-in maid, Eldemira, who spoke no English and a Filipino houseboy named Gina, who followed me around everywhere and became my confidante. We furnished the house rather minimally with a couple of beautiful teal and turquoise Swedish hand-woven shag rugs, a white brocade sofa and loveseat, Danish modern dining room table and chairs and he bought a big TV for the kids who were over the moon watching cartoons. Louie brought home mattresses to lay on the floor without box springs for the bedrooms. It was a complete change in our lifestyle. I figured he must have won big at Numbers or Ruella had gotten him a big loan. I wasn't asking.

Nito finally had a high chair, but he had not taken his first steps at a year old and was still silent. He watched everything with his big brown eyes shaded under his long curling eyelashes though. One day he came down with a fever, delirious with white spots inside his mouth. Louie rushed us to Children's Hospital only to discover that he was severely anemic. It was a shock, but given how long we had starved and he'd lived on just milk, no surprise. I was sure we were all anemic. We were given iron supplements and baby vitamins with a specially planned diet. And we bought chewable multivitamins for Nita and Rico on the way home too.

It must have really gotten to Louie, because he began doing family things with us, even taking us all out to a drive-in movie in his newly acquired metallic bronze Jaguar XKE. He confused me. On one hand he seemed to love doing things as a family and seemed to genuinely care for the children. He always made sure I had a diaper service and always showed up with food eventually. He even took us all fishing once and delighted in pan frying his catch over an open fire. We had wonderful moments although they never lasted. Without warning he'd revert to an impenetrable, terrifying monster and I was always kept off balance.

Someone asked me if I loved him. It caught me off guard, because by then I had no idea. My life with Louie was just day-to-day survival, while protecting and caring for the children. I was so numb by then that I had no feelings at all it seemed except love for the children and a deep paralyzing fear of him. I moved forward every day without thinking beyond our immediate needs. So, love? What's that?

Louie set up his photography studio in our new house. He filled it with all the most updated equipment required for a professional photo studio - tripods, backdrops and lights. He had an office desk and phone in the corner. It looked very posh and business-like. I expected him to book models and begin his business officially. But as time went by, there were very few models that he photographed, except me on occasion - nude, holding the baby. When I looked at the color transparencies, I was horrified to see how emaciated I looked. I could see my ribs and hip bones protruding, even my teeth looked bigger. I had gone from 110 lbs. when I met Louie to 72 lbs. I wore Boys size 12 corduroy slacks.

I began to suspect that the studio was his cover for something but I didn't know what. He would have meetings with his new assistants behind closed studio doors. I'd overhear them discussing strategies, but I never could decipher what it was they were planning. If I opened the studio door everyone ceased speaking and I'd get *The Look* from Louie. It was safer not to intrude. I wondered where all the money was coming from, since we'd only recently lived in a slum without enough food to go around. The questions were always on my mind, but I dared not ask. In truth I was so relieved to have a roof over our heads and food on the table that I was willing to let it go. The last two years had exhausted me beyond words, both mentally and physically. The kids were thrilled to have a big TV and could watch Sesame Street in Spanish. I had a roof over my head, a maid, a house boy, a car and food. I tried not to make waves.

Louie got his conga drums out of hock, which was always a reason for celebration with drumming, dancing and home cooked Cuban food. I was grateful for every moment of distraction. Moe and his friends from John Cassavetes' film acting troupe all came up to celebrate. Rupert Crosse, Seymour Cassel and John himself. They enjoyed our gatherings. No one had a clue any more than I did what might be going on behind the scenes. They were there to eat, dance, smoke weed and play music.

Moe became like a brother to me all the rest of his life. When he came to my eldest daughter's wedding in 1998 he told me he knew nothing then of Louie's abuse or criminal activities. He said his first clue that Louie was not on the up-and-up was when one day he was asked to go along to pick up Louie's car. All was normal until suddenly they were crouching and stalking down an alley in South Central L. A. carrying baseball bats. Moe said it hit him hard and he distanced himself. I wish he'd told me and taken me with him.

Louie introduced me to a woman who lived in an old English-style stone manor house a half a block below the Sunset Strip whom he coincidentally knew and she turned out to be a Madame in the dark, glittering underworld of *Beverly Hills Call Girls*. Her clientele included the top echelon in show business. He'd introduced me to her as the new *"Miss September 1963, Playboy's Playmate of the Month"* and I thought at first it was a show business introduction, now that we were finally settled. I didn't realize that she was a *Call Girl* and they were intending to use my Playboy celebrity as their selling point. Using his familiar form of coercion, through violence and his new form of cruelty, holding my children hostage at home by the maid and a guy named Buddy since Ruella had disappeared from the scene, Louie and his Madame friend sold me to celebrities. He delivered me to her house and I remained to see clients with her until he came to pick me up and collect his money. They were big names - actors and comedians that the world, my folks and I had revered. These *clients* were not only in the film industry but were well known in the political arena, as well. I went through the motions feeling disillusioned and sicker by the day.

They had me *turning* at least five *tricks* a day, seven days a week, and on occasion there were evening cocktail parties with elected national political officials at luxurious Beverly Hills hotels. I saw things and was forced to participate in things I could never have imagined; things that tainted my view of life and of the society I had been raised to respect. I soon understood how a person can become so detached from their feelings that they feel nothing at all, and need more and more stimulus in order to feel anything. I had to put my emotions in a little locked box and tuck it away inside myself somewhere impenetrable.

There was only one client I enjoyed. He was the alcoholic son of an iconic movie star from the Thirties and Forties. He paid $50 just to sit and talk for an hour in his cottage high in the Hollywood Hills. He never laid a hand on me. He was a lonely mess and died at 43 in the late Sixties. Someone said it was suicide. It was a reprieve for me not to have to have sex and to talk about books, theater and loneliness. I never told him my story. I was being paid to listen to his.

Louie continued to restrict my movement outside the house with the children to ensure my return home with the cash. If I was 30 seconds late, I would get backhanded and knocked to the floor, or he'd grab me by the throat with his fingernails gripping my windpipe. It would leave little half-moon cuts in the skin on my neck. I would drive home terrified, dry-retching out of the car window, as if I needed to lose any more weight. I'd lost my appetite once he began pimping me. If there was heavy traffic or if I got stuck at a red light, there would be even more hell to pay and I would begin shaking uncontrollably.

One afternoon I was literally one minute late walking in the door. My insides were shaking badly, but I put on my indifferent *no expression mask*, trying to act like nothing was wrong and laid the cash on his desk. He lowered his reading glasses to the tip of his nose and stared at me silently. His cohort, Buddy, called my name. He was now a permanent fixture around the house and assigned to be my bodyguard when Louie was out. Though Ruella had seemed to disappear, it didn't mean she wasn't somewhere behind the scenes hustling money for him. I turned my head to look towards Buddy and then immediately back to Louie.

"Where's the money?"

"I put it right there, on the corner of your desk!"

"No, you didn't! Give it to me!"

"I gave it to you!"

"No, you didn't! You're just *putting out* for free. You're just out there giving it away!"

"I am not! I put the money right there on your desk!"

His voice began its usual crescendo and when it reached the peak of its intensity, he lashed out. I was backhanded on the side of my face. My head whipped around and I landed face down on the asphalt tiled studio floor. Buddy just stood and watched indifferently, then left the room. This was Louie's way of showing what a tough guy he was keeping his woman in line. There was never any effort to help me get up. I dragged myself into the bedroom and was unable to get out of bed for a day or so until he made me get up and go back to work. It occurred to me that it was me who was now primarily supporting our new lifestyle - the lifestyle I was unable to enjoy.

I was so severely damaged psychologically, emotionally and physically that I had reached the end. I had no appetite even when there was food to eat. I had managed to gain a little weight and had gone up to about 80 lbs., which was some improvement, but with my pale skin, dyed black beehive, I looked like a hollow-eyed wraith with Sixties eyeliner - at least to me. I couldn't find any of the beauty that clients told me I had.

1. 2. 3.

1. Mom and Daddy Jim's Wedding
2. Sgt. James Arthur Bartlett off to WWII.
3. My mom and me while Daddy Jim was away at war.

4. 5. 6.

4. Grandma Refa
5. Auntie Te
6. North Genesee, family home

7.   8.   9.

7. Mom, Uncle Bill, Aunt Emmy
8. Daddy Jim as a Teen with Grandma Grace
9. Mom, Daddy Nino and me. Our 1st date.

10.   11.   12.

10. Me at 4 1/2 in Nevada the summer I was hogtied.
11. My 2nd Birthday.
12. NYC after Mom began losing her hair.

13.   14.   15.

13. Auntie Paula in NYC on Broadway.
14. Me at 7 or 8 with Mom and her new wig.
15. Daddy Nino and I at Sopos Creek summering in the Catskills, New York.

16.   17.   18.

16. Summer in Bonaparte, Iowa where our family lived for generations.
17. Me with my 1st cat, Bagheera, in Connecticut.
18. Cousin Anne and I after she came to live with us in Connecticut.

Chapter 44
Mommy!

I would call Auntie Nor Nor whenever I could to let her know where I was. I never revealed everything. Over those two years with Louie, she was my only point of contact with anyone related to my family after she'd told me that Daddy had announced to the family that I was disowned. On one of those rare calls, I learned that my parents had recently moved back to Hollywood and Daddy had gone back to work as a background artist in the animation studios. She gave me their telephone number and address. I wrote it down and stashed it away in my wallet. It almost felt like a sacred talisman. They lived in an apartment building just a few blocks away from the bottom of the canyon where we lived. My heart leapt in some kind of faint joy just knowing they were near. I needed to see where they lived, but was afraid to call. There was a surge of hope realizing they were no longer nearly 3,000 miles away. I casually told Buddy I was going to the store with the children one day while Louie was gone. He was stoned, napping on the sofa, so he let it slide. I was astonished at how easy leaving with the children had been. I had been so caught in the grip of terror before that I never attempted to test it out, but having my parents close by gave me that extra little boost of courage. My heart was pounding. I was so afraid I'd get caught. I tried to act normally, but my heart was doing back flips.

I drove down the canyon to Hollywood Boulevard, cruised slowly up and down the street until I zeroed in on the address. It was a small building that looked as though there were only four apartments; two upstairs and two down. I parked across the street from their building and quieted the kids while my eyes searched for the windows that might be theirs. I yearned for my parents, the safety and familiarity of my family home. Wherever they were, no matter how dysfunctional, they were my home. I wondered if they still loved me or if they would still even want me in their lives.

I rolled down my driver's side window and looked up at the second-floor apartment window on the east side of the building and just then Mom looked out. We locked eyes. She gasped in disbelief, "Ooooh Vic! Stay there! Stay there! I'll be right down!"

Mom ran outside and practically flew across the street to my open car window. We chatted for a minute as she leaned in my window. I told her I needed to get back, but she insisted that we come inside. My courage was bolstered by her presence. She fixed tea and cookies and I introduced her to my children. Clearly, she didn't know what to do with my three brown babies, though she tentatively held her first grandson, Nito, on her lap. Nita and Rico were immediately enamored with my glamorous looking mother, her exotic eyeliner, her big gold ear bangles and multi-ringed, red nail polished fingers - and the homemade cookies and milk helped.

I tried to pretend that my life was just lovely; photographer husband, live-in maid, big house, new cars. I invited her up to my home in the canyon for tea one day. I needed to show her that I was okay even though I was far from it. I don't know who I was trying to convince more. Maybe I thought that if my mother visited Louie would be put on notice - delusional thinking on my part, but... Mom came up the following week. It was extraordinarily uncomfortable. She sat tensely at the breakfast bar gripping her purse tightly on her lap. Louie came out from the photo studio barefoot, wearing his black jeans with no shirt. He loomed over her and flashed his bare, ebony, muscular torso close to her, deliberately designed to intimidate. He spoke to her in demeaning tones. It was clear that he wanted to get her out of there as soon as possible. She felt it and left shortly thereafter. He gave me his usual warning look that sent chills down my spine.

I remembered in the beginning of our marriage when I had felt so defensive of him. We were pulled over by the cops one evening when we were driving out at night with the children. He was told to step out of the car and was then thrown against the wall while I was forced by the LAPD to sit with the children on the curb. They called me N-lover. I responded to the cops snarkily asking them what they had stopped us for and why they had searched our car, glove compartment and trunk, then ran a *make* on us when they found Louie's Maalox tablets for his ulcer in a bubble pack. I was on his side then. I stood up for him. "We thought your brake lights weren't working," the cop said.

I remember feeling indignant when he was driving his chess partner, TV star Michael Parks's new Jaguar. Michael's girlfriend, my neighbor, Sally Kellerman and I rode in the back. We were pulled over by the police speeding on the 101 freeway and herded off at the next exit. We were all expected to get out of the car. Sally and I stood there making smart ass comments to the cops, because we were shivering cold. Louie was thrown against the wall and frisked. Michael was asked for his autograph. I bridled at the injustice of it all. I bonded to Louie more closely in those moments. But after he had stripped me of all my inheritance, my Playboy earnings, beat and sold me, I had no compassion left for him at all. I just desperately wanted out. My dilemma as always was the children. I loved them with my life. They had no idea that I wasn't their real mother. But, what could I do? I knew I had to make a decision. I felt like I was dying. I needed ME back, whoever that was. I hoped I could find myself again.

After seeing my mother my need for my old family life intensified. I just wanted to go home.

Just being in her presence, in her apartment amongst the old familiar furnishings I'd grown up with gave me a moment of identity. The antique Chinese red and cobalt blue wool Oriental rug in the living room that we had bought in the Forties in Manhattan before Mom lost her hair, the faint scent of sandalwood incense that she always burned after she finished cleaning the house that lingered in the air, the familiar music issuing from her radio, all gave me a yearning so deep that I was in physical pain. Her solid presence gave me a flicker of hope. It jolted me back to the person I used to be; the identity of my own people, my clan, my tribe. I knew in my bones that if I didn't get away from Louie I really would die. It wasn't a melodramatic statement. It was a fact. I had to find a way.

I became so weak one day I just laid down in bed. I told Louie that I was too weak to stand up, which was pretty much true. I'd collapsed - physically but more than anything else - spiritually. I laid there for days drifting in and out of sleep. I'd sneak into the bathroom so he wouldn't see me standing up and force me out to work again. Listless, hopeless, I was unable to eat. I was. Seeing my mother gave me back what little will I had left to live. I kept thinking of her just down the hill, safety within reach.

One day the phone rang. Louie answered it and brought the phone to me where I laid in bed. It was one of my clients - a very famous comedian who was well known for entertaining the troops during his USO tours. He had been very kind to me and we'd had conversations about his career. I had indicated that while I had gone to the American Theatre Wing to be an actress, I had found myself abandoned with three children and was doing what I needed to do to feed them. He was sympathetic but he was still a client - a *John*.

"Hello?"

"I heard that you were sick. Is there anything I can do to help you?"

"No, I'm fine," I mumbled weakly. "Thank you for calling. Goodbye, then."

Louie stood glowering over the bed so I couldn't scream *"Help! Get me outta here!"* Louie grabbed the phone out of my hand, gave me a dirty look and slammed out of the bedroom leaving me alone. I wished I had the comedian's telephone number, so I could call him back later, but Louie's Madame friend controlled all of that. I needed a drink of water; my mouth was so dry, but I couldn't find the strength to move.

For a couple of weeks, actor, Rupert Crosse, from the Cassavetes gang, called me every day after he discovered I was ill. If Louie answered the phone, he used the pretense that he was just calling to jam with him. I finally revealed to him that I was being beaten and prostituted. The concept of being *trafficked* hadn't entered my consciousness or vocabulary in those days. I was just considered a *Beverly Hills Call Girl*, a *hooker*, a *Working Girl*, in the vernacular of *The Life*.

Rupert bolstered my courage daily. He'd tell me how strong I was, how smart, how beautiful, how much better I was than what I was being forced to endure. He told me I could make it; I could get away. He gave me a slowly growing courage and determination. He told me something that I still pass on to others who are emerging from horrifically abusive situations. He said, "Just remember, once you get out of the shit pile, don't expect not to stink for a while."

It took me years to quit 'stinking,' suffering the symptoms of that abusive dehumanizing experience. And to this day I still deal with some of the physical injuries as well as untangling the residual emotional and psychological detritus. Transforming one's pain into wellness doesn't come easy and it doesn't come quick... but it comes.

Speaking out in 2014 about Cosby's rape unearthed a lot of archeological debris that I thought I had cleared out a long time before, but instead I had just buried it. It was like a pocket of infection still festering in some dark fossa of my bones. Finding my voice was in so many ways a much more effective organic form of intensive psychotherapy that I never expected to face head on in this way, at this time of my life. I had just put it away, staying busy and moving forward.

One night around 10 p.m., out of complete desperation I made up my mind that it was the night that I was going to take the baby and escape. I had to face facts about Nita and Rico. They were not mine as much as I had sacrificed for their survival and as much as I loved them. I'd been thinking about it, mulling it over for a long time. It had been slowly coming to a head. I just hadn't figured out the logistics. Now knowing my mom and dad were living just a few blocks away from the bottom of the canyon, I felt that safe harbor was finally within reach. I had somewhere to go.

Louie had taken the sixteen-year-old babysitter home, but I thought maybe he'd stay a bit longer, since someone mentioned that he was screwing her, too. I banked on the chance that it might be true I might have extra time.

When he left, he took my white Mustang instead of the XKE because he knew I couldn't drive a stick shift and I'd be unable to leave. Buddy was left to guard me as usual, but he was passed out on the sofa in the living room, snoring gutturally. I could hear him. I tiptoed to the bedroom door, peeked out and saw him on the sofa facing away from the doorway. Very quietly I closed the doors leading out of the hallway bedrooms to the living room. I wanted to make sure that I had an added layer of sound protection.

I wrapped up what clothes and baby gear I could in a sheet; bundled it and tied it in a knot. I stealthily took it out the back door, crept down the brick steps and hid it behind a bush. I ran back upstairs barefoot so I wouldn't make any sound and picked up my sleeping baby. I sat on the bed next to Rico and Nita's innocent sleeping forms and tucked their blankets around them. I wept and prayed over them. I kissed their foreheads and prayed they'd forgive me one day, even though I knew they would never understand. I knew they'd be confused, frightened, feel abandoned and cry for me, but I didn't know what else to do. I didn't even dare tell the maid I was going. I knew I had no choice if I was going to survive. I prayed the next 'Mommy' that Louie recruited would love them as much as I did.

Even with his warped psyche, in his atavistic way, he loved them very deeply. I knew he would never abandon them no matter what; and without a shadow of a doubt, he would make sure they were cared for, even if by the maid, the babysitter or (shudder) Ruella who I suspected was still lurking in the wings. Louie always had several women on the string doing his bidding. I hated the thought, but I knew at that point leaving with my baby was a matter of life and death - my life - my death. If I took Nita and Rico, it would be kidnapping and I knew, too, that if I took them, he would hunt me down and kill me. That was a given.

I rushed out the back patio door behind the house balancing my baby on my hip. My heart was pounding so hard in my chest I barely could breathe. I felt like I was going to wet my pants and my guts were turning to water. Shaking, I ran down the long brick steps to the street in the dark looking for a place to hide until the cab arrived. I ran to the large, dense-foliaged bush downhill below the next-door neighbor's house where I had stashed my bundle. It wasn't much cover, but it was all I could find and still be able to see the cab when it pulled up. Had I known the neighbors I might have sought refuge there, but I had never seen them and their windows were dark anyway. I hid behind the tall bush trembling uncontrollably. I waited until I thought I was going to pass out from fear.

My stomach was cramping, I was sure I was going to shit my pants. I had to pee so badly but I couldn't do anything about it. I kept talking softly to Nito so he wouldn't cry. I prayed that the taxi would hurry up and get there. I thought I should have called my mom to come pick me up but somehow, I hadn't thought of it in time and now it was too late. "What is taking that fucking cab so long?" I kept listening for the sound of an engine, but all I heard were crickets and an owl hooting in a tree nearby. I was getting so weak from fear and my arm was tremoring from the weight of holding my fourteen-month-old baby in an awkward position. It felt like it was beginning to give out.

At last, the cab zipped uphill past me. He pulled in towards the garage door on an angle under the yellow overhead light. I was delirious with relief. I rushed out from behind the bush and started running uphill towards the taxi. I was afraid if he didn't see me standing there that he'd leave without me. I started waving my arm at him, crying, "Help me! Please! Help me!" The taxi driver heard me and got out of his cab and began walking downhill towards me. He was in silhouette. As he got closer, I ran towards him faster - and then my heart stopped.

I recognized the familiar off-angled walk, his tight black jeans, his narrow-brimmed hat, his tweed sports jacket - his features came into focus. I froze. The yellow light over the garage had made my white Mustang look yellow. In my terror I had mistaken it for a Yellow Cab and acted too quickly. I stopped dead and looked up at our neighbor's houses - all strangers - all darkened windows. It was after midnight with nowhere to run. I was all alone. No sanctuary and paralyzed with fear.

Louie reached me quickly and immediately grabbed the baby out of my arms. He took a handful of my hair in his hands, pulled my head backwards, leaned forward. For one nanosecond I thought he was going to kiss me but he opened his mouth and his teeth engulfed my entire mouth as he bit me. He jerked me forward by my long hair and yanked me off balance then dragged me up the street, up the long brick staircase to the house. I couldn't get my footing. My shins were scraping on the sharp edges of the brick steps and I felt my skin tearing. All I could do was hang on - dreading what I knew would come next. He dragged me around to the back patio and through the sliding glass doors into the studio. He banged my head against each door jamb as he dragged me through. I was in shock, dizzy and dazed. He pulled me into the doorway of the children's room and threw my baby carelessly onto the bed next to the still sleeping children, then he pulled me through the living room where Buddy groggily turned over, looked at what was happening and yawned. Louie slammed me against the wall by the front door and was strangling me. He gripped my windpipe between his fingernails clamping off my air so I couldn't make a sound. Buddy turned away facing the back of the sofa and returned to sleep.

Louie forced me back downstairs and pushed me into the passenger seat of the Mustang, then he slammed the door and drove it into the garage. I sat there accepting finally that I was going to be killed, just like Aunt Emmy. I still remembered Grandma screaming at me when I went out with Auntie Nor's son. It had played over in my head like a curse so many times since then I couldn't shake it. "You're going to turn out just like Aunt Emmy!" Maybe she was right. I remembered Louie saying early in our relationship, "I take people to the City Dump." I hadn't understood what he meant then, but I finally got it.

The taxi arrived and honked just as Louie turned off the ignition and I was sitting in shambles inside the locked car in the garage. I wanted to run and cry for help, but I was afraid to move. My baby was upstairs and I couldn't leave him. What would happen if I did that? Would the taxi driver choose not to get involved and drive away? Then, what? I just sat there frozen like a rabbit in the hunter's gun sights, letting whatever was going to happen, happen. I accepted my fate.

Louie walked over to the taxi driver. I heard him say, just as cool as if he'd had a lovely day, "They already left," he said. The cab hung a U-turn and sped back down the hill. I saw my last hope of salvation drive away. The bottom of my stomach dropped into my feet. I began separating from myself. I began seeing things as if from a distance, as if everything was very far away in miniature. When Louie opened the passenger door and grabbed me, he dragged me back up the stairs, through the patio sliders into the studio. He banged my head into every door jamb we passed through as hard as he could. I was dazed and limp and couldn't stand on my own. He held me by the hair and kept hitting me in the face. Finally, he let go of me and I fell flat on my face on the asphalt tile of the studio floor. He grabbed me by the arm and flipped me over on my back, straddled me and kept slapping me in the face with a vengeance he hadn't released on me before. I choked on something and managed to turn my head to spit it out. I saw on the floor a piece of my front tooth. I felt as though at that moment there could be no return. I thought, "What if I still had braces on my teeth?" He pulled me up, dragged me through the studio door into our adjacent bedroom and threw me onto our bed. He kept hitting me in the head and face, shoulders and arms until I was babbling incoherently. I started deliriously crying, "Mommy! Mommy! Help me, please!"

Abruptly, he stopped hitting me - just stopped. He looked at me as though he had come out of a trance. He wrapped me in his arms and cradled me. He rocked me and softly crooned, "No, no... You're not a little girl. You're a woman. You're my wife. You're the mother of my sons." As I slipped into mindless babbling delirium and slid into a dark spiraling void, crying for my mommy, my last prayer, he raped me.

I woke up sometime the next day. I looked over onto his pillow and thanked god he wasn't there. I didn't know if he was still in the house and what would happen when he surfaced. I laid there in so much pain. I ran my tongue over the ragged edge of my upper front tooth. I couldn't move, but I had to pee so badly I knew I had to try. It had been hours. I literally crawled into the bathroom and pulled myself up onto the toilet. I was so dizzy I thought I was going to fall on the floor. My head was spinning and I felt nauseated. After I wiped myself, I managed to stand up and look in the mirror to see how badly broken my tooth was. I hardly recognized my own face. The chip off my left upper front tooth was triangular. I had had a perfect smile for the first time since my grown-up teeth had grown in once my braces were off and seeing myself with a broken front tooth sent me to the bottom of whatever deep pit I was already in. There was nothing left of me. I closed the bedroom door and slid back onto my bed and passed out again. I drifted in and out of consciousness for a long time. I lost track. Beaten and bruised, I was probably suffering a concussion. For the rest of the day and all the next night I was feverish and delirious. Every muscle in my body ached. My front tooth throbbed and my lips were cut inside and swollen. When I emerged from unconsciousness from time to time, I tried to think about what was going on outside my closed bedroom door. I tried to hear the children's voices, the baby crying, the maid tending to the children, but I couldn't unscramble my thoughts. I reverted to my most primal need. I wanted my Mommy.

Finally, I dragged myself out of bed again. I peeked into the other rooms and tiptoed into the photo studio as far away from the living room as I could where Buddy remained on guard. I peeked to see the babysitter in the kitchen fixing the children's breakfast. I saw the maid changing the baby's diaper in the next room. I knew I had a bit of wiggle room. I hid in the closet to muffle the sound and called my mother. I wasn't going to tell her what had happened. I just needed to hear her voice. As soon as she heard mine, she knew something was terribly wrong. Whatever differences my mother and I had, we remained intuitively connected all of our lives. "Vic? What's wrong?" Against all my initial intentions I broke down blubbering, sobbing and blurted everything out. "I'm coming up with Daddy right now and we're bringing you home."

"No, Mom! If Louie comes home, he'll hurt Daddy. You can't bring Daddy up here! I have everything under control. I know what to do." Of course, I had no idea what to do but I knew Daddy's Sicilian temper and bluster. I felt I had to protect my Daddy. I'm sure Mom completely saw through me and knew better. So, she talked to Auntie Paula who had also moved back to California and was still her confidante and advisor. Auntie Paula of course told her to call the police right away. I guess she hesitated and waited until the next morning. I was completely unprepared.

Chapter 45
Busted
October 1964

I stayed in bed all that day and the ensuing night. I was so bruised, swollen, in pain and in a brain fog that all I could do was lie there half-awake or unconscious. The next morning, I was awakened by the phone ringing in the studio. I surfaced through deep layers of confused images and stiff muscles. I looked to see that Louie wasn't in bed next to me and I headed for the phone, hoping and praying it might be Mom. It wasn't. It was a client wanting to book an appointment. I told him that I was no longer available. I became aware of someone standing in front of the desk. Thinking it was Louie, I panicked and looked up only to see a big tall Los Angeles cop in full uniform standing in front of me. I was bewildered. He said, "Ma'am, come with me," and directed me into the living room. I had no idea what was happening.

When I arrived in the living room, I was surprised to see several people, most of whom were strangers to me, lined up on the white sofas. In their midst was Louie glaring at me. The TV was playing Sesame Street and the children were sitting on the cozy rug confused about who all these big uniformed gun-toting guys were who were standing in the middle of our house.

Apparently, the cops answered my mother's distress call, knocked on our front door and four-year-old Rico answered. When the cops saw racially mixed people hanging out, crashing on the sofas, they thought that on top of my mother's report about my beating that it was suspicious and they just walked in. They frisked everybody and found a marijuana joint in the pocket of some guy who had tagged along with one of Louie's friends.

One of the cops, a big black guy recognized me and asked Louie, "Was her mouth like that when she was in Playboy, Man?" Louie gave me the *evil eye*. I was terrified at that point thinking the cops would leave and he would finish killing me.

They didn't leave - and they didn't save me either. Instead, they destroyed what was left of me - and my children.

Chapter 46
Juvie, Hollywood Division, Lincoln Heights and Bill Jennings

When they asked us where we were growing marijuana I sarcastically said, "Yeah, up in the rock garden." It was so preposterous, but all the cops rushed outside lusting for a big drug bust. They found nothing. They told us to stand up and they handcuffed us all behind our backs.

Female cops arrived and without explanation grabbed all three of my children who were in their pjs and whisked them out of the house. They were all terrified and screaming. I was handcuffed behind my back along with every other adult in the house, including the sixteen-year-old babysitter. It was the last I ever saw of her. I hope she had a better outcome than my children and me.

I couldn't reach out to comfort them. We were placed in the backs of several different squad cars lined up at the curb. First, I was taken down to Juvenile Hall where my terrified children were allowed to be with me in an interview room but then were snatched screaming and literally ripped out of my arms. The cops said, "We're feeding them breakfast!" I kept thinking that the cops would realize there was a mistake and the kids would be back in my arms and we'd be released. Then I wondered where would I go from there?

They questioned me at West Hollywood Juvenile Hall about the children, their personal data and I couldn't give them anything other than birthdays and their birth parents' names. All I could tell them was my own baby's info. Once done at Juvie, I was taken across the street to Hollywood Division. I kept asking where they were taking my children. They threw me in a cage with one of the women who had been at our house with her husband. I cried and cried and became hysterical. I had just started my period the night before and had no tampons with me. When I asked to go to the ladies' room, I was taken upstairs by a big tough woman cop who stood there and made me strip in front of her and then directed me to remove my blood saturated tampon and place it on a paper towel that she had placed on the floor in front of me. I was allowed to use the toilet but only with the door open within her view. I felt so degraded. I was not given a replacement tampon nor a sanitary napkin even. After I was allowed to put my clothes back on, I was taken back downstairs and handcuffed to a chair while I bled through my pants. The cops said they were awaiting directions about what to do with us next.

Still handcuffed, bruised and in pain, I was taken in the back of a squad car with the other woman downtown to a tall, glass windowed building, upstairs to the Narco. Division on the 4th floor. The cops discovered they had taken us to the wrong place and took us back downstairs and driven somewhere else. They didn't tell us anything more and we were still painfully handcuffed behind our backs forced to lean forward in the back seat of the car. I was already in so much pain anyway this was added torture. They really should have taken me to the hospital. Finally, they delivered us into a dark horrid pea-green-gray painted dungeon where we were led through the booking process. I learned later that it was Lincoln Heights, the worst women's prison in the country.

As I was being photographed and fingerprinted, I was shown a mug shot of Louie under an entirely different name. I stood numbly, bleeding down my legs. I shook my head and didn't mention that I recognized that name - William Jennings. He told me once that he went by Bill Jennings when he jumped ship from Cuba evading Immigration Officers. It just added to the mystery of who he really was, because the photo didn't look like a man that much younger than he was when we met. I have never found out the truth and probably never will.

When I was allowed my one phone call, I called my mother frantically. "Please, Mom! Go get my children!" She said tensely, "It's too late." "What do you mean 'too late'?" She said something about papers being signed. I had no idea what she meant. Bottom line - they didn't want the children, certainly not brown children. We both knew she was lying. I hung up and was taken to a degrading public shower in an open hallway. Still no sanitary napkins or tampons offered, just a rough gray prison dress that didn't fit. I was thrown into a felony cell with an open toilet that had no seat on it and a concrete platform that looked like a tub with no mattress, sheets or blankets. I was shivering. I moaned, sobbed and wailed for my children for twelve horrible hours lying on the floor of the cell directly across from the other woman with whom I'd been busted. This was the felony section I learned. It was nothing more than a wind tunnel with cells along both sides. I felt feverish and was inconsolable. My co-prisoner sang old Negro Spirituals to me, for which I'll be forever grateful. A Trustee came to mop the floor and smiled salaciously at me, hinting that I could have a mattress if I was nice to her. I pretended I didn't understand. "I want my babies!"

Chapter 47
Bailed
October 1964

Late that night we were bailed out, by an attorney who Louie knew who also pimped his own wife and other Call Girls and sent many clients our way. The bail bondsman took us over to the men's prison where we sat while the bondsman spoke to the people at the desk. The bail bondsman indicated that we were expected to be responsible for their bail. I immediately realized what that meant. We would be sent out to turn tricks to pay for it. Louie, Buddy, and the husband of the woman who I was with, arrived in a glass cage expecting to be released. Louie glared at me, giving me the *Evil Eye*. Chills went down my spine. Something snapped in me and I called the bondsman over and told him, "NO! I will not bail him out." I don't know where I got the strength and conviction, but I knew he couldn't hurt me again if he was behind bars and there was no way I was turning another trick ever again. I saw the cops behind the counter muttering to each other and then walking over to Louie and his pals. They turned them around and walked them back through the security door. The look of astonishment and hatred on Louie's face burned a hole in my brain. I didn't think beyond that moment of relief and narrow escape.

I knew I had done the right thing. I had saved my life. I felt a weight lift off my head and heart, but I was shaking inside reacting to the sheer guts of what I finally did. I felt free for the first time since he had overtaken my life two years before. And with my mother and dad close by I felt I had somewhere I could go at last where I'd be safe. But I had no idea what would happen next. Where was he taking us? What would I do? I had no idea where my children were, but I knew I had to figure that out, but would my mother help me? I sat in the bondsman's car with the other woman in limbo. I decided to call my houseboy, Gina, who fortunately had not been at the house during the bust. She gave me her friend's address on Hollywood Boulevard and said she'd meet us there. As it turned out her friend was a trans hooker and lived in an apartment building somewhere on Hollywood Boulevard several blocks east of my folks' apartment building.

She met us at the door in sheer, fuchsia baby doll PJs. She had long brown hair, and was very pretty, petite but with an indifferent expression on her face. She told me I could sleep on her couch. She had nothing in the apartment to eat, nothing to drink but cheap sweet wine. The place smelled of pungent perfume and a lot of funk. I thought I'd jumped from the frying pan into the fire. The other woman with me called a friend who picked her up, and then I called my mother. Mom said I couldn't come over until the next day after Daddy had left for work at the studio and my little 8-year-old half-sister had gone to school. It hurt but at the same time I understood and it would give me a few hours to be alone with my mom.

I was so hungry. I didn't remember the last time I had eaten. The prison food had been shoved in on a tray through a slit in the door and was inedible. I had been too upset to even try more than a couple of disgusting lukewarm bites of tasteless split pea soup and that had been it for days. I accepted a glass of my hostess's icky sweet wine and fell asleep on the couch with a massive headache.

The next morning, I walked all the way to my mother's apartment building. She was glad I was safe and fixed me tea and toast - and listened to my horror story of the last several days. It was clearly more than she could handle, so she began cleaning the kitchen counter while I tried to talk to her. I wanted to see her face, her eyes, have her respond with something like concern, but I got her turned back. When Daddy came home, he was gruff. My sister was timid at first after not seeing me for four years, but once she knew this strange scarecrow of a woman with the dyed black hair (courtesy of Hugh Hefner) was her big sister she was cautiously thrilled to see me.

It was so odd being back in my parents' space again with the old comforting familiar ambience. The food was familiar and everything smelled of home. My parents looked more or less the same - a bit older. Daddy was sleeping on a single bed at the foot of Mom's double bed. That was odd but the excuse was that Daddy was too hot for Mom to sleep comfortably. I knew I had changed. I was emaciated with a broken front tooth. I had no toiletries, no change of clothing, no sanitary napkins, disheveled hair and what residual mascara and eyeliner I'd had on was long gone. I could see how bad I looked reflected in the strained expressions on my folks' faces. They had no idea what was next any more than I did.

The next day was an ordeal trying to find out where the children were. They were in Maclaren Hall, I was told, a place for children who were removed from unsafe homes or parents who were in custody. Once I was able to navigate this new territory, I found out that I could visit the children, but I needed a ride. Auntie Nor Nor drove me and waited patiently for me in the car but was not allowed to accompany me.

Once I was there, I was told I was only allowed to visit my baby, not my stepchildren. Rico was in a separate unit for boys his age and Nita was in another area for girls her age. I was devastated. I tried to explain that I was the only mother the children knew, but my pleas fell on deaf ears. As I was escorted down a hallway towards the room where the institutional cribs were lined up, I suddenly heard a shriek. "Mama!" I looked up and it was my little girl struggling to fight free from the grasp of two attendants trying to hold onto her. She finally broke loose and ran to me as they chased after her. I scooped her up in my arms and we both sobbed sitting on the floor. Her hair that I had been used to brushing and carefully caring for with Dixie Peach, putting it up into a little *chignon* on the top of her head was all nappy, unbrushed and wild. She had a wrinkled dress on her that was at least two sizes too big. It was a nightmare seeing her like that. She was a child who loved dressing pretty and neat.

The attendants thankfully felt compassion for us and Nita was allowed to stay with me as we both visited Nito in his jail-like crib. She clung to me as she had when her father first brought her to me, terrified of strangers, wetting on the floor from fear, and here she was again. We were chaperoned and the time given us was strictly limited. I never caught a glimpse of Rico as they separated us again. How does one explain to a three-and-a-half-year-old? We were pulled apart in tears again and I was powerless to do anything.

Once the court date had been set, I was placed in a chair across a large noisy, people-filled room where I couldn't hear or understand anything being said and no one explained the proceedings to me. They put the baby on my lap perfunctorily and walked away. Then Nita and Rico were brought in through a door on the far side of the huge room, crying and resisting. Rico hung onto the door frame with his fingers clenched tightly. They were pulling him and trying to peel his fingers away, but he held on. Nita saw me and ran towards me. Then Rico saw me too and he ran to me as fast as he could and clung as close to me as was possible. I was enveloping them in my arms as best I could. We huddled around the baby on my sagging lap, but once the proceedings were completed, all three children were dragged away again, all of us in tears.

I never understood what was happening nor heard a thing the judge was saying as they decided our lives. No one offered an explanation and I had to ask the Social Worker what was happening as they extricated the children from my arms. It was the most horrifying experience. I could only imagine what the children were experiencing, understanding even less than I. We were all traumatized and I knew in my heart we'd never completely recover.

I learned that my case was dismissed, but the court decided that the children were to be placed in a temporary foster home somewhere in the Valley, before a more permanent placement could be found. I was allowed to visit, but I wouldn't be allowed custody of the children until I showed that I could provide a safe, healthy environment for my baby. No one mentioned Rico and Nita's fate although all three were placed together in foster homes. The first foster family was lovely. The foster mother in her compassion for our situation was arranging for me to rent a room in her next-door neighbor's house and wanted to help me find a local job. My heart leapt in gratitude.

Mom and Auntie Paula drove me to see the children regularly. Sadly, by the time I was allowed to see them again after the court decision, I had missed seeing my baby take his first steps. Since Social Service had placed all three children in the same home, I was able to take gifts and visit them all at the same time until I could surreptitiously move next door. Then suddenly the foster mother apologetically informed me that they were being transferred because her husband, a railroad man, was being moved to a new locale out of state. My hopes plummeted.

The Social Worker moved them all to a new foster home up in the high desert over an hour's drive from Hollywood. I was frantically trying to hustle rides on my free days since I no longer had the leased Mustang. I went when I could and would take them gifts and clothes. It was painful for us all, especially when I had to leave them there. The African-American foster family lived in a poor dark shabby house in a shabby dust flat. My kids had been surrounded by Afro-Cuban culture, and these people didn't know one word of Spanish. Social Service had color coded my kids instead of placing them in a Latin family based on their home culture.

Chapter 48
On My Own
November 1964

In the first few weeks after escaping Louie, Daddy was bellowing at Mom and me whenever we stayed up late at night talking in the living room. He said he couldn't sleep until everyone was in bed for the night. He had returned to work as a background artist at the animation studios in Burbank and had enough problems of his own without mine. He made it very clear that I was an interruption and an added expense. I needed to find a job quickly. Losing my kids the way I had traumatized me in ways I can't ever accurately describe. It was hard for me to get my mind wrapped around what I had to do now. I knew it traumatized my folks too, but by calling the authorities without warning me, everything was taken out of my hands. The children and I were all at the mercy of the system. *The children, now in their sixties, never recovered.* Recovery for me took on many layers. I discovered I had gonorrhea, an abscess in my groin and a dry abscess in my gum from my broken tooth. Not only was I a psychological mess, I was physically very unwell. I looked skeletal and obsessively tried to tell Mom everything that had happened to me after they threw me out. It was not something she wanted to hear, nor could she absorb. Furthermore, her sensibilities were shocked beyond words. But I wanted her to be shocked; Shocked as I had been. I wanted her to understand how much I had suffered. I needed her empathy. I needed her apology. She couldn't give it. She chronically mopped the kitchen counters with her back turned while I told her of the last two years' nightmare. I didn't even begin to go into what had happened in New York.

"Don't dwell, Vic. Don't dwell."

"I need to say it out loud, Mom. I need to tell someone. You, I need you."

During the brief stay with my folks, I was trying to get my health issues resolved and I needed to find work. Daddy made it clear that he couldn't afford to take me on nor my additional expenses. Mom's downstairs neighbor knew a guy called Shelly Davis, who along with Elmer Valentine, was part owner of the new hot club on the Sunset Strip, *The Whisky a Go! Go!* Shelly gave me a job as a cocktail waitress. He treated me like a daughter and was endlessly kind to me after he heard my story. I loved the energy in the club and felt cautiously revived.

Johnny Rivers was playing LIVE blasting *Blueberry Hill* night after night and the dance floor was packed. Famed hairdresser, the late Gene Shacove whose life the film *Shampoo* was based on, was a frequent customer. Go-Go Dancers in their fringed costumes and white high-heeled boots were dancing in suspended cages above the stage by the back wall where the service bar was tucked away. We wore black pantyhose, high heels, short black skirts and striped t-shirts. We were costumed to look like French *Apache* dancers. I weaved my way through shoulder-to-shoulder crowds carrying my tray above my head. I learned the calling order of drinks and was able to memorize them in correct order so the bartender would accept them and then remember who and in which order they were to be delivered.

One-handed, I wove through the crowds of drinking, partying patrons, tallying the drink tabs in my head all the while balancing my tray high above the crush with folded paper money wrapped around my fingers. It was empowering learning that I could count money and make change on the fly.

Mom had always intoned, "I was never good at arithmetic and you never will be either. You won't need it, because your husband will take care of your money." I think that may have been the only time she ever indicated that she thought I would marry. When the other girls in high school were carefully filling their Hope Chests with their mothers, plotting their college careers in hopes of finding a good provider husband, my mom was telling me I needed my eyeliner a little bit more uplifted on the outside ends, making me look more exotic. For an innocent little country girl that did not stand me in good stead. And, of course, my husband did take care of all my money. I never saw a penny.

Liberated and stronger by the day, my dental, neck, spinal injuries and gynecological issues continued to plague me. I always kept my mouth closed when I was working because I was packing white candle wax over my front tooth so the break wasn't visible. Customers would always say, "Why don't you smile?" I would smile enigmatically like the Mona Lisa. While I was enjoying my new freedom, every day remained a challenge.

I borrowed $140 from Daddy to move into a one-bedroom apartment just below the Sunset Strip walking distance from my new job. After being systematically starved and confined for so long I was truly malnourished and had no idea how to grocery shop, cook for one, or eat healthful foods anymore. Just the freedom to taste things I hadn't tasted since I left home in Connecticut was miraculous in itself. I'd even concoct weird mixtures like 7-Up and heavy whipping cream just to savor different flavors and textures. Everything tasted luxurious. I kept eggs, butter, bread, Cheerios, milk and not much else.

The cops had sliced our mattresses open and tossed the Canyon house finding no drugs so I had minimal salvaged furniture. My folks had taken me up one time to collect what I could, but there wasn't much left undamaged. Daddy kept the Hasselblad camera purchased with my Playboy money and all the camera equipment as collateral for my loan. I managed to retrieve the Scandinavian shag rugs, a couple of small antique tables, a couple of matching chairs and a studio couch that I slept on in my new apartment's living room. There were no paintings on the walls. I didn't even have a chest of drawers. Scavengers had stripped most of my furniture from the Canyon house. I had a couple of plates, a small frying pan, a saucepan and I found some silverware. Nito's crib was placed in the empty bedroom awaiting the day when I could bring him home and that was pretty much it.

I bought myself some very conservative looking, frumpy clothes in a thrift shop that covered me up as much as possible. Even though I sweltered in the L.A. heat, I didn't want anyone looking at my figure and I was fearful of being recognized.

While I was living my new life, I worried constantly about everything - my kids in the foster home, Louie getting out of prison and trying to take revenge. I was getting calls from the prison Chaplain telling me that Louie was begging my forgiveness and to please come get him out. I wondered how he got my new telephone number. I ignored him. The FBI was making visits to me, but never indicated why, so I suspected Louie was into something more serious than I knew about. I was deeply depressed dealing with the past years of trauma but the job, the music, the money and a couple of new friends and my nice clean one-bedroom apartment kept me going.

One of the waitresses I was working with at the Whisky told me that she heard that the Playboy Club was scheduled to open on New Year's Eve and it was going to be fabulous. They were hiring girls to train as Bunnies. She said we were sure to be able to make a lot more money there. So, she and I went over and applied. Since I was a relatively recent Playmate, I was sure that I'd be a shoo-in as they wanted as many Playmates as possible to open the Club. We both got hired.

It was the first Playboy Club on the West Coast so there was quite a big buzz about it. We were all excited to be there. The anticipation of its opening was the talk of the town. The Bunnies were already Stars on the Strip before Playboy even opened their club doors. Local guys considered it a feather in their caps if they could get the phone number of one of the Bunnies.

One of my Bunny Instructors was Francesca, a beautiful, hip, sassy, black woman from New York who became my friend. Playboy brought her out to Los Angeles from one of the 'back east' clubs, along with Hope Parker, another lifelong friend who recently died. They were to train all of us, the new Bunnies, on the intricacies of how to wear the costume, how to serve and mix drinks at the table, "backwards and in high heels." There was the "Bunny Dip" to master, and the "Bunny Perch." We weren't allowed to sit.

We were assigned two costumes, a white collar and cuffs, a black bow tie and silver cufflinks with the rabbit head logo imprinted on them. And, of course, our quintessential Bunny ears and fluffy white Bunny tails. We were instructed to make sure the Bunny heads were 'kissing' when we put our fists together. We wore black panty hose and our heels had to be regulation 3-inches and match each costume color. They couldn't be scuffed and we couldn't get a run in our stockings. We had wigs, false eyelashes and false fingernails. The bodices of our costumes were built a bit lower than our breasts so we had to put bust pads inside and sit ourselves on top making us look much bigger than natural. That's why we were trained to serve and mix drinks backwards, otherwise we'd fall out on the tables, not that the customers, the *Keyholders*, would complain.

I remember one funny moment when Bunny J.J. told a Keyholder that he could have a piece of tail for $50. He enthusiastically agreed. She went back to the Service Bar, pulled a piece of yarn from her Bunny tail, tied it around a Bunny head swizzle stick and saucily returned it to him. He paid up! It was a good laugh and we all were impressed by her *chutzpah*.

It took two weeks before we were considered ready to meet the public. We had to be perfect. We represented the image of Playboy - the Girl Next Door, "Look but don't touch." We were expected to be perfectly trained in order to be presented by New Year's Eve for the big Celebrity Gala opening.

When we first opened the Club in '65, Francesca (Bunny J.J.) and Bunny China Lee, worked in the club's Living Room. China became the first Chinese Playmate in Playboy history. Bunny Anna, who now owns a home next door to Fran's lovely historic Victorian in Selma, Alabama, along with Bunny Gwen Wong, who later became the second Chinese Playmate, worked with me in the Playmate Bar. My Centerfold was backlit on the wall above the bar, as all the Centerfolds were. Mine was hanging over the cash register. Our favorite bartender, Mario Maglieri, went on to become owner of The Whisky a Go-Go and The Roxy on the Strip.

The two-week training was stringent. The rules and regulations were rigid. Our dress code was strict. Our Bunny costumes had to be checked in and out by the Wardrobe Mistress who took care of them, dry cleaned them, and made sure we were flawless at the beginning of each shift. And, the Bunny Mother oversaw everything from her office off the dressing room.

Each and every infraction carried a demerit. Thirty demerits, any significant weight gain, scuffed heels, ears weren't worn properly, a dirty tail or any other straying from the rules and we were out. We were, however, allowed to earn back merits by participating in Playboy Promotional events. On one such attempt to earn back merits I participated in a televised Arthritis Telethon in which I danced with the legendary Dick Van Dyke. I emceed a Bunny baseball game at Dodger Stadium during halftime with the now deceased Honorary Hollywood Mayor, Johnny Grant, with both our names high on the marquis and posed for many photo ops with celebrities.

The trays were probably a minimum of twenty-five pounds if it were only a table of four. For one scotch and water, there was a 'rock' glass with ice cubes, a jigger of scotch and a carafe of water. So, you can imagine how heavy the trays were when there was a table of eight or ten Keyholders. It was not an easy job. This club was more like work than the Whisky had been. We arrived at 2 in the afternoon to be ready to go down on the floor by 3 p.m. It took a lot of time to be fabulous!

We were trained to please men. It was our job to be objects of men's desires. In those days, women understood that in order to succeed, we had to be smiled upon by the male power structure. At Playboy, it often manifested through either marriage to a Playboy executive or one of Hugh Hefner's cronies or celebrity friends. But, at the very least, we were to be appealing and sexy at all times… and appear to be, but not, available. Naturally it didn't apply to Hef's inner circle of VIPs, his cronies. We were allowed to mingle with them. While we were Hef's Private Reserve, there was no pressure to perform for them other than our routine work shifts. Everyone had a choice.

There were Wilmark agents, private detectives who posed as Keyholders to make sure the Bunnies didn't accept dates from members. The policy was in place to protect us from abuse and all about keeping us on a pedestal. While we were only making $2.03 an hour, our tips were in cash and they were so great that we often had to be reminded to pick up our paychecks. Needless to say, we earned every penny.

In those Bunny days, we still glorified in our own objectification. Women were at a turning point in their social and political evolution. For the most part we hadn't defined what we were doing as objectification... yet.

Many of the Bunnies were working their way through college, saving money to buy a house or start businesses. But many, like Francesca and me, were single parents just trying to make ends meet. I was struggling through all my post trauma and focusing on trying to maintain a responsible job so I could get my boy back and I was still dealing with my dental issues from the broken tooth. There were fun moments but underneath the public smiles I was a basket case - and desperately lonely.

We were pals with all the entertainers who played the Playboy Club circuit, Red Foxx, Jackie Gayle, Richard Pryor, Gary Crosby and Bill Cosby. We never saw them as a threat. We'd get off work and go across the street after work to have 'breakfast' at Cyrano's, as all fellow employees did.

When feminist, activist, and author Gloria Steinem, became an undercover Bunny in the New York Club in 1986, exposing the chauvinism, the misogyny, and the paternalistic control of women, I was already gone. But her famous quote and book title really speaks to me. "The truth will set you free, but first it will piss you off."

She was researching how Bunnies, and all women really, were mere objects for men's whimsical sport. She wrote about it and didn't endear herself to Hef at all. They became arch enemies and faced off in television interviews from time to time. She confronted him publicly and became a chronic thorn in his patriarchal side.

While I simmered and felt resentful about being treated as just a sex object, I didn't know yet how to define my nebulous resentments. I didn't know how to frame my anger in a constructive way in order for it to become effective rather than self-destructive. I still felt inhibited about being labeled a feminist - *those women who want to act like a man!* Women were disdained for being Women's Libbers. Even my mother looked down on them. I remember fearing being ostracized or ridiculed as a feminist. It's embarrassing to admit, but though I loathed being reduced to a collection of body parts, it was the only way I knew. I resented the fact that there was no respect or concern for my intellect, yet I didn't see a way out of it. I was intimidated by men's invalidating denigration of women, because they were the controlling power structure. My entire financial survival depended on my compliance. *Quid pro quo.* Pay to play and vice versa. Compliance for a living wage with the dangling promise of something better on the horizon - albeit vague - glittering and nebulous.

I'd still say sarcastically to guys whose eyes were glued to my boobs when we were introduced, "Hello, I'm up here," and I'd guide their glance to my face. They'd look up embarrassed. They knew I was calling them on their trip. An actor's agent took me to a party where he wanted me to be *seen*. Before we arrived, he said to me, "Just stand there and look pretty. Don't say anything intelligent and spoil it." I seethed, but at twenty-two, still felt powerless to stand up against what seemed to me an impenetrable system of male dominance. It was just something I didn't have in me at the time. I was continuously rebounding from my traumatic experiences, and every day I was just in survival mode.

My therapist from USC who was offering free counseling for his research project about prostitutes put moves on me and a decade later I saw his face on the cover of *Psychology Today*. My Beverly Hills dentist wanted to trade dental work for a little *hanky-panky* and when I refused, he turned me over to a collection agency. The physician who lanced the boil in my groin suggested that he schedule another procedure and put me under a general anesthetic so he and his doctor friend could explore my situation a bit further. I never went back. It seemed that there was no one I could trust.

As a teen in the *Father Knows Best* Fifties, raised in a very patriarchal family structure by narcissistic parents, I was untangling a lot. I had not yet found my strength of conviction nor my words. I couldn't stand up against it. I didn't even know I could. I had no voice. My experience taught me that when I voiced my thoughts, feelings and opinions, I got whacked across the face. I'd gotten used to being dismissed or spoken to platitudinously. I bridled against the little patronizing pats on the head as though I were such a clever little child speaking idealistically out of my ass. I'd been fired for less. While I remained silent for years, my *thinking* was very loud inside my head. My cynicism grew and my sarcasm became increasingly sharp-edged. I was simultaneously, haltingly beginning to soothe my old wounds. I acted indifferent and above it all. I didn't ask anyone for anything. I just kept my head down, my mouth shut and soldiered on alone.

I acted, modeled, became an acting intern at MGM. I dated and was in love with actor Jim Brolin and later, producer Aaron Spelling after his divorce from Carolyn

Jones, but sabotaged each love affaire because I couldn't tell them about what had just happened to me - and that I had a racially mixed toddler in foster care who I was planning on bringing home as soon as I could. How could I explain any of what I had survived? I imagined they would reject me and I so I rejected them first. They never understood why I broke it off. I still remember their confusion and hurt. Aaron said, "Are you sure?" I said "Yes," without elaborating and hung up the phone. I couldn't even look him in the eyes and tell him to his face. That hurt for a long time. Writing songs became my outlet. I could say things poetically to music that I couldn't say straight out to a person's face. And who could hit me when I had a big guitar on my lap?

Chapter 49
My Dirty Diamond

In 1965, I was beginning to make some good money at the Club - and got to keep it all myself. I was beginning to feel tentatively independent and relatively courageous. I recall getting a postcard, an ad, in the mail, saying "You have won a diamond! Just come on down and pick out your setting! $50!"

After I'd lost everything I'd ever owned, it seemed particularly tantalizing to buy myself a diamond ring. Looking at my Playboy candid shots in borrowed clothing holding my guitar across my swelling belly and tight waistband, I needed something to uplift me. It felt like a dream to be able to buy something beautiful for myself and call it my very own. It was my little secret celebration of renewal and I never told anyone. I was embarrassed to admit it.

So, I went downtown to check out this *free* diamond. I was too naïve to know it was just a marketing ploy, though I sensed the salesman suppressing his amusement. I didn't look up into his eyes. I felt timid and self-conscious, but I tried to appear sophisticated and blasé as if it was nothing too important - just a new trinket. I'm sure I was pretty obvious.

Looking at all the settings, the one that drew me in was a lovely delicate gold rose. I was captivated. My eyes returned to it, over and over. I chose it for my *free* diamond set in the center. It would take two weeks for it to be ready.

I was barely able to contain myself. When it was ready and I finally wore it home I couldn't stop looking at it on my ring finger. I held it one way, then the other. The diamond sparkled in the light, twinkled in the night. I was mesmerized. I felt so proud of myself for being able to, actually, pay for it with my own earned money. I felt grown up, glamorous, elegant. It looked so pretty glistening on my finger that I simply couldn't stop looking at it.

One day, a fellow Bunny looked at my hand admiringly and said, "Oh, what a pretty ring!" Puffing up a bit, I said, "Oh, thank you!" in my best, casually sophisticated voice. I think I may have stood a bit taller and straighter in that moment. *"But your diamond is dirty,"* she said. *"You really need to clean it. How do you clean YOUR diamonds? Now the way I clean MY diamonds..."*

I was caught off guard - flustered, embarrassed, crestfallen, deflated - all of it. I may have even turned red. I know I shrank and was tongue-tied. My face felt hot and I didn't know how to answer her. I had never noticed it was dirty and no one, not even my jewelry-diva mother, had ever told me that diamonds needed to be cleaned. It hadn't occurred to me. It was all just as beautiful in my eyes as it was on the day that I wore it home. But, suddenly I saw my precious diamond in a different light. I realized that it had, in fact, gotten dull after all. I just hadn't noticed. I'd been blinded by a brief superficial flash and I'd become oblivious to its diminishing sparkle. In the end it was stolen.

I saw my lost and dirty diamond becoming a metaphor for my life. Have you ever had one of those days when you wake up in the morning and wonder where the sparkle went, the spontaneous joy - and when did it leave? Most importantly, how do you get it back? How DO we clean our diamonds?

We need to clean our diamonds - our soul gifts - like our windows or our mirrors - routine maintenance. We must make time for our daily reality checks, our personal inventory and quiet times of self-exploration and self-care. Sometimes just a walk alone in nature, a quiet day in bed with a good book, a cup of tea and a nap with our fur babies - a day to care for ourselves and no one else - is the perfect therapy. We need the Light to shine through. We want OUR light to shine through.

Like so many young people, I had received precious jewels of opportunity, talent, and spirit. Not having my special gifts valued by the very people who were supposed to teach me how to honor and protect myself, I never learned how to value my gifts, nor recognize my own true worth. From not understanding the true value of the gifts I was given, I allowed others to devalue them, to devalue me, my worth, my diamonds - and so they became dulled, dirty, stolen and lost. Worst of all I entrusted my diamonds (my crystalline inner being, my light) to those unworthy of my trust.

I began understanding the Yin and Yang of life. The shadow and the light that are all part of the whole. I began to understand that tragedy and triumph are often dished on the same plate. Without sorrow, we can't fully comprehend let alone appreciate joy, nor to place value on simple, unfrilled contentment. Without darkness there is no gratitude for the Light. Ralph Waldo Emerson in a collection of his essays called it Compensation. Balance. Counterbalance.

I learned to call it LIFE.

I have learned to set healthier boundaries, something my youngest daughter, Meaganlark, taught me. "Mama! Healthy boundaries!" she admonished me once when I needed to hear it. She was surprised and pleased when I told her it was, she who taught me that. The child becomes the mother. The mirror is held up.

My life now is about what I will and will not allow to drain my energy, my time, my personal space, and my precious resources. In some ways I have returned to who I was when I was a child. I am often the silent observer, taking stock, assessing, finding balance.

My children and my 'Baby Grands' are my most precious jewels... my diamonds... my most lasting treasures... my true legacy as a woman, as a human being. It is not that the product of my biology wins out in the end but - I get to see the future in their eyes. I get to celebrate their brilliant facets. I get to perhaps offer some inspiration, some guidance. I hope to teach them how valuable they are to the world - and to take every stumbling block tossed in their path as a lesson so they may become deeper souls, more empathic and wiser. I'll teach them how to keep their diamonds clean.

I heard someone say, "You can't have a diamond without a volcano, but not every volcano produces a diamond."

Diamonds are not necessarily born with their facets fully polished. They are created under pressure, a pressure they don't necessarily choose. Like a diamond under pressure, we can choose to crumble or shine.

We must choose to shine.

Playboy and Glam Shots

19.

20.

21.

22.

19-21. Model photos by Harry Drinkwater.
22. Sculptor's house when I lost all my belongings.

23.

24.

25.

26.

23. The Centerfold - Miss September 1963
24. Trading card series - Top 100 Centerfolds of the
Century (The 20th)
25. Photo by Harry Drinkwater

Reentering Life After Being Trafficked
1964 – 1969

26.

27.

28.

29.

26. Daddy, me at 98 lbs. with Anne at Grandma's right after I escaped - 1964
27. Playboy Club Opening Sunset Strip with Ryan O'Neill- 1965
28. Playmate Promo Arthritis Telethon with Johnny Grant and Dick Van Dyke-1965
29. Bunny "Vicky" - 1965

30.   31.

32.

30. Go Go Dancing - Las Vegas -1965
31. Acting Headshot - 1966
32. Singing Anti-War songs, Hollywood Canteen. Back-up guitar, Richard D'Agostin -1968

Chapter 50
Vegas a Go-Go Go

I worked at the Playboy Club for the first six months after it opened. But I was so tired of the long late-night hours, standing and serving in three-inch heels that when I heard about an audition to dance in a Go-Go line in Vegas, I jumped on it. I loved dancing.

I signed a six-week contract and I figured that since my housing would be covered and I was making union wages, I would send all my checks home to Mom to save for me. I'd keep just enough to live on while I was away. I needed to save up to buy a car.

The production company flew us up to Vegas the night we auditioned. We were tucked into our motel rooms and were told that we would be taken over to the Thunderbird Hotel in the morning for our first rehearsal. We had to begin at 6 a.m. We'd go for costume fitting and then our first of three shows would be that very day at 1 p.m. in the hotel lounge with a rock n' roll group called The Crickets. We'd have 45 minutes in between each of the three daily shows. It was all pretty exciting. I slept alone in my room that night and was told that I would have a roommate but she would meet us in the morning at rehearsal.

I arrived in the rehearsal hall ready to work. My new roommate and chorus mate came over to me and what a surprise! It was Carmen, from my trip to Aspen, Colorado with Hoyt - Travis Edmundson's then ex-wife. The rehearsal hall was crowded with dancers and choreographers, musicians and performers they had pulled from the evening show who would dance topless since we would not. In the midst of all the high energy I heard a man's voice saying, "Victoria Valentino! We meet again!"

It took me a minute. I was stunned. There was "Porsche Guy" weaving towards me through the crush of dancers, a long way from a Venice Beach phone booth. I couldn't believe it. Long white ponytail and the same serene crystal blue smiling eyes. He introduced himself. It was Otho Pettijean, and his wife, Angelique, was one of the dancers from the evening show who would be dancing with us. What a reunion this was turning out to be.

Angelique Pettijean was tall, svelte with a little French boy haircut, huge eyes framed by Otho's intricately painted eyeliner designs. She had perfect breasts, danced with style and added a definite elegant glam to our chorus line. From then on whenever we could, Otho, Angelique and I hung out by the hotel pool sunbathing after our shows.

During the first week we were moved to the night shift but then eventually moved back to the day shift. While the other girls were sitting and gambling with guys in between our three shows, I was sitting in the Oyster Bar writing letters home to my mother and enclosing my earnings.

After we had gotten into our dance routines and adjusted to our new schedules, we were able to enjoy ourselves a bit more. We were dancing in black leotard tops and bottoms with white tassels and white high heeled Go-Go boots. The band behind us turned out to be a lot of fun - *The Crickets*. We were dancing to *"Walking the Dog," "Oh, Johnny B Goode," "Natural Woman,"* and every good classic

'60s hit song you can imagine. It was lively and we had a great response from the lounge audience. Our contract was extended for another few weeks.

I met a nice guy named Norman through Otho and after I sprained my ankle and had to take a break, I began spending every spare bit of time with him. I walked around with an ace wrap and limped. He didn't seem to mind, and thankfully didn't notice when my temporary front tooth got stuck in my cheeseburger during lunch. I covered up pretty quickly, but I was still under so much ongoing stress getting my broken tooth repaired, I never could completely relax and feel confident.

Norman turned out to be Robert "Bobby" Goulet's personal manager when Bobby was married to the singer Carol Lawrence. We regularly hung out with them along with many other big stars on the Las Vegas Strip. Norman used to love to go watch Don Rickles perform in the lounge of the Sands Hotel. We'd be joined frequently by singer Abbe Lane who was no longer married to Xavier Cugat but during the time I knew her she was married to a guy named Perry Leff. Perry had a tall spiky dark crew cut, with a very distinctive white streak blazing through it.

Whenever Norman, Abbe and I would enter the Sands Lounge to see Don, he would stop his routine for a rapid-fire delivery of one-liners.

"Here's Norman Rosemont, Robert Goulet's manager! Hope you get a cold in both your throats! Norman's here with the little gimp from the Thunderbird, looking like she just stepped off a box of Fannie Farmer Chocolates! (The ace wrap on my ankle and the white cotton Mexican dress with cotton lace bell-shaped sleeves that

Mom had given me completed the image.) *And Abbe Lane! Where's your husband - The Last of the Mohicans?"*

Don was always outrageous and unflappable. So, when Norman gave Bobby and Carol their second wedding anniversary party on the rooftop terrace at the Sands with every major star on the Strip in attendance - Ed Sullivan and his wife, Polly Bergen and her husband, Freddy Fields, Frank Sinatra, Jr., Shelly Berman, Norm Crosby, Jack E. Leonard, Mort Sahl, Abbe and Perry, of course - it was a fabulous night. But Don Rickles couldn't make it, because he was performing his late-night show downstairs in the Lounge.

Bobby had the idea that we should all parade downstairs together and see if we could rattle Don. So, with our *leis* around our necks, our umbrella-drinks in hand, we all piled into the elevators and arrived at the closed door of the Lounge. We lined up outside. Bobby and Carol, in the lead and behind them every mega-star in Vegas - and Playmate me. We could hardly contain ourselves imagining Don's reaction when we walked in.

The doors were opened and we took a beat, then promenaded down the center aisle, walked over the little bridge that crossed the sunken stage-side bar, and directly onto the stage. We circled Don at the mic without looking at him or saying a word and marched off into the wings.

Don just stood there silently, then looked at the audience never missing a beat and in his typical blasé manner said, *"See? They have to come here to get noticed."* The audience broke into peals of laughter.

The next morning in the dining room where we were all hung over and having breakfast, there was a constant reliving of that moment. We were sitting with comedian Shelly Berman who was bemoaning his flagging career. He was so downcast that he could barely lift his head up. He complained, *"No one even knows who I am anymore."* As we tried to reassure him, he lifted his head to see a girl in the doorway of the restaurant scanning the crowd. Suddenly she appeared to make contact and rushed over to our table.

"Shelly! She said, *"I didn't recognize you!"*

It was his personal assistant. He said, *"See!"*

It was finally time for me to return home to Los Angeles and say goodbye to everyone. I learned that Norman was married, so I accepted that this was it, but I was sorry to go. I didn't want to return to the Playboy Club and I didn't think I could live or raise a child in Vegas, so I was going to have to come up with something else when I got back to L.A. I just wasn't sure what that would be.

"Feathers fall around you and show you the way to go…"
--Neil Young

Chapter 51
Saved

I returned to my apartment, got another cocktail waitress job and had one more run-in with Louie. I never could figure out how he always found me. One day while I was waiting for a girlfriend to pick me up to go to work, there was a knock on the door. Thinking it was her, I opened the door widely with a big smile on my face, which faded immediately. It was Louie's thug, Buddy, standing there. He pushed his way inside and, in a few seconds, there was another knock on the door. Buddy opened the door to let in Louie and a big mean guy with scraggly long hair and a beard that almost reached his waist. I knew I was in trouble.

Louie forced me down on my studio couch and began his familiar ranting. He had just gotten out of prison along with Buddy and this other goon and they were there so Louie could claim his pound of flesh. His voice began crescendoing in volume as he worked himself up to hitting me. I knew his pattern all too well. Suddenly my phone rang. It was sitting on the couch and I lunged for it before Louie could grab it. On the other line was my condo neighbor, Frank Sinatra's *valet charmante,* George Jacobs, whose great parties I often attended. I had confided in George so he knew my story. I answered deliberately in an uncharacteristic tone of voice and he said, "Are you alright?" I said, "No." He asked "Do you want me to send the cops?" I emphatically said, "Absolutely!" In two minutes, there was a knock on the door and I heard "Police! Open up!" Louie opened the door and started telling the cops that I was his wife and I had been a street corner hooker that got our children taken away. The cops didn't buy it and asked him if his name was on the rental agreement. I jumped in and said, "NO." They were escorted out. I was so relieved that I almost collapsed. I called George back and told him that he had saved my life. Louie never returned. I began looking for a new apartment close to Grandma's house.

After a year's time, I had work, an apartment, the approval of the Social Worker and the FBI, and I was shown to be fit. I was informed that I could take my son home, but Nita and Rico had to remain until their father could pick them up. I knew that would happen since I had no legal claim to them, but it didn't make it any easier on any of us. As an adult I understood, but the children never would and I knew they'd be traumatized once again. I dreaded the moment.

My mother agreed to drive me up to the foster home way up in the high desert when it was time to bring Nito home. All three kids had been placed together, which had not been a smart thing for them to do. Daddy wanted me to give my baby up for adoption to the foster mother who had been pressuring me to let her adopt him, so he made retrieving my baby as difficult as possible. I fought him all the way. He didn't want *his daughter to have a Negro child*. I told Daddy, "This is *my* son! He has *my* eyes. I will *never* give him up."

He told Mom she was not allowed to drive me, and left her with an empty tank of gas and no cash. To her credit she determinedly walked from their Hollywood Boulevard apartment all the way down to Grandma's house. She borrowed just enough gas money to fill the tank and then walked all the way back. It was a horribly long drive through the hot high desert. Since air conditioning wasn't standard issue in cars until the Eighties, my parents had none. When we got there the foster mother had the baby's belongings all packed and ready to go. Nita was restless, acting unsettled, picking up on the vibe. Rico was in kindergarten that day and I was not allowed to wait till he got home to say goodbye. I had no chance to offer an explanation that might sit easier in any child's heart and mind, even though I knew nothing really could.

For decades I was plagued by my last memories of Nita who was 4 ½ years old by then. She clung to me crying once she understood I was leaving with the baby and not her. The foster mother had to separate us. Her fingers had to be peeled off the car door handle. I was dying inside. As my mother pulled away, I saw her in my side view mirror running after the car. I sat in the passenger seat holding my two-year-old Nito in my lap, my mother at the wheel, trying not to just make my mother stop the car and go grab her and deal with the consequences later. She was running and screaming, "Mama! Mama! Why are you taking the baby and you're not taking me?" My mother kept driving and looked straight ahead without a word. She never discussed it with me for the rest of her life. It never ceased to haunt me.

That image played over and over again all my life. I hoped that one day our paths would cross again and I could explain that I was given no choice. I had to let them go. I imagined that perhaps one day we might be reunited in love and healing. But I knew that as long as Louie was alive, I would never see them again. For years I laid awake thinking about them. I wrote letters to them on the ceiling at night when I couldn't sleep, begging for their forgiveness, praying they were alright. I must have written a million letters to them in my head. I wondered if I'd ever see them again and if they'd even remember me - and if they did, would they hate me… I had no doubt in my mind that if Louie had anything to do with it, he'd see to it.

Once I had my baby home, I decided to change his name. I wanted to distance myself and him, as far from Louie and past experiences as I possibly could. The African-American foster parents had been calling him Raymond. That was not going to stick. Rico and Nita called him "*Choo Choo*" because he loved trains…

I chose Antony Lucien. Daddy's name was Antonino and I wanted to give my son a name of my choosing and my own family. Daddy had been called Tony when he was young but he grew into Nino after he grew up and became a professional artist. So, I called my little man, Tony. He also bore Daddy's last name as I did. After I escaped from Louie, I reverted to using my maiden name, Daddy Nino's name, the one I grew up with in school. I didn't return to using Valentino professionally again until after I learned that he had died and I became involved with Playboy again in my Fifties for their 40th Anniversary festivities, and only because of my fans.

Chapter 52
The Single Mom Shuffle

Daddy did indeed find me a car with the money I'd earned dancing. It was a red and white Nash Rambler that his mechanic vouched for, though it did not exactly suit my mood, nor style, people always saw me coming. It took every penny I had saved. Tony and I moved into a one-bedroom apartment a block south of Grandma's house on Genesee. Tony went to pre-school and I took a couple of waitress jobs and piecemealed my life together. I got an agent who got me the occasional magazine ad modeling job, Mexican beer commercials; I performed in the occasional play and modeled for another Playboy layout using Playmates as Zodiac signs. I was Taurus in toreador pants, a matador hat and a cape with a big bull head mounted on a board. It paid our rent that month.

I became a Screen Actor's Guild member by being Maureen Arthur's "*fanny*" double in the film, *How to Succeed in Business Without Really Trying* with Robert Morse and Michelle Lee. Maureen had played the lead on Broadway and was now the star of the film, but they needed someone with a well-shaped *derriere* who could do a trick walk. I got the job. When they wanted me on set, they hollered, "*Fanny!*" So, when you see the camera pan on Maureen's fanny walking down the center aisle of the typing pool, it's me!

Maureen was not pleased and was kvetching to Michelle that having a body double was not in her contract.

I overheard her and walked up to her, bent over and said, *"Here! Kick it!"* We all laughed and it cleared the air.

I had Nelson Eddy's dressing trailer on the set with his name on the door while he was out for a week. People were always stopping by expecting to chat with him, so I put a sign above his name on the door. It read, *"I am* NOT... Nelson Eddy." I loved every minute.

I also got a bit part as a Greek secret agent on Man from U.N.C.L.E. and was being considered for a recurring character when the series was canceled. I always felt as if I was on the verge of modest regular employment only to have it crash. I was hired as a Can-Can dancer in the chorus line of Franz Lehar's *The Merry Widow Waltz* and we performed at the Wilshire Ebell Theater. We were doing high kicks in ruffled skirts, cartwheels into splits and I could sing at full volume. It was the kind of theater I had been trained for in Connecticut and New York - and I loved it with all my heart. As a SAG member I could get paid for being on *The Dating Game* so I was happy to do that. It wasn't about the date. I chose the date who in turn would introduce me to Tamar, the mother of a baby named Peace. *Peace on Earth Goodwill Towards All Men Hodell.* She and her entourage of two young gay guys found an apartment that occupied the entire second floor of a big old house in Echo Park. We decided we'd all live communally and share expenses. It was 1967 and the beginning of the Hippy Movement; the Peace and Love movement, the anti-Vietnam protest movement and the Black Power movement. It was an exciting time to live in L.A. I saw lots of changes and I found so much happiness within myself during that year. I was writing a lot of songs. Tony was a loving free spirit always at my side as we lived our eclectic life. I hand-sewed his little tunics, his *dashikis* and his hair was becoming a righteous Sixties Afro. He was gregarious and loved people and they in turn loved him.

While living in our commune, I was contacted by journalist Joe Hyams to be interviewed for a *Cosmopolitan Magazine* article - a retrospective on the Playboy Playmates. Joe arrived in front of our big old shabby two-story Craftsman house in Echo Park. It was a poorish area of L.A. on the south west section of Sunset Boulevard. When his driver parked his big Rolls Royce right in front it caused quite a stir. The old, bleached blond, heavy-set, landlady who lived on the first floor gawked through her window wondering what in heaven's name a Rolls Royce was doing in front of her house.

Joe wrote a great article describing me sitting on the floor in my under-the-eaves room draped with white lace tablecloths for bed curtains, dipping dried shrimp in my Japanese tea bowl. He said I was the lead in his article and thought I was so funny. Funny would never have been a word I'd have used to describe myself then. I realized while I was alone in my head other people were seeing a very different me. It was startling.

That year during the *Summer of Love*, I met a couple from Santa Barbara who were involved in the Peace Movement. Regine and David. David was an Art History professor but wove his passion for left wing politics into his art lectures. Regine was a former Parisian ballet dancer.

After being inspired by then KPFK talk show host, Elliot Mintz, Regine came down to L.A. the summer of 1967 and showed up at an advocacy group meeting at the West Hollywood Presbyterian Church, looking to get involved.

Elliot reported daily on the Hippy Movement. He let all the Hippy kids in town know where the Love-ins were and how they could access health care, feed-ins and crash pads. Regine crashed at my place and we became an extended family. Their home in Santa Barbara became Tony's and my get-away from L.A. when city life overwhelmed us. Regine became Tony's Mama Regine. He'd spend time with them and he went to a progressive summer school up there. Their friends became ours. An English lord and his German wife had two children Tony's age, so when we were there, he spent every free moment at their house. Santa Barbara and our friends gave us so much normalcy, affirmation, inspiration and soul renewal.

Those summers included our excursions to the Renaissance Faires in the Agoura Hills, north of L.A. Regine choreographed the period dances while Tony and I enjoyed stepping into another period of history. We were living quite a marvelous, open-hearted, loving existence. I continued to write songs, perform at *Hootenannies* now called Open Mic Nights. I acted in multiple non-union movies to pay the rent in between union gigs and we frequented *Love-ins* and peace rallies. It was healing and the best time of our lives.

Chapter 53
Peace, Man!
1967

Tony and I were free spirits almost growing up together. He was four when the 1967 Summer of Love took over the consciousness of young people everywhere who were tired of the war in Vietnam - tired of racism - tired of sexism - tired of the hypocrisy and uptightness of the Fifties, the decade from which we had so recently emerged. Everyone was marching in the streets protesting and I was no exception. Tony rode on my shoulders chanting along with me and everyone else - "*Peace NOW!*"

Hippy kids from all over the country were making a rush on San Francisco and the Haight- Ashbury District, but flooding also into L.A. It was a thrilling time in my personal history. It was an energy-infused, highly creative period of my life. I was acting, singing, songwriting, meditating, dropping acid, experimenting with mescaline and chewing peyote buttons, reading Carlos Castaneda's *The Teachings of Don Juan: A Yaqui Way of Knowledge* - and cooking for lots of hungry scraggly kids daily at the church. Tony sat on the counter as I stirred huge cauldrons of rib-sticking chiles, spaghetti and stews. Tony greeted each of them as if they were family, or long-lost friends. Tony was our welcome committee. That year was the best therapy for me. I never had a *bad trip* and I wrote inspired songs. Reconnecting with my spiritual core, I became a meditator. I burned incense and lightheartedly danced at "Be-Ins" and "Love-Ins" wearing my beads, bells and headbands, carrying flowers, holding out hope for Peace and Universal Cosmic Love. I went to the Monterey Pops Festival with a friend. The Monterey Pops was the Woodstock before Woodstock. We sat right in front of Janis Joplin looking up into her lunging body as she sang *Ball and Chain* with Big Brother and the Holding Company. Ravi Shankar played his sitar. Girls were putting flowers into the barrels of the sheriffs' guns. I witnessed *The Who* smash their guitars on stage the same day before Jimi Hendrix came out and anticlimactically smashed his in the last set of the evening. Humping the wreckage to the tune of the *Star-Spangled Banner*. It was the final memorable political statement of the night.

We couldn't find a place to camp that Saturday night after Day 1 of the concert. All the road turn-outs and the campgrounds were packed and rumors of the Dead showing up at random campgrounds doing guerilla performances were rampant. At 4 a.m. we finally snuck into the grounds of the Esalen Institute in Big Sur, tip-toeing carefully through the deep wet grass and thick fog in the dark. Thinking we were alone in the big field we laid our sleeping bags down contentedly and crawled inside. When dawn came, the rain began and we peeked out only to discover that we were surrounded by a plethora of other people in sleeping bags. Not only that, we were very close to the edge of the craggy cliffs that dropped off into the churning sea. I had no idea how we managed not to step on anyone in the dark. It was part of what would become an iconic event - Rock n' Roll history in the making. And - in case you were wondering - Grandma's oatmeal cookies were great.

As my parents once had, I too sang at the USO in the Hollywood Canteen on Hollywood Boulevard. The late Richard "Dick" D'Agostin was my back-up guitar. I, however, sang anti-war songs and was not invited back! A psychodrama was being produced at the West Hollywood Presbyterian Church, my grandmother and great aunt's church. Dean Martin's daughter Deana Martin, Peter Fonda, Dennis Hopper and I performed. Dennis and I spent hours sitting on my living room floor with our many friends talking all night, sorting out what we believed to be our enlightened anti-war and deep life philosophies. Dennis and I began our brief *affaire* during those intense, iconoclastic, brainstorming, marathon convos.

I remember one day after I hadn't seen him for a couple of days, I was driving down Sunset Boulevard heading east. I came to a halt at a red light directly in front of Hollywood High School. Dennis, in his full-on fringed, rough-out regalia and long stringy hair was leaning into traffic with his thumb out. I swerved over and told him to hop in. "What the fuck are you doing hitchhiking for God's sake? Geez, Man!" He was high as usual, reeking of weed. He laughed. He said, "I'm heading over to the studio to see the rushes on this movie I'm making. Wanna come along?" "Sure."

We arrived in the projection room a mile or so down Sunset, only to find Peter standing there alone looking at the rushes of "*Easy Rider*" on a very big screen. I don't think either of them had a clue that it would become an iconic film journey that would take many of us along for the ride.

Chapter 54
Capitol Records
July 1969

To keep myself occupied in between *takes* on a film I was acting in, I'd been picking a little guitar. I sang in one scene and a fellow actor kept telling me how much he loved my voice. "I know an agent who's looking for talent for a music producer at Capitol Records. Are you interested?" "Hell, yeah!" He made the appointment and pretty soon I was sitting in front of the producer Vic Briggs, the former lead guitarist with Eric Burdon and the British Rock group *The Animals,* in the most iconic building in Hollywood - the Capitol Records building that looks like a stack of 45s. I had my guitar and played him a tune or two.

"You wanna make an album?"

"Sure!" Inside my head I was thinking, "Are you fucking kidding me?"

I called my guitarist immediately in utter excitement and disbelief. "Richard! You've got to play back-up with me!" So, Richard D'Agostin accompanied me when I auditioned singing Donovan's bluesy song "*Sunny Goodge Street.*" *"On the firefly platform on Sunny Goodge Street, a violent hash smoker shook a chocolate machine. Involved in an eating scene…"*

Vic stopped performing to produce other musicians before leaving the music business for a while. I was so jazzed that he wanted to produce me. The contracts were drawn up and my film producer friend, Ned, found me an established, well-known music attorney to negotiate my contract. I was feeling that at last I'd been heard. It would be my music, my lyrics, my voice that would be acknowledged - not just my cleavage and my fanny.

During the time my contract was being negotiated, my attorney Martin Cohen and I connected. We started dating. Tony and I spent lots of time together with him at his house, swimming in his pool, feeding his pet goats and tending to his organic vegetable garden. He was planning a pool party at his house to celebrate his new wine cellar and the successful negotiation of my recording contract. He let me know that if I was open, he wanted to announce our impending engagement.

I hadn't given him a firm answer yet. It was a heavy decision and I wasn't really sure how I felt. I was looking forward to a fun day full of promise, but that was it.

So, on September 6th, 1969, we planned to arrive at Martin's house in the Hollywood Hills ready to party.

It had been a busy week. Tony had become a Screen Actors Guild member from the "Wonder Bread" commercial he had acted in the previous summer and he was going for a "McDonald's" commercial on Friday the 5th. It was shooting on Monday.

On Thursday the 4th, the day before his audition, I took Tony to "Little Tokyo." We'd had a fun day, except that I had less than $10 on me. My dwindling finances added to my stress levels to say the least, but I tried to keep a smile on my face. He was having so much fun I didn't want him to know how anxious I was. Our new house that we'd moved into had eaten up most of my advance money from my Capitol contract and I was pinching pennies.

He wanted to buy every colorful trinket he saw and a pack of *nori nori* - dry sheets of seasoned black seaweed. We stopped for a small treat in a cafe and I watched him enjoy it as I drank my cup of green tea. Tony loved *nori nori*. He'd spent that day mischievously pasting the black sheets on his front teeth and smiling broadly at everyone he passed as he skipped behind me down the street. We giggled at the expressions on the faces of the passersby. He had such a quirky sense of humor that no matter how *down* I might be feeling he always made me laugh. We were totally pooped out when we got home and went straight to bed so we'd be rested for his morning audition.

The morning of Friday the 5th we drove out to a big park with massive red rock boulders in Chatsworth, California where the audition was held. We were happy as larks, singing our silly song we always sang in the car together until we giggled ourselves into utter exhaustion. It was a bawdy song we had picked up at the Renaissance Faire. And was our usual road song. We sang at the top of our lungs in our best, comic, exaggerated attempt at a Cockney accent! He had gone with friends to see the film *Oliver* that year so he had become infatuated with the sound of it. He'd run around chirping, *"Olivah! Olivah!"*

> *"Roll me ovah in the clovah,*
> *loyk you nevah did befohr!*
> *Roll me ovah! Roll me ovah!*
> *And ye'll nevah be a mayden anymohr!"*

The sun was shining, and we sang and we laughed, and we felt on top of the world as we sailed out the partially opened new 210 freeway heading west. There was hardly any traffic and we were jubilant. Tony got the audition and was booked to shoot the commercial on the coming Monday. That night we went to dinner with Martin and his other client, singer Linda Ronstadt, to a Chinese restaurant. Tony was smitten with her. After a very tiring day, he laid down with his head on her lap and fell asleep - then peed. I took note. He had wet the bed well into his fifth year, but had stopped when we moved into our new house. He loved his new room, proudly making his bed with his antique crazy-quilt that I was still repairing and adding velvet patches to, but lately since we began spending weekends with Martin, he was beginning to wet at night again. He never peed during a nap. I recognized that with all the changes in our lives, he was feeling insecure. This was a sign I needed to take seriously.

The next day we were expected to go to Martin's house, high in the hills above the Hollywood Bowl for the big pool party, but the following morning, Saturday the 6th of September, an avid fan of mine, a young Japanese dental assistant who was kind of crazy about Tony and me, invited us to spend the day with him doing lighthearted stuff. He pleaded his case with tempting outings - a picnic, a day at the beach, a movie, whatever our hearts desired, driving in his yellow Corvette convertible with the top down. It would be a fun free-spirited day. His name was Hiroshi, but he was called Hiro. We were about the same age and he utterly adored Tony. I was tempted to ditch Martin for the day and take Tony to go play with Hiro. It would put off my need to make a decision about moving in with Martin. But Martin's insistent telephone calls urging me to hurry up before guests arrived made me turn Hiro down. Martin wanted to know when I was arriving so we could go to the feed store to get hay for the goats. He said there was a cougar in a cage that he thought Tony would love to see. He insisted that we hurry because people would be showing up for the party and he needed to get all the chores done first. I felt obligated.

Martin had a nickname, too, "Mutt." I chose Mutt over Hiro.

Chapter 55
September 6, 1969

I grabbed our overnight bag and wrapped myself in my dark blue Nigerian-patterned cotton sarong over my bikini. Tony insisted on wearing his new jeans. He was outgrowing his African-style *dashikis* that I'd handsewn for him. He was wanting to dress more like the other boys in t-shirts and jeans. He had recently also insisted on having me shear off his massive afro. So on Thursday the 4th before we went to Little Tokyo, I sat him down on a stool in Grandma's kitchen and did the deed. I cut it all off with Grandma supervising while she stirred her pot of oatmeal on the stove. Tony was so happy and ran across the street with it all in a paper bag to give to Auntie Nor Nor. She'd told him that when he cut his hair, she'd save it and stuff a pillow with it for him to keep. He looked so fresh and neat. His *'fro'* had gotten so big that he hated having it brushed out. I used to tease him that I was finding little mouse nests in there. *"Oh, Mommy! There are NOT!"*

On Saturday late morning, with his fresh haircut, we ran out of the house in a hurry but forgot his swim trunks. When we arrived, Martin said not to worry, because he had his son's trunks at the house to wear in the pool for later. Martin had two young kids we hadn't met yet; a boy and a girl who lived with their mom. They left lots of their pool gear at their dad's house, since they visited and swam in the pool regularly.

Piling into Martin's car we headed to the feed store. Tony had a great time and as Martin predicted, he didn't want to leave the cougar. We had to rush him into the car or he would have stayed all day and Martin was beginning to get uptight. I rushed Tony into the backseat and slammed the door right on his fingers. He howled. I freaked. We got ice. We checked for anything broken and thanked God nothing was. I felt like utter shit for not being more patient and careful - and for allowing Martin's uptightness to frazzle me. I fussed over Tony all the way to the Frosty Freeze where Martin took him for an ice cream cone to calm him down and make his '*owie*' go away. It worked.

We got back to Martin's house, the house he wanted us to move into should I accept his recent proposal. I was still vacillating. I wasn't crazy in love, but he was earthy, said what was on his mind, and made me feel secure. He was offering Tony and me a safe, stable, normal home life and Tony would have a responsible father. Martin had power and control and that in itself was quite an aphrodisiac. We would go to music industry parties and he liked having me sit on the arm of the chair next to him. I would roll, sniff and light his cigars and drape myself sensually against his shoulder in my vintage 1930s olive green silk, deeply-décolletaged, wrap-around dress. I was his glamorous rising star. We made an impression.

Tony climbed into Martin's son's swim trunks and headed out to the pool with the little white styrofoam surfboard Martin had given him. That day there were masses of drowning baby grasshoppers coating the surface of the pool. He'd squat on the outside edge of the pool and gently scoop them *en masse* to the edge to safety. He was on a mission.

Tony had swimming lessons at the local YMCA but was still not as secure in the water as we would have liked. He was getting there as we were spending more time at Martin's pool on the weekends. We'd be in the pool and encourage him to scoot his butt all the way down and jump into our arms, then we'd swim him around the pool while he kicked and practiced his strokes. It was great fun and Tony loved it. But that day he didn't want to go in the water. He just wanted to save grasshoppers.

The pump that sent the stream of water down the center of the slide leading into the pool had been in the shop for repairs on the previous weekends, but Martin never mentioned that it was fixed in time for the party. He was out puttering poolside with his newly constructed wine cellar readying it for the case of wine that his sister-in-law was bringing over shortly. I was standing watching Tony poolside when Martin told me to go in the house. I thought he wanted me to make sure things were ready for arriving guests. I felt a bit conflicted and I vacillated, but I obediently went inside, because Martin was right there puttering and keeping an eye on him. Being a dad of young kids who were at the house playing in and around the pool all the time, I didn't really worry. I told Tony *"Now, be careful!"* Running with a purpose and smiling happily he said, *"Ok! I will, Mom!"* I went into the house.

When I got inside, I saw that nothing was really needed of me. I wondered why Martin told me to go in. I looked around the kitchen and the front room, but it seemed as though there was nothing for me to do. I finally assumed that Martin wanted me to be able to open the front door when his sister-in-law arrived with the case of wine. So, I casually glanced over the titles of the books on the floor to ceiling bookshelves adjacent to the big sliding glass door leading out to the patio and pool area. I took _Midnight Cowboy_ off the shelf. It had been a recent best seller and I hadn't read it, or seen the film. I randomly opened to the part where the young boy was questioning which of the men who came and went in the house might be his dad and which of the blond women might be his mom. I was overcome with an urge to run out and give Tony a big suffocating hug, but controlled myself. My mother's voice played inside my head, "_Oh, Vic, don't be so emotional._" But, in that moment, I made up my mind to accept Martin's proposal.

Martin ambled into the den through the sliding glass door from the pool just as Suzie was at the front door. He ran to open it and took the heavy case of wine from her arms and set it on the kitchen counter top. As we watched, he lifted up each bottle appraising its label ... and then he asked casually... almost too casually, when I think back, as he lifted another bottle out of the case... "_Where's Tony?_"

Chapter 56
Saving Grasshoppers

Where's Tony?

My eyes widened. I looked at him. My heart caught in my throat... sharp intake of breath... I raced outside, looking here, looking there, running to the goats in their pen, anywhere but where I must have intuitively known I would find him... and then... my gaze settled unavoidably on the black bottomed pool... tender baby grasshoppers floating, struggling - pale green tendrils encrusting the placid surface. Sun-gilded fluttering wings in last desperate efforts to fly free. Small white island aimlessly floating in their midst - a post-modern Monet - a still life.

My eyes adjust - not an island - Tony's small white styrofoam surfboard floating.

My feet, heavy-rooted as if in concrete, unable to move as dread seeped into my throat like bile. My eyes began to focus beneath and beyond like those pictures in which you have to squint as alternate images emerge. My vision became acute, blinded me, numbed me, paralyzed me. I focused on what laid beneath. Silently - my beautiful little man, Tony, just turned six...

Frozen, paralyzed, yawning horror... unspeakable anguish... strangled agonal screams... whose voice?

From a reservoir in the core of this very earth is stored the ancestral wailing of every mother who has ever seen her dead child at her feet... and from each mother's throat all mothers' screams rush forward, toppling over each other to be heard...and heard once more never having been silenced in the heart, or in the memory of the universe...

From the core of the earth, they come like a herd of stampeding wild horses... they come... Through the layers of clay and granite, through the tangled roots of human consciousness they come. Through the soles of a mother's feet consuming every fiber of her body gushing through her conduit throat and finally out of her gaping mouth that is not wide enough to contain so much agony... they come. They come to broadcast it beyond the impenetrable veil to recall that child from the beyond - to beg, to plead, to grovel at the feet of any ancient god for some miracle... to rewind the moment, rewrite the ending... How many shrieking, begging, pleading prayers before it might come true, but never does?

Martin ran outside, saw Tony face down at the bottom of the deep end of that ominous black pool. It was as if he had gone head-first down the slide on his surfboard, straight to the bottom, and never came back up.

Martin dove in, bringing him up, laying him down on the concrete on his back, flailing his arms, trying to give him mouth to mouth resuscitation. Tony's Frosty Freeze came pouring into Martin's mouth and he ran to the pool and vomited. Tony lay limp, blue-beige, unmoving. The firemen arrived and began their pumping, but no matter what they did, there was no response. I stood frozen, waiting to see him open his eyes. It would all be a horrible mistake.

"Oh, dear God, this can't be happening... not to Tony... not to Tony... not to Tony..."

Martin's sister-in-law took me gently by the elbow and guided me to a bench at the picnic table, made me sit down, sat across from me trying to calm me, but I knew at that moment I had become instantly insane. No Hollywood ending. No magical recovery. No hope. No life. Nothing would ever be the same again.

If I'd just gone out to hug him when the urge to hug him overcame me...

If I'd gone out with Hiro. Yet I chose Mutt...

If - if - if...

Did I really see his belly inflate like that? It seemed like it was his leg, but that's not possible, is it?

If I could hold him in my arms and warm him back to life...

If I could sleep embracing him and wake up to find it was just a bad dream... he would look up at me and ask, "Can I have my Cheerios, Mommy?"

Oh, God, I didn't love him enough. No, no, maybe I loved him too much. Yes! Yes! That's it! I loved him too much and God took him away. I didn't deserve him...

Chaos around me. Fireman came to me, "I'm sorry Ma'am, he was in the water too long. Should we lay him in there on the bed?" I said, "Yes," in a fog of incomprehension.

People, strangers swarm the house talking to everyone - but me. Mouths move but sounds make no sense. Stricken. Some kind of paralysis.

I slipped unnoticed from the room to Martin's bed where they'd laid my beautiful boy. I laid down next to him, embracing his cold, damp body. I touched his curls, the curve of his face. I touched my lips to his cool cheek. I pulled him tighter to me and was overcome with a fatigue I'd never known... I closed my eyes and was gone into some blissful

oblivion where reality couldn't touch me. "If I could just die
now...

"Where did she go?"

Rough hands grabbed my arms and yanked me off
the bed away from the sweet embrace, my last embrace, with
my precious baby boy... my angel son, my wise child who
had only love and understanding for those around him...
"Please don't take me..."

"Crazy bitch! She's in bed with him! C'mon! You
have to answer questions from the detective."

I was dragged into the den. I stood confused,
wavering on sticks of jello-weak legs. Not comprehending
my purpose. *What was wanted of me? Why couldn't someone
else do it?* The detective sat at the counter looking down at
his paperwork, never once looking at me, tonelessly asking
me Tony's name, Social Security number, family names,
telephone numbers, addresses...

"What happened? How did it happen?"

I began feeling the darkness close in around me. The
weight of my body pulling me down - too heavy to hold up.
I couldn't bear it anymore. My brain couldn't hold it. I
crumpled backwards to the floor. Through the mist, I
heard... *The crazy bitch has taken drugs. Check the
medicine cabinet!* Lifted by strangers, I was carried to a
guest room and placed on a bed. I lay as though some dense
layer of subterranean clay with the weight of an entire
mountain range was pressing down on my inert body.

In what seemed a few moments, my parents were
standing at the bedside looking down upon me. I wondered
how they knew - how they found me. I looked up at them
silently, my eyes dead, mute. No arms stretched out to hold

me. No hands reached out to stroke my face. Mom looked down on me, straight backed, clutching her own hands, twisting her linen hankie, as she always did when she was upset. Her lips tightened. Her jaw tensed. Her lips blanched around the periphery of her faded red lipstick. She nodded tersely to Daddy to see if he wanted to go down the hall to see Tony's body. He shook his head, no. She went, then the coroner arrived.

She returned to my bedside wordlessly, holding herself tight, looking down at me, judgment etched in her eyes. Daddy in his gruff Brooklyn Sicilian way, said, *"What didja leave'im alone by the pool for?"* I had no answer.

It was only in the last three months of Tony's life that he had acknowledged Tony as his grandson - at least in my presence. We were at Grandma's house on Genesee and they were sitting side by side on Grandma's sofa when Tony climbed up on his lap, kissed his cheek and said, *"Grandpa, I love you."* He mumbled something to Tony. I've forgotten what, but he very clearly said, *"Grandson..."* and then glanced up at me.

I knew they loved him. It was just awkward for them. They had to get past their feelings about me - and my son's color. Tony was easy to love. He had an irrepressible scrunched up smile and a gentle nature. He never doubted that he was loved, or loveable. We used to holler at each other from different rooms in our house while I was cleaning up and he was playing in his room.

> *"I love you!"*
> *"I love you too!"*
Just to stay in touch.

I looked to the doorway where the coroner was wheeling my baby's shrouded body on a gurney down the hallway past the open door of the room where I was laid. I wanted to run to him, stop them, love him one more time, but I couldn't move my leaden limbs. I couldn't cry out. I just laid there and watched my precious jewel pass the doorway. I was powerless, gutted, limp, listless and felt a heaviness I couldn't overcome… a mute apathy.

I think of Neil Young's lyric … *"I was feeling like a burned-out basement... with the full moon in my eye... I was hoping for a replacement..."*

And this is where my life ended...

And, this is where it began... a childless mother with no name.

If not Mama, who, then?

Chapter 57
A Childless Mother

There are moments in everyone's life in which there is one defining moment. From then on, one's life story is forever told from a *before* and an *after*.

My life became that - before Tony died and after Tony died.

My journey *after* led me back to myself - eventually. It took years to see it, to sort it out, to understand it. I see it very clearly now (I think.) Time will tell. But, the me that was, died that day alongside my son.

Tony Days

33.   34.

35.   36.

37.

33. Tony, 2 years old, when he returned from foster care.
34. Tony at 3 years old.
35. Tony wearing his *fave* rough-out jacket.
36.Tony and me.
37. Tony's Kindergarten photo.

38.   39.

40.   41.

38. Dressing my son.
39. At Chuck Barris Productions.
40. On our way to Plummer Park.
41. Renaissance Faire.

42.

43.

44.

45.

42. Breakfast in Santa Barbara, home away from home.
43. Tony's photo of me with his new camera.
44. Photo Cosby held
45. Tony's 6th Birthday party, his last photo.

Chapter 58
Later that Day

Mom and Dad drove me home from Martin's to their house in Glendale. They must have, though I remember nothing of the ride from lying on that bed to climbing every one of the sixty-two rough stone steps up to the house. I must have told them to call certain people, otherwise they wouldn't have known their names or numbers. They really never knew my life and friends, preferring to make assumptions based on their own prejudices and misperceptions.

The rest of the evening I laid on Mom's sofa. The two people who came to the house were loyal friends, both of whom were producers at Chuck Barris Productions, Larry and Catley, who used to say to anyone passing in the studio hallways when Tony would escape his office, *"Hey, anyone see a little kid about this tall,"* as he held his hand about waist high. *"Looks just like me?"*

They sat at the dining room table all evening talking to my parents, while I drifted in and out of consciousness on the sofa in the living room after my mother had given me a Valium. I have no idea what they discussed. I was semi-comatose most of the evening, well into the night and the next day. I had images of my own while floating in and out of distorted dreams, reviewing the last weeks of my baby's life. Every minute, every choice I had made leading up to the moment, the irretrievable moment, agonizing over what I could have done differently that would have led to a different outcome.

Larry and Catley put in a call to the long-haired muse who had changed my life view through the books and music with which he had gifted me - Herman Hesse, Kafka, Kahlil Gibran, The Beatles, Donovan. He opened a place within me that I'd left behind in my Connecticut childhood along with my innocence.

We had all met when I was a guest on *The Dating Game* in the mid-Sixties, but he had moved across the country by then. When we originally met, he had wooed me with sweet words in French. He was sublime, I was enchanted. We sparked a little fire between us. On dates, he would take Tony and me on the back of his motorcycle, or in his British convertible roadster. I began to believe there just might be a god after all. But as these things often are, it was a case of mistaken identity. He adored my son, as they all did. He was much younger than I. Jaded as I was at the grand-old age of twenty-four, I self-sabotaged. I yearned for him but I couldn't let him get too close. I couldn't risk him discovering my past, become horrified and reject me first. I could never have told him, or anyone else, what I had been through. I didn't even understand how to make sense of it myself. Therefore, I kept silent and denied myself any opportunity for happiness.

Now as a medical professional and advocate myself with increased clinical knowledge and understanding of post-traumatic stress, I realize that my symptoms were classic. I understand that I was ricocheting off of my myriad rape traumas and violent beatings. I have gained so much understanding since then through my shared experiences with other sexual assault and trafficking survivors. Since I have spoken out about my rape experiences as a result of going public about Cosby, I have interacted with many trauma-informed professionals. It has been very educational and it has provided me with invaluable personal insight. It has also given me the ability to assess other survivors' symptomology more accurately and provide them with more informed care.

So even though I was free of the events themselves, I was not free of the damage. I was living my life on a Post-Traumatic Stress Disorder (PTSD) rollercoaster for years. Something I did not understand, nor did the medical community. PTSD was not even identified as a legitimate diagnosis. I was just always bouncing from one emotion to the other, one reaction to the next and trying to act on the surface as if I had it all together. Behind the scenes I was a basket case without a shoulder on which to cry - without a soul to whom I felt I could confide.

In spite of my parents' disapproval of me, I knew they had loved Tony. Seeing him dead must have been horrid for my mother, though she never said a word about it, ever. She handled trauma the way she always had, tight-lipped, straight-backed, cleaning the house furiously, and then a migraine. She, nor Daddy, ever reached out to me with a much-needed embrace. I felt as though I needed someone to keep all my fractured pieces from floating off in different directions. A hug might have helped to hold me together. In looking back, I realized that absolutely no one hugged me. How weird. I still wonder why my friend, Francesca, wasn't there. Where were my friends, Joe and Signe? Where was Auntie Nor Nor? They would have hugged me. There are so many details from that time I can't remember. It's a blur. There are these cameo memories that, still after all these years, I can't sort out. Certain images I recall in great detail and others are just gone. I am still never quite sure of the chronology of things and now there is no one left to ask.

I remembered back when Allen, Fran's husband, scooped Tony out of the deep end of the pool 3 ½ years earlier when Tony was only 2 ½. I'd recently recovered him from the foster home. We were at a Bunny pool party hosted by the late Bunny Hope Parker and her childhood friend, Shelley Feinman. Tony just walked up to the edge of the pool, looked in and fell forward. We screamed and Allen, who was swimming underwater, scooped him up onto the side of the pool. Allen pushed down on his back. Tony sputtered, got up and ran off as if nothing had happened. A portent of things to come? The question begs to be asked, *"Was he trying to leave us all along?"*

Karmically, Allen died many years later on Tony's birthday... August 22nd.

I had been waiting interminably for the coroner to release Tony's body from the morgue so we could see him one last time before his cremation, and arrange his funeral. It had taken so long because it was *"a drowning."* The coroner had to perform the autopsy, write his legal report before Tony's body could be declared accidental and released for burial. I dreamed every night about him lying alone in a freezer in the morgue.

My mother pressured me to go ahead and have a memorial service without Tony's ashes. It became evident that she just wanted it over as soon as possible. She made me feel that I was being an inconvenience. She wanted to get on with her life - or maybe she thought it would help me to get on with mine. Not sure, but I resisted nonetheless.

I wanted a graveside service with Reverend Greek from my grandmother's church officiating. A lifetime before in that church at four years old, I had recited the *Night Before Christmas*. I wore the Royal Stewart plaid taffeta dress that Grandma had sewn for me with her crippled hands. It was a sacred place. Rev. Greek, from his huge heart, had baptized Tony with the name I had given him, Antony Lucien, so he could enter Kindergarten. The school required either a birth certificate or a baptismal certificate. I panicked. It was something I hadn't thought of when I changed his name. I never legally registered it.

Reverend Greek and his wife supported us over the years in so many ways when my own family did not. My mother loathed Reverend Greek for reasons I never understood, but he had been good, kind and deeply compassionate to Tony and me. I insisted he officiate.

At last, the autopsy was completed and I was informed that Tony's body had been delivered to the mortuary. I was asked what kind of coffin I wanted to view him in. I was horrified. "None! Ever! I will never *ever* see my son in a coffin!" They told me to bring clothes to put him in. "Why? He loved being butt naked." There was so much about this death business I simply didn't understand. I didn't realize for many years this was considered A *Viewing*. I'd never been to a funeral in my entire twenty-five years of life. The vocabulary still makes me shudder... *Cremains!* *Why not, simply, ashes? "Ashes to ashes, dust to dust..."* I couldn't take it anymore.

When we arrived at the Viewing Room, it was Mom, Francesca, Auntie Nor Nor, Auntie Paula, my uncle's second wife, Trudi, and me. None of the men would go, nor did they go to his funeral. Daddy didn't allow my twelve-year-old sister to go either. They had been joyful, high-energy playmates who used to beg to get together to play. She was only six years older than he was.

Tony was laid on a gurney with a white sheet pulled up to his chin. I wasn't really sure what to do, but I slowly approached and stared. I wasn't even sure if I was allowed to touch him. Auntie Nor Nor took the lead and lifted the white cover sheet and peered under it just from morbid curiosity. She said she'd heard that men have erections when they die. I was in shock. I screamed and flung myself backwards into someone's arms. Have you ever seen how they whip up the V-shaped autopsy incision on a corpse's chest like nothing more than a piece of horsehide? There is no finesse.

My beautiful, precious, tender child - kissed by the sun. His long curling eyelashes sleeping on cheeks pinkened by some well-intentioned mortician - lips carved of caramel... He was stitched up like some crudely repaired, rag doll. No one thought to offer a prayer.

That night I dreamt I squatted over a black man's cold dead body on a steel slab. I slowly lowered myself and felt his frozen stiffness penetrate my very core... yet, he would not breathe...

Chapter 59
In the Wake

Mom drove me once more to Martin's house to collect Tony's left-behind clothes from that weekend. I stood on his doorstep like a beggar, refusing to go inside. He was angry and brusque with me and couldn't understand why I was unable to continue our relationship and move in with him. How could I ever go into that house again or ever look into that black bottomed pool without seeing Tony face down in the deep waters. For some reason, that concept escaped him. Instead of a lover's compassion and a father's empathy, it was almost a reaction of someone having been thwarted.

Finally, I had to face returning to my house. It took all my courage. I felt crushed by being there. It was empty, lonely and my shoes echoed as I walked across the hardwood floors. The silence deafened me and I knew then that I couldn't stay. I stood alone in Tony's room remembering him getting up every morning, neatly making his bed, and then calling me to come see how neatly it was done. His books and toys were lined up in his bookcase with his antique wooden sailing ship, fitted out with canvas sails and riggings on the top shelf of his red painted bookshelf. Red was his favorite color and I'd painted his rattan headboard red, too - even his new two-wheeler was red. He had ridden it himself all the way over from our old house, two blocks away on Genesee to our new little home on Stanley. Tony was so sure of himself, so responsible, mature, capable and wise. I was so proud of him as I watched him grow and spread his wings.

My precious little man, always playing Superhero. *"Mighty Mouse to save the day!"* Tony the Tiger! *Grrrr....* Tony's bedroom was flooded with light through the small-panes of the floor to ceiling French windows. The bushes and shade trees outside gave him privacy from the street. He spent every minute at home in his room, when he wasn't out running with his new friends in the neighborhood, or riding his new red two-wheeler. I could see him growing in stature.

We'd found his wooden sailing ship in Mendocino when we were on location filming Roger Corman's film, *Dunwich*. It was a beautifully crafted memento of our magical time there that last Spring of his life, and reminded us of the freedom of the deep woods. Tony was flown up with the crew and as he disembarked from the crew bus, he ran out exuberantly shouting and laughing, *"Hi! I'm Tony! I'm a Leo!"*

He and actress Sandra Dee's son, Dodd, ran free and played endlessly in those verdant expanses. She had brought her son on location with her mother to watch over him. Dodd was a year older than Tony and I watched them both blossom. The vast openness of emerald green fields and the rhythmic crashing of the sea on its stony cliffs called us to return forever. I told Tony that one day we would return to live there. It was a dream I wanted to turn into a reality.

Tony was not quite six when we first moved to the Stanley Street cottage and was preparing for first grade. We bought his new clothes for school, his first pair of bell bottoms, the new '*in*' style that year, with his Nehru jacket from kindergarten being replaced with a new favorite, a rough-out jacket with long leather fringe. His sixth birthday party was held in our backyard decorated with balloons and streamers in the fruit trees, fun hats and a big cake. All of his friends from his Genesee Street gang came - and his special little love, Carrie, the only other racially mixed child in our neighborhood. Carrie was Chinese-Jewish. Her family lived next door to Grandma's house and her mom, Kathleen, was my mom's best friend. The two little ones were both bird-bone-delicate. Tony would protectively drape his arm around her shoulders as they walked down the street together and her deceptive Oriental flower fragility belied her deep sultry voice. In my dreams I already had their marriage arranged. Even Hoyt, dropped by wearing his big ten-gallon cowboy hat, so he could show off his brand new big black Cadillac. Tony innocently ran to meet him, and Hoyt playing "Mr. Big Shot" flipped him a silver dollar. Hoyt still wanted me to eat my heart out that I'd left him.

Someone gave Tony a pair of Groucho Marx glasses, the ones with the bushy black eyebrows, big nose and mustache. I think it was his favorite birthday present. He put them on as soon as he saw them and refused to be photographed without them. I pleaded with him to take them off for a photo, but he wasn't having any of it. So, the very last picture of him ever taken, was in those glasses. *"Leave 'em with a smile!"* the old comedians used to say...

In the days and weeks that followed Tony's death, I thought about him constantly. I obsessively went over everything I had done with him, not done with him, anything I could have done with him or done differently. Healthy boundaries I should have

established for us both but didn't. I whipped myself
mercilessly. People who I thought were friends
distanced themselves from me. I saw reproach in their
eyes. It never ended, but there never could have been
more emotional guilt-flogging than what I did to
myself. I felt more and more alone and desolate. I
thought over and over about the last few days before
his last day on this earth - the last few hours, his final
moments - before he swam away from me. Tony - my
son - my reason to breathe.

It was only a month or so before he died that Tony
had been hit with the cruelty of racism for the first time. But
laughter had saved the day, at least for that moment. He ran
into the house crying. When I asked him what had happened,
thinking perhaps he had skinned his knees falling off his
bike, he sobbed, *"Adam called me a Negro and I told him I
was not! I was a Nigger!"*

We looked at each other and simultaneously realized
he had gotten it backwards. His eyebrows wiggled, the
corners of his mouth began to twitch, and we started to
giggle. We laughed until we fell into each other's arms on
the floor with tears pouring down our cheeks… well, maybe
only MY cheeks.

He looked at me as if seeing me for the first time and
asked, *"Mama, why are you so light and I'm so dark?"*

I was initially stumped, because we'd never talked
about it before. We just were who we were. Our friends had
racially mixed families, so to Tony it was always natural. I
wanted him to grow up feeling that way. I'd never planned
what I might say if he asked.

"Ok," I said, as the analogy popped into my head, *"You know how when you pour cream into black coffee?"* He said, *"Yeah...?"* *"Well,"* I said, *"Your daddy was as dark as black coffee and I am the cream! So, when we got together, we made you! You're our coffee with cream!"*

I was waiting for the next logical question - "Who and where is my Daddy?" Thankfully, it never came. Tony was so excited that he ran five houses up the block to Grandma's house to tell her. *"Grandma! Grandma! I'm coffee with cream!"*

While he went to Grandma's, I strode across the street and knocked on the little Catholic boy, Adam's front door. When his mother opened the door, her face went blank as I sternly recounted what had transpired. I said in as restrained a manner as I could muster so as not to lose my righteous authority, *"Since you take your son to church every day, you might want to teach him that Nigger is a bad word and he hurt my son's feelings. Maybe you should be teaching him the Golden Rule!"*

I turned on my heel before she could say a word and strode away. I'll never know the effect it had on her or on her boy. I hope he grew up to be a better man. I wish I'd suggested she bring him over for an in-person apology and turn it into a teachable moment, but I was too upset to think of it.

Not too long after that Grandma told me that Tony had slipped into her kitchen and sat up on the stool next to her as she was rolling out the dough for her baking powder biscuits. She made them every Sunday morning till the day she died. She'd always save a piece of raw dough for us, because we loved to eat it. Annie and I always called it *'dough-dough.'* Tony always called Grandma's biscuits *'puffs.'* Being paralyzed on her entire right side from polio since she was four, she managed to find ways to do almost everything she ever wanted and needed to do. She was an inspiration and example of the strong, pioneer women on whose shoulders I stood. She'd nestle the crock bowl in the crook of her crippled right arm, then mix everything with a long handled wooden spoon gripped tightly in her strong left hand.

Grandma said that on this particular morning he had come directly into the kitchen and seemed very subdued. He sat quietly on the stool as she rolled out her dough on the cutting board. His head was hanging down and he was quieter than usual. He seemed troubled.

"What's the matter, Tony?"

"You know, Grandma, I'm half Negro."

"Well, yes, Tony, I know that, but it doesn't matter what you are as long as you are a good person." She said he brightened up after that, but oddly he never discussed it with me.

Even with all her old-generation-Iowa-white woman biases, Grandma came through in the end.

Three weeks after Tony died, Grandma died. She'd told me as I sat next to her on her bed the week before how much she'd grown to love him and that she couldn't stop crying.

Mom: *"That's not true!"*

Me: *"Grandma told me so."*

At my mother's memorial service decades later in 2011, a red-headed, middle-aged man I didn't recognize crossed the room to speak with me. He introduced himself and said that he was one of the boys on the block that Tony had played with as a child. This is what he told me:

"*I was ten and Tony was five. He looked up to me as if I was the older, wiser person, but it was he who changed my worldview. I heard what grownups said about the two of you, because you were a single white mom with a black child. I saw the difference in the way they talked about you and the way you really were, since I played at your house. I knew who you really were. As I grew up, I carried those memories with me. It changed the way I understood life. Tony was a serious little boy with deep thoughts.*"

He and I would sit on the curb and he would ask me questions like, 'Is there a God?' and 'What happens to people after they die?' It made me start thinking about those things too. I had no real answers. My family was Catholic. We lived that life and I had never questioned it until Tony and I became friends. Now I'm married, my wife is Jewish and I have become a healer. I have Tony and you to thank for that. That's why I came today. I have always wanted you to know that."

Chapter 60
Unconditional Love and Other Ideas
1969

Walking now, all night through the old familiar West Hollywood neighborhood, up and down Genesee, Stanley, Spaulding, Curson, Delongpre, Poinsettia Place, up and down and around... can't sleep, can't put water on my face... images of water rushing into Tony's mouth, his nose, his lungs flood my thoughts... can't find... can't find... What am I looking for? ... familiar scent of night-blooming jasmine, achingly nostalgic, old friend, filling my senses... walking, walking, walking - and morning dawns. Confused, still wandering in my thoughts. I am standing at the open door of Grandma's church. How did I get here? Is it Sunday? Standing there unsure... I just stand... go in? Leave? Sermon in progress.... sudden silence... Reverend Greek stops preaching. He walks down from the pulpit to the back of the church where I stand unsure. Suddenly surrounded by arms... dissolving, sobbing, being rocked... "Sit here," says Mrs. Greek, leading me by the hand to her pew, patting the seat next to her, holding my hand, not losing touch. Her husband returns to the pulpit... resumes his sermon and changes direction. He speaks of unconditional love.

Auntie Te had been in a nursing home with dementia and Diabetes by then. Auntie was our inspiration, our teacher, our poet, our muse. She gave her quiet life supporting her widowed sister and her three little children during the Great Depression. A poorly paid elementary school teacher, she sent half her wages and hand-me-downs to them. She took responsibility for the children's summertime education and introduced them to natural science while walking with them in the woods. She introduced them to different cultures through her many different traveling assignments. Auntie Te made up children's stories on the fly to distract me from things I didn't want to do, like put on my shoes. The scientifically correct but fancifully invented story of the <u>Rain Fairy</u> evolved from that. She taught us how to rhyme and write poetry. She taught me how to crochet. Without Auntie Te none of us would have had the scope of learning that we did. She was our backbone, our humble and silent motor.

Mom: *"Go visit Auntie. She's asking for you to come read to her. But you can't tell her about Tony because it'll be too upsetting for her."*

Me: *"How can I see her and not tell her? She'll ask how he is. She'll know that something's wrong, Mom."*

Auntie Te and Tony shared the same birthday, August 22nd. She told Mom that she sensed Grandma had just died and would know beyond any facade of mine that I was lying to her about Tony. If she asked how he was I'd break down in tears - so I never went. Soon they would share the same grave.

Mom: *"Auntie always asked why you never came to read to her as you promised."*

Me: (*Silence*)

Chapter 61
Sleep With the Angels, My Son...

The day of Tony's funeral was a gray, overcast day. Friends began gathering around the open grave at Valhalla Cemetery in North Hollywood. I stood stiffly next to my mother and the aunties, wearing the full length, Edwardian-collared, silk linen, bone-colored, hand knit dress that I had originally chosen to wear for my album cover. It was the most expensive dress I'd ever bought. Otho Pettijean, *Porsche Guy*, who somehow remained in my life in his sudden appearances driving down Hollywood Boulevard, beeping and waving cheerfully, from his same old white Porsche convertible, who sometimes stopped and visited, insisted on taking me shopping to find the perfect outfit to wear for my album cover. Since I'd lost all my things during the Louie days, I was still wearing everyone else's hand-me-downs or thrift shop purchases. That dress was symbolic of Tony's and my impending success, but instead, I would be wearing it to bury him.

Richard D'Agostin, played acoustic guitar that day and sang a song he wrote with the refrain *"and brown shall live again..."*

Christos, my young Greek folk singer, former boyfriend, played guitar and sang a Greek lullaby...

"Sleep, go Nani Nani -
and like Christ when He was asked to carry His cross, we,
too, must say,
'Yes. I can.'"

Reverend Greek officiated and led us in the Doxology, *"Praise God from whom all blessings flow..."* and the *"Glory be's."* I read from Kahlil Gibran's, <u>The Prophet</u>, his essays, *"On Children..."*

"Your children are not your children.
They come through you but not from you.
And though they are with you yet they belong not to you...
*
Their souls dwell in the house of tomorrow...
You are the bows from which your children as living
arrows are sent forth."

... and *"On Death..."*

"You would know the secret of death.
But how shall you find it unless you seek it in the heart of
life?
*
For life and death are one, even as the river and the sea
are one.
*
What is it to die but to stand naked in the wind and to melt
into the sun?"

I stood devoid of feeling, emotionally frozen in the chill, gray day. But I stood proud, tall and strong for my son...

All of Christos' family were there. They told me that they were proud of me and that I was like an ancient Greek woman, brave and stoic. I was numb. Francesca and Allen were there, the only ones dressed in black. I had asked everyone to wear bright colors to celebrate Tony's life. My friends Joe and Signe were there. Signe told me later that one time when she was babysitting Tony, an ambulance had gone by. He asked her so many questions about it and then asked her, "Signe? Will you come to my funeral?" It was almost as if he had a premonition.

Tony's funeral was a large gathering. I wondered if my mother was surprised to see that we had so many friends, or any friends at all. Martin stood apart in the back, separate from the crowd. He paid for the cremation and the memorial plaque but Auntie Te had purchased the plot for herself. It was next to Aunt Emmy's, never imagining it would be used first by her great-great grandnephew. How could any of us have imagined that?

While Mom was physically present, she was emotionally unavailable. "Aunt" Trudi, who was always more understanding and caring, was there. Her husband, my Uncle Bill, my mother's brother, my actual blood, was not. Auntie Nor Nor and Auntie Paula stood by me there as family.

I wonder if there was some reception expected afterwards? I hadn't thought of that, new to the death game as I was. But I couldn't pretend to be sociable and politically correct. After I spoke to everyone, Christos and I ran off leaving everyone in our wake and found the closest bar.

Why the shunning, the exclusion from the people who really mattered to me? Those who had meant so much to me throughout my entire childhood continued to shun me, judge me, criticize me even during the horrific loss of my only child. Because in their minds everything was my fault?

Because what - because they thought I was a whore? Because I had a racially mixed child? Because I had been a Playboy Playmate? Because they had listened and believed my mother's malicious gossip? Because I didn't live life on their terms? Because they never made an effort to clarify, verify, or simply reach out in kind and uplifting ways. *It was all quite vague to me, but their absence was very real.*

The crazy thing about it was that it was the people who were *not* blood related, who *saw* me, who knew my heart, and loved me unconditionally. Yet, those who *were* my blood, who *should* have loved me unconditionally, withheld their emotional support. They were, however, unfailingly generous with their judgements, rejection, exclusion and condemnation.

Grandma died three weeks later. Then Auntie Te on the heels of that, and then Auntie Nor, without warning, literally dropped dead four months later. She had an aneurysm that burst. One minute she was there and the next minute she wasn't. I was bereft and had no one left even in my extended family to lean on.

Life After Tony

46.

47.

48.

49.

50.

46. The Dress - Album Cover Shoot.
47. After Tony died.
48. The Dress again Album Cover Shoot.
49. Outside my dirt floored garage in Topanga Canyon where I lived for a year.
50. Jay "Bobby" Willis & good dog Moby who took me home to his "*Mamom*" and blessed me with my daughter, Erinbrooke.

Chapter 62
Beyond the Coil

When I got my recording contract at Capitol Records in July of 1969, I thought Tony and I had gotten past the rough times. Things were falling into place. I began seeing some promise of financial security, some promise of a real life, peace, easier times, a career doing what I loved - a home and family. It had been such a long journey trying to establish equilibrium ever since my escape from Louie, trying to forget about it and heal. Even though I still had a long way to go, there was hope on the horizon. But then, once again, everything blew my world apart.

At twenty-five I had never been to a funeral, yet here I was attending funeral after funeral for all the people I deeply loved, the pillars of my tenuous temple. As a child I had knelt in prayer with red rough-skinned knees at the little graves I'd dug for the dead birds I'd found. I'd laid down stones and wildflowers through my tears for those little lost lives. How was I ever to know what to do with a dead child? How could I carry on? Within three months, I'd lost the main foundation in my life and felt like a little boat made of dry leaves without an anchor, adrift on a swirling, churning river with no destination.

Francesca and I were at my parents' house after returning from viewing Tony's body before the funeral. I broke down sobbing in my mother's living room. I heard Mom say from somewhere behind me, *"What are you crying about?"* Francesca leaned in and whispered in my ear. *"I see what's going on here. You're coming to stay with me."*

Chapter 63
Under the Eaves
1969

Fran was living in Laurel Canyon with her late husband, Allen, and her three children, Debby, Leslie and Geoffrey Charles. Her girls were from her first husband, and her little toddler son was Allen's and hers. Their great, big, rustic, three-story house had French doors that opened onto a front deck. A great stone sunken fireplace dominated the high-ceilinged Great Room. All of the bedrooms were on one side with a staircase leading upwards along the wall. I was given my own little room under the eaves on the third floor. It was a perfect sanctuary for me to hole up in and try to sort things out. Nothing was required of me. Nothing was requested except that I be safe and try to heal. I could just be.

I was unable to sleep at night. The spirits conspired to enter my dreams, so I stayed awake sitting cross legged on the floor in my cozy room, hand-sewing the patchwork quilt I had been working on for Tony when he died. It was an antique, crazy quilt I was restoring. Late at night I sewed in candlelight and focused on my stitches, fabric colors and textures. It allowed my mind to wander freely, and the shadows in my soul were kept at bay.

When I thought of someone who had been particularly kind to me and my son, I would just pick up the phone and call them to say 'thank you' without any idea of the time. It might be five o'clock in the morning. There were a lot of confused, groggy responses.

"You're welcome, Victoria, just go back to sleep. It will be alright."

I'd sew until I was sleepy and my eyelids drooped, then I'd lie down and pull the quilt over me feeling protected in my son's arms. All through the night there were crickets chirping in the dark corners of my little bolt hole. Listening to them, I began to believe that they were conveying messages from my son. I was sure he was trying to communicate with me through them and it gave me comfort. I wasn't alone.

Over these many years, my children and family friends and I have had unique, karmic-seeming grasshopper sightings between Tony's birthday, August 22nd and the day he died on September 6th. I have come to believe, and we have all come to accept, that in that moment when he lost his life saving grasshoppers, his spirit and theirs merged in those waters and shared some form of communion. They have since become his messengers. I continue to draw comfort and affirmation from every visitation. There is sometimes more truth in the unexplained phenomena than in the tangibles in which we come to place our faith. When the grasshopper visits, I now say, "Hello, my son."

Fran had arranged for a friend to take me places. He guided me by the elbow and drove me where I needed to go, because for a good while I was too distracted and unsafe. My dad was harassing me to go to the DMV for my car registration at a time when I felt as though I was walking underwater in slow-motion. I was disoriented most of the time and things had an unreal other-worldly quality. I was trying to navigate in a new distorted reality.

I remember one night, I had returned from wandering the canyon roads aimlessly. I walked to Fran's front deck, to find the French doors all open with white sheers wafting ethereally through them out into the night air. I stepped through into the living room. The little girls had gone upstairs to bed, but her two-year-old little son was asleep facing the back of the sofa. I decided I'd better shut the windows and put him in his crib. As I scooped him up in my arms, he rolled over towards me. The printed message on his little t-shirt read, *"He ain't heavy, he's my brother."* I began to sob uncontrollably, and carried him all the way up three flights of stairs to his room, barely able to see through my tears.

Chapter 64
Let It Be

In the blurred bubble in time after Tony's death, while I was still staying with Francesca, a friend or two might invite me to go places with them. On one such foray out into the world, we drove out to the beach. It was a bitterly cold night with slightly drizzling rain. We had the heater blasting, listening to the radio. They pulled into a Qwik Stop and went in for cigarettes - *always a trigger.* I stayed in the car with the motor running to stay warm. The radio was barely audible and my thoughts were spinning. Grandma had just died. I was still barely functioning. Running on empty, feeling utterly desolate, I stared blankly at my lap outside in the bleak, run down, depressing mini-mall. In tears I suddenly cranked up the volume on the radio to shut out the noise in my head. The lyrics that penetrated the night air saved me that night - *"...when in times of trouble, Mother Mary comes to me, speaking words of wisdom, let it be..."*

That is when my love affair with the Madonna first began, even though I relate to both the Marys - Mary Magdalene, the misunderstood. I was sure Grandma was sending me a message. Grandma had lost Aunt Emmy, her middle daughter. I had lost my only son and the Madonna had lost her blessed son. Who could be better than them to understand my grief?

Now I had someone in Spirit with whom I could confide, some talisman I could cling to - some comfort, although intangible, was all I had. It was that wispy cobwebby thread that held my shattered mind, heart and soul tentatively together. I grasped at whatever I could to make sense of what had happened to my child, and what could possibly make sense of my life from then on.

Chapter 65
Out of Body, Out of Mind

Francesca and I were invited over to our friend Larry's house to watch a home movie of *The Dating Game.* Frannie had dated Chuck Barris. We'd all remained friends since. Larry had invited Fran and me over to watch a film of a winning *Dating Game* couple whom he had chaperoned to Spain. Larry and Catley, were setting up the home projector and screen in the living room, while Fran and I were in the kitchen getting a glass of wine. The grief hit me like a sledgehammer in the gut. I doubled over convulsing in sobs. Frannie said, *"You'd better pull yourself together! "* I forced myself to stop weeping and followed her out into the living room. I was quiet, but desperately wanting relief from the visceral all-consuming pain. I was convinced it would never end.

They sat me in a rocking chair and positioned themselves around the projection screen with their wine glasses. Off went the lights and the movie began. Larry narrated. It was lighthearted and he was thrilled with his trip to beautiful Spain. I sat with my arms folded across my chest, rocking, and tuning everything out. I prayed with every fiber of my being and with every ounce of my soul to be taken to my son. I ached. I yearned. I begged to be with my child, my baby, my reason for being. *"Please God! Take me…"*

Without warning, I felt this swoosh through the top of my head and suddenly, I was above myself looking down. I was eye level with the crown molding. While the entire room below was dark, there was a strata of soft, golden light around the molding that filled the ceiling. I was stunned but immediately understood that this was a response to my prayers. I looked around expecting to see someone - Tony, a spirit, some kind of guide - to reach out to me but no one was there. It was bewildering. I kept expecting someone would appear, take my hand and tell me what to do next. It never occurred to me that I could go through the walls, and I didn't see anywhere else I could go from there. I recognized that while I was out of my body, I was still *me*. My personality was intact. I could think, see, analyze and feel emotion.

I looked down on my body below sitting in the rocking chair wondering why my arms were still crossed if I was no longer in my body - no longer in control. I concluded that it was because of leverage, the way I had placed my arms. Then, I remembered something I had read once about astral travel. I remembered reading that there was supposed to be a silver cord connecting the astral body to the physical body during astral projection. I remembered reading that if that silver cord was broken, the soul couldn't return to the body. I looked to see, but saw nothing, and panicked. I thought how devastated Fran, Larry and Catley would be if the lights went up and my dead body was found slumped, rocking in that chair. One more gruesome event to add on to their year.

In that one moment of panic, the fear that I would not be able to return to my body, I was instantly sucked back in through the top of my head. There was a dramatic change in atmospheric pressure, as if I had closed the sunroof on my car, and just as suddenly as I'd left, I was back inside my body. I was sitting in the rocking chair with my arms across my chest just as I was when I'd lifted out. I had no idea how long I'd been out, but certainly long enough to look around, have a view from above and think about things. It was uncanny.

I was immediately washed with a flood of guilt. I felt cowardly. I felt as though I'd failed and not continued on to my child when I had been given the opportunity. It felt as though I'd been given an answer to my prayers and then been too chicken to go. Even though I hadn't quite figured out how to navigate while I was hovering above myself, I still felt I'd flunked the test.

I said to myself, that if I had to be alive, I had to make my life worthwhile in some way. I had to do something to make myself worthy of being alive. I had no idea what that might be, but it seemed clear to me that I had been shown that I could leave my body at any time I chose. I had been shown that the spirit remained intact outside the physical body and I as a person remained intact. But I had chosen to remain for a reason.

Then, my internal cynic said, *"What a cop-out. You're just a coward!"* I countered again and said to myself, *"I must have a purpose here, then… a destiny."*

I just had no idea what it might be, but from that moment forward, one major thing in my life changed. I ceased to be a spiritual seeker. It was my '*Aha*' moment.

I had always been a spiritually-inspired child, maybe from being alone in nature listening to the cicadas chorusing at twilight as I pondered life… maybe from discovering

Mahatma Gandhi, as a kid, who knows. But I began returning to a sacred place where Tony and I used to go whenever we could. The Self Realization Fellowship Lake Shrine out near Malibu was always one of our favorite places. I paid homage at the World Peace Memorial there, which housed a portion of Gandhi's ashes. I sat near the sapling that had been grafted from the original Bodhi tree where Buddha had achieved enlightenment. It was so peaceful. I hoped some might rub off on me. I imagined Tony running those paths along the lake again, feeding the Koi fish and watching the swans gliding on the water. I could almost hear his voice in the ambient sounds of nature, bird song, flute music and Hindu chants wafting through the lush foliage.

When I had been initiated into Transcendental Meditation in 1968 at UCLA I thought I 'got it' in one of those '*Aha!*' moments that the Buddha teaches - that moment of enlightenment. Meditation was the key. But nothing gave me more clarity than the moments when I was out of body. Losing Tony challenged everything I had experienced thus far. I came away with what I thought was a message from the other side, wherever that may be. What was made very clear to me, however, was that I was still myself with all my faculties intact. I was given the gift of understanding that the body is akin to a suit of clothing that may be shed, but does not diminish nor detract from the wearer, the soul. The wearer remains fully intact without its clothes.

I understood that any physical object, be it wood, metal, glass, or flesh, that could be destroyed by fire, flood, hammer, or buzz saw, was not truly everlasting. The one element that remained intact was the personality, the essence of the being, the living spirit that is untethered and unbound by material limitations and superficial characteristics - the Soul. I understood that God is not a person, a gender, an anthropomorphic being assigned to a particular sect of humans, God dwells in the space between '*this and that*' where the universal truths of love and light exist - infinitely.

I believed I had been shown that my son still lived, yet in a transformed state of energy and consciousness. While it did not stanch my grief, it made it more bearable. I still missed him and his loss was excruciating for a very long time - the pain got softer around the edges and visited less frequently, but even with the knowledge I had gleaned, The pain when it came remained acute... and always will. No one truly ever recovers from the loss of a child.

Chapter 66
Meeting Cosby for the First Time

I was running out of my advance money from Capitol for my album. I wasn't able to sing anymore. I was a hollow shell and I'd lost my music. I worked a couple of days here and there on a film just to get by. Working on a film at Metro, Andy Warhol's black-haired French star UltraViolet and I met and became friends for a while. We'd drive around together and that kept my mind busy. She had a lightness about her. Sometimes I'd do hair and makeup on my friend Ned's film, but it wasn't enough or consistent. I needed something substantial. I told Fran I needed a good paying Screen Actors Guild job - a union job. She mentioned that she knew Bill Cosby from when he was playing the Playboy Club circuit along with lots of other comedians and singers who played the circuit. She thought that maybe he'd give me a part on his show if she referred me.

I only knew about Cosby because my parents watched *I Spy* when I went to visit. The show had been a big deal as the first series in which a black actor had starred. Lost in grief, I had taken up crocheting to keep my hands occupied, since I was unable to play guitar, write songs or sing anymore, but I thought I could at least parrot other people's words. That didn't take the same energy and emotion. Show up, hit your mark and say your lines.

I had absolutely no idea what shows Cosby was in at that time other than *I Spy*, but I needed a gig. I was willing to audition for whatever I could get. She told me how nice he had been to her when she was struggling before she and Allen got married. He had invited her out to dinner, but when she declined his invitation because she had to be all day in the food stamp office, he sent his driver to her house with an envelope filled with ten $100 bills and a note saying - "Just so you don't have to do anything you don't want to do. Love, Cos"

She had lost her job at Playboy and was a single mother of two little girls, so his kindness and generosity left a big impression. She hoped that he would be helpful to me as well.

As I was walking out the door to go to my audition Fran said, *"Take that photo of Tony with you and tell him what happened."* So, I did. Once I arrived at the studio gate, I was directed to his trailer. It seemed odd to discover I'd be meeting him in his trailer instead of in an audition studio or office, but I figured since he and Fran had a causal relationship, he was forgoing formalities. I didn't question it more than that.

He answered the door in his sweats and let me in. I told him I was a Screen Actor's Guild member and basically ran down my resume as I handed him Tony's 8x10 black and white headshot and sat down on a chair across from him. As he looked at Tony's photo, I began telling him my story. I told him that my little boy had just died and I really needed an acting job.

Tony's photo was stunning. He was looking directly into the lens of the camera, soulful, serious and deep. There was destiny speaking through his eyes almost as if he knew the depths of the viewer's soul. Cosby's eyes were suddenly riveted on the little person in the picture looking back at him.

He held Tony's picture in his hands and sat staring at it in silence. He sat there with no expression on his face, just staring. I felt as though I were talking to a cardboard cut-out instead of a man. There was just nothing there, but I think Tony's eyes touched a childhood memory of his own. Something happened there.

The silence became increasingly uncomfortable. I talked more and more as I do when I'm stressed to fill in the gaps, so I was rattling on and then ran out of things to say. He was not looking at me or responding to anything I said. I began to suspect that I was not going to get an audition. Of course, I blamed myself. I was sure he was thinking that I was too much of an emotional basket case to hire. I kept waiting for him to say something, but he didn't say a word. Finally, I stood up abruptly, excused myself, took Tony's photo and left. He had a blank look on his face. He mumbled something unintelligible and that was it. I never expected to see him again and I left feeling as though I'd flunked another test, whatever that was. So, I just went on with my day-to-day struggle, wandering aimlessly as if through some gelatinous viscosity that had taken up residence in my brain. I couldn't shake it. I forgot about Cosby and figured I'd blown any chance of a job. I needed a job but I needed to find peace even more.

Chapter 67
Return to Genesee

When Grandma died three weeks after Tony my head was still reeling, compounded by the subsequent deaths of Auntie Te and Auntie Nor Nor. Cousin Annie moved in for a short while with her girlfriend, then they moved. Mom and Uncle Bill asked if I'd like to live there. Going home was just what I needed. Every piece of furniture was just as they had left it, not at all fashionable but familiar and comforting. My earliest memories of home called to me and tugged at my heart. This was the house where I was taken home from the hospital when I was born. Cousin Anne had been born there. Her mother had died in front of it, and Grandma had died there. It was Mom's and my mantra for home. The address was imprinted on my consciousness as if it had been fire branded on my brain.

It's a designated historic district and our house was the first house built on that block that once had been a meadow. Not much had changed since I was a child - except the people. My great-great Uncle Alf built it in the early part of the century and it was a typical early 1900s California Craftsman bungalow with three cozy bedrooms a block and a half south of Sunset Boulevard. It meant a lot to me that they were offering me the house, but it was expensive by 1969 standards and I didn't have a regular job. I needed roommates. I asked JD, an actor friend of my Stanley Drive neighbors who I was casually seeing, if he wanted to move in with me. He did and he invited his two friends, Ed and

Em, a couple of aspiring actors, to join us. It made the rent doable. Eben, Em's Alaskan Malamute had pale white-blue eyes that matched her own. Her eyes were so startling that once seen, they were rarely forgotten.

I reclaimed my back bedroom overlooking the fruit tree-filled backyard. I threw open the windows and let the nostalgic, comforting fragrances of orange blossoms and night blooming jasmine fill the room. I could almost still imagine my first tire swing hanging in the apricot tree. Being there let me breathe again, even though my grief was still fresh and hit me without warning in crippling waves.

While I was referred to Crisis therapy to sort out my grief, I was assigned to a therapist who was very green behind the ears. She was a young college girl who had no kids, no apparent trauma in her life nor any life experience that could help her begin to grasp the level of my trauma. She was working towards acquiring her required hours for her Master's degree and was offering free crisis therapy in exchange. She wanted me to perform in her Master's thesis film, which I did with no appreciable therapeutic benefit. So many efforts to help me seemed like pointless exercises. No one knew what to do with me.

Cookie cutter modalities were not meant for someone with such complicated grief and trauma issues. My complex mix of traumatic experiences had never been fully addressed, or even shared in their entirety, because no one had time to listen to it all. I had no outlet. At the end of fifty-minute sessions I was just getting started, then I was left without a safety net free-floating with all my raw emotions just beginning to surface. I was a ragged mass of feelings and knee-jerk reactions. I had no sense of how to process or verbalize any of it. Sorting it out seemed impossible. I felt increasingly hopeless; emotionally isolating myself more and more.

Now as a hospice nurse of many years I've learned that in grief just a silent patient presence, a hand on yours, an ear, a shoulder, is the only thing that helps. There is no timeline for grief, no correctness in its manifestation. It is a season unto itself that runs its course. Dawn comes after the long depths of restless shadow-haunted nights. Self-rescue was the only way for me. I kept returning to the healing of the natural world and the knowledge of its constancy. I reminded myself that Spring always follows Winter. And I continued crocheting...

Chapter 68
Meeting Cosby Again
End of '69

In the midst of all this soul shattering grief and familial death cluster, I unexpectedly met Cosby again. Em, my roommate, suggested we go to the *Café Figaro*. I thought that if it was anything like the one in Greenwich Village in New York I was going to love it. The *Café Figaro* in the Village was where I did my homework when I was in high school. There was low lighting with French newspapers orange-shellacked to the walls and they showed *Laurel and Hardy* movies at night. This L.A. version didn't have the soul, however. It was a *very* cleaned up version on the border of West Hollywood and Beverly Hills.

We each ordered onion soup that was to die for and shared a basket of hot bread, with a half carafe of red wine. That day was an extremely difficult day for me. Without warning the grief had just gripped me. I felt like a horse kicked me in the gut. I couldn't stop crying no matter what I did and tears were dripping in my soup when Cosby came to stand at our table. We were sitting at a '*twoey*' opposite each other against a wall divider. I didn't know at the time that Cosby was part owner. I don't know whether Em did either.

I'm sure her startling eyes caught Cosby's attention and since he already knew my story, my sobbing presence gave him the perfect opening. I didn't want to look up, or engage in conversation. I was a mess. After my previous interaction with him I really wasn't interested in connecting anyway. I just tried to tune them out while they talked. Because I was still sobbing, I kept my head down, and of course, he understood why. He expressed concern and suggested to Em that it would do me good to have a steam bath and a massage at a Finnish spa down on Santa Monica Boulevard and that he'd like to treat us. While it seemed a very nice gesture I couldn't have cared less. Getting naked and wet had no appeal for me. My hair would frizz up and I was in no mood. I would have preferred him comping us to another carafe of wine - and then leaving. Em, however, seemed enthused by the prospect of Cosby's offer.

He put her in charge of me, gave her the money to pay for everything and gave her his direct line on a scrap of paper. He said, "When you're done, call me and I'll send my car to pick you up and I'll treat you to dinner." It really did sound like a gracious offer. And in show business it's always about who you know and the connections you make, not necessarily how talented you are. I remember thinking, "I wish I had the energy to care."

Chapter 69
That Night in 1969

It was early evening and still light when Cosby's chauffeur picked us up at Grandma's house. With a little hope, and a modicum of gratitude in our naive hearts, we were delivered to the parking lot above the Whisky-A-Go-Go. Sneaky Pete's, the new cool steakhouse on the Sunset Strip was right next to it. Cosby walked across the parking lot to greet us with a welcoming smile and escorted us downstairs to our table. He was quite gentlemanly.

We sat at a linear banquette-style table along the aisle near the front entrance. He had positioned himself to the left of Em, and I was to her right. He had obviously arranged to have her all to himself. She seemed politely interested in him, at least just being politically correct. It was obvious that I was clearly just the tag-along in this scenario. Since we both had live-in boyfriends, our interest was definitely platonic, professional and we were being polite after his earlier kindness.

Em was a vegetarian therefore her conversation with Cosby and the waiter orbited around what she could eat in a steak restaurant. Cosby and the waiter were accommodating and our entrees were ordered with red wine. I have no memory of what I ordered but I wasn't really hungry, or feeling particularly sociable, so I idly rearranged the food on my plate and barely sipped the wine. I was trying to tune them out until we could politely finish and return home. Cosby was trying to entertain us. I wasn't amused by his attempts at humor, or able to really hear him over the ambient restaurant noise, so I wasn't joining into the levity he was trying to create. He was making mush-mouth jokes which made him even more difficult to follow. I guess he wasn't getting the glowing response he had hoped to get from me, but it was what it was. I had heavier things on my mind.

Cosby reached across Em and placed a pill next to my wine glass. *"Here! Take this! It will make you feel better. It will make us* ALL *feel better!"* His message was clear. I was a wet blanket. He put another pill next to Em's wine glass, then he gave the impression he was also taking one. He put the pill up to his mouth with one hand, and covered his hand with the other hand and acted as if he'd swallowed it. He successfully guilted me, so trying to be a good sport, I thought I'd show a little camaraderie. It occurred to me that it was a *diet* pill - an *upper.* The way I was feeling I thought an *upper* might just be the ticket. I really did want to feel better, so I popped the pill.

In retrospect, I should have done what he did, fake it.

Shortly thereafter, he reached across Em and put another pill directly into my mouth and directly into hers. It didn't take long before my head was nodding. I was struggling to keep my face out of my plate. I was not feeling better at all. In fact, my head was spinning and I felt nauseated.

I heard a voice, pretty sure it was mine, say, *"I want to go home now."* He easily agreed.

Cosby escorted us as we staggered back up the stairs to the parking area. I noticed his car and driver were not there and asked him where his chauffeur was. He said, "*Oh, he had something else to do.*" I remember thinking how odd that was. Wouldn't a chauffeur be obligated to do whatever his boss wanted him to do? But Cosby kindly offered to drive us home himself. I was too out of it to press him further.

Grandma's house was just below Sunset Blvd. and a few blocks east of where we were on the Sunset Strip. So, of course, we expected to be home in about five minutes, and believe me, that's where I needed to be. I was dizzy, my face felt hot and at the same time it felt as if a cold mask was sitting an inch in front of my face. I was pretty sure I was going to be sick to my stomach any minute if I didn't get home quickly. I focused all my energy on trying to control my spinners and my stomach.

Em was assisted into the front seat and I sat in the back with Cosby behind the wheel. He turned left out of the parking lot taking us up into the hills instead of turning right down onto the Strip leading to Grandma's house. I was immediately unnerved, but feeling too sick to talk. I concluded that he must be taking some shortcut onto Nichols Canyon, which then became Genesee, once south of Hollywood Boulevard. I thought maybe he didn't want to be recognized on the main drag. But I just wanted to get home and climb in bed.

The car kept weaving up and around curves on those narrow winding hills. My stomach was lurching. I kept rolling from side to side in the back seat, praying he would just stop, and then he did - abruptly. The nose of the car was pointing uphill and when I opened my eyes, I discovered we were parked in front of a narrow multi-story building. Cosby got out, opened the passenger door, reached in, took Em's arm and helped her out onto the sidewalk. She was slumped over and wobbly. *"I want to show you girls my awards in my office."* All I could think of was, *"Oh, God..."* It was truly the last thing I wanted to do.

With all my Bunny adventures and having been trafficked to mega-stars revered by the public but less than celestial in their private lives, I was not impressed by Hollywood. I was sick of all the actors and their associates bragging about how fabulous and important they were. A New York theater girl at heart having grown up amongst true craftsmen, Shakespearean actors, opera singers and Broadway performers, I was unimpressed by the idea of seeing Cosby's awards. Fleetingly, I thought I'd just wait in the car, since Em seemed to have a connection with him that I did not. But, then, he opened the back door, reached for my arm and assisted me out. We staggered into the building. I hoped I could manage to muster some polite *Oooohs* and *Aaaaahs* over his awards so we could get home quicker - even though I felt like I was collapsing. Being polite was always my downfall, *and I'm told, still is!* What I should have done was ditch, but how?

What we have all since learned through speaking out and joining forces is that this was his grooming pattern. He was allegedly an experienced predator, and serial rapist already, but just hadn't perfected his drugging yet. That was still in evolution.

So, like lambs to the slaughter, we were herded into the elevator. He unlocked the door to his second-floor office and it became immediately apparent that it was no working office. Against the wall to the right of the door there was a little writing desk with a small table lamp on it that provided soft and muted. Next to the lamp there was a cream-colored, French Provincial-style phone. There were framed posters of him and Robert Culp on the walls in *I Spy*. The only other furniture in that room that I recall were too smallish loveseats, one parallel to the front door about five feet from it. The other one was against the wall to the left, separate but perpendicular to the other. Em staggered to that one, sat down heavily and keeled over on her right side. She pulled her knees up and passed out.

I sat down on the one parallel to the front door, laying my head back and closing my eyes. Suddenly I jolted awake. It had become so silent that for a minute I thought they had left me because I'd passed out, or perhaps they had slipped into an adjacent room that I hadn't noticed. I panicked and looked around, then saw him sitting next to Em adjacent to her hips. His gaze was fixated on her like a raptor preparing to pounce on its prey.

The unmistakably intense look on his face and the bulge in his jeans was making it obvious what his intentions were. She was completely unconscious and I became frantic. My memory of being sedated and raped by my abortion doctor years before was not easily forgotten, nor my D.C. experience with Omar. I wasn't going to let it happen to her. I leaned over and reached my arm out towards him trying to get his attention. I wanted to distract him, but he was beyond my reach. I tried to say something, but my words came out garbled. I was making sounds, but they made no sense. My thoughts weren't connecting to my tongue and I couldn't make myself understood. I had this vision of myself like Frankenstein with groping arms, making guttural sounds.

He ignored me as if I was a gnat, but I was persistent. By the look on his face, I could see that I was annoying him. Finally, when I continued to interrupt his concentration, he became so angry and exasperated that he stood up and came towards me. The expression on his face terrified me so much that I thought he might hit me. I stood up quickly - too quickly, and my legs wobbled and I buckled. I reached out grabbing onto him to prevent myself from falling. The next thing I remember, I was on my knees on the floor. He was sitting on the loveseat unzipping his jeans. He grabbed my hair and forced himself into my mouth. I was gagging, afraid I'd vomit. Maybe I should have done. I passively tried to please him so he wouldn't hit me, hoping it might be over with quickly so we could just get out of there and get home. I must not have done a very inspiring job because he stood me up, bent me forward facing away from him and raped me *doggie-style*. When he was finished, he pushed me back on the couch like a piece of trash, zipped up, and headed out the door.

I garbled, "How are we going to get home?"

He stopped and without even looking in my direction, he nodded disdainfully towards the phone. "*Call a cab!*" Then he turned and slammed the door shut.

The most mortifying thing is that I remember saying, *thank you,* as he walked out the door. All I can imagine is that in my drugged state of mind, I was just grateful that he hadn't raped Em while she was unconscious - grateful that he hadn't hit me for distracting him from the one he wanted. I was the sacrificial lamb - collateral damage.

In my mind, being violated was just one more punishment for not being there when my baby boy needed me most. Thinking about how afraid he must have been in that moment when water flooded into his mouth, nose and lungs played over and over in my mind constantly. Wondering if he tried to call out to me and I didn't hear him. I felt I deserved any and every punishment for not being there when he needed me most. Even though Cosby's rape became the epic headline, for me it was a blip on my radar compared to the devastation of my child's death. I was already destroyed. It was simply the last straw broken on my already broken back - my shattered spirit.

When Cosby's only son was murdered in 1997, the first thought that came into my consciousness was 'karma.' I wondered if he ever thought about what he had done to me after my only son died. The back room gossip from the girls at the Playboy Mansion was that he had allegedly drugged and raped a mobster's wife and his son's murder was payback - except the hit was for him. His son randomly borrowed Daddy's car that day.

I practically crawled over to Em on rubbery legs. I shook her repeatedly. Hysterically I said, "We've gotta get outta here!! We've gotta get outta here!!"

When Em came to, she seemed to understand immediately that we were in peril. I never knew if she was ever aware of what had actually happened to me and we didn't discuss it. I felt too denigrated to talk about it. We started moving towards the phone, but realized we couldn't call a cab because we had no idea where we were! We were still so drugged that we couldn't think clearly. We thought perhaps if we called her boyfriend at home, he could figure something out. We picked up the phone and there was no dial tone. Em said, "It must have come out of the jack," so she got down on her hands and knees, crawled under the desk and discovered there was no phone jack. We looked at the phone cord but it was one of those old cloth cords that had been cut. It was a prop. In a panic we understood that we'd been duped from the very beginning.

We ran out of the door straight to the elevator. Then, had a moment of shared horror at the prospect of the door opening, finding Cosby standing inside and being trapped. We found the door into the stairwell and hurriedly clattered down the two flights of stairs in our high heels. We ran through the small lobby and burst out onto the street. It was no longer twilight as it had been when we arrived. The twinkling jewels of the city lights lay far below us; wistfully luminous, after the painful outcome of our evening. Em began running downhill. We hoped that we'd find a street we recognized. I ran after her, feeling the hot breath of evil on my heels driving me forward as fast as I could run.

Em reached the Strip first. I was sure she hollered up at me, *"We're behind the Marmont"* as she ran onto the boulevard. She hailed a rare passing taxi. We jumped into it and finally took our first free breath. I don't think we even spoke on the way home about what had happened.

When the BBC interviewed me a few years ago
about that night, I forced myself to retrace my steps

after forty-six years, to look for that building. I avoided that street for decades, barely able to look where I thought it might be. I'd look the other way every time I drove past the Chateau Marmont on Sunset Blvd. But this time I forced myself to face old fears and overcome old demons.

I remembered from other experiences in my life that often the traumatic memory of a bad experience is just ordinary and small when confronted in the present. I thought of my daddy who was such a fearful tyrant when I was little, but whose confidante I became in his old age - shorter than me by then, and no longer frightening at all.

I took the BBC crew into the little parking lot where Cosby's chauffeur had delivered us, above what had been that steakhouse where Cosby had taken us in 1969. I took the same left out of the parking lot as he had and drove uphill. I curved around and cut from small streets to winding lanes. I came out behind the Chateau Marmont - and recognized nothing.

The BBC was oddly more interested in getting establishing shots of Sunset Boulevard's stereotypical palm tree lined streets. In their documentary they never even mentioned that I was a bereaved mother and took the pill because I was suffering. I was sadly disappointed.

Em and I arrived at home and rushed up the front walk, onto the porch and through the front door. We were welcomed by Em's waiting boyfriend. There was a flurry of upset words, but I have no memory of them. He embraced her comfortingly, wrapped his arm around her shoulders and they sallied off to their room - my grandma's former bedroom. I ran back to my room, my safe haven; the room I shared with my mother when I was a baby, when my birth father was away fighting and dying in World War II. Here I was all grown up in the same room fighting my own war. We were both blown to smithereens.

Alone in the house a couple of nights later I sat cross-legged on the floor in the corner of that same room screaming hysterically, gripping Grandma's dull, antique, sewing scissors slashing at my wrists. JD arrived home and saw me, slapped my face, grabbed me roughly, threw me on the bed, screwed me angrily, then grabbed his duffle bag and walked out. We were done. I lay there staring at the ceiling in hopeless despair.

A few days after the event, the debacle, the rapes, both of them, (*I am finally learning to call them both by their true name...*) Em wanted to go back to the Figaro. I didn't, but I had the car so I finally agreed. She convinced me there was no chance we'd see him there again. But I always wondered if she really hoped we would see him so she might sort out what had happened that night, and why.

I parked. She got out, walking quickly down the sidewalk and through the restaurant door. I dragged my feet, dreading the possibility of seeing him inside... and then what? So, as I walked slowly towards the café entrance, I heard people on the street begin to scream, "Look, there's Bill Cosby!" I froze... Fight or Flight?

I tried not to look and call attention to myself as a big shiny black limo slid up to the curb. *"Should I run into the restaurant to grab Em and escape?"* *"Should I run back to my car? No, I can't leave Em. She's already inside! I have to go in.*"

Panicky, frantic, then pissed off, some switch flipped on in my brain and I rallied. I walked up to the dark, tinted, back window of his limo, pressed my nose up against the glass and stuck my tongue out. I waggled my hands with my thumbs in my ears, like some bratty little kid. To this day, I have no idea what possessed me, but impotent as it was, it was the only protest I could muster. Through the darkened window, my eyes fixed on her, his wife, Camille, who was sitting next to him - beautiful, elegant, sleek, hair swept high on her head with a little chignon on top. She was a queen - above it all. I felt even more grubby, powerless, aimless - and worst of all - ineffective. Hell, I couldn't even successfully slash my wrists.

"Anything that can be faced down,
can be dealt with..."
--Mary Pipher
Author, <u>A Life in Light: Meditations on Impermanence.</u>

Chapter 70
Seeking the Light

A couple of weeks later, I was sitting at the big round oak table in Grandma's dining room with a friend who was throwing the *I Ching* coins. They're thrown six times and with each throw - heads or tails - represents a straight or broken line that adds up to a hexagram. That hexagram correlates with a spiritually philosophical rendering, a prophetic foretelling in the *Book of Changes.*

J.D. unexpectedly walked through the open front door to collect the remainder of his belongings. He saw us throwing the coins and mocked us. He, with his drifty right eye, picked up the coins and with all the false bravado of a Vegas gambler, threw them on the table.

When my friend looked up and read the *I Ching* hexagram she froze and looked at me. It began like this, "*A one-eyed man who thinks that he sees, a bravo who thinks he speaks the words of wise men.*" We were dumbfounded. J.D. dismissed it like brushing so much dandruff off his collar. My friend and I quietly nodded in acknowledgement.

In time, it became a song I wrote in three different chapters of my journey over the next three years. The 'I Ching Git-It-On Boogie Blues.'

It was from this physical place - this place in my spirit - that I understood I needed to seek my own healing path in a place of simplicity, in revitalizing, predictable, seasons of nature away from the artifice of the city if I was going to survive. I packed what I could into my parent's garage. I loaded my guitar, my dog and whatever I thought I might need to live on for a while into my old green Chevy. And with my son in my heart, I left Los Angeles on the first leg of my journey seeking myself - my authentic self. It was a *walkabout* that lasted twelve years and brought me through many life changes, a return to college twice, two more children, and a family that showed me unconditional love.

Chapter 71
In for a Penny, In for a Pound
2014

When I began my journey as an unwitting activist in November of 2014, I never imagined that I was about to change my life forever. It was liberating to call my sexual assault by its name at last. When I sent off a comment to the Washington Post about my 1969 experience with Bill Cosby, I was convinced that I'd never get a response. To my surprise, within the hour, I received a call from Adam Kushner at the Washington Post. I couldn't have imagined the journey I was about to begin.

Over the years I had never told anyone all the dirty details, but many close friends and my two daughters knew something untoward had happened back then shortly after my son died. I would sneer, make sarcastic comments, change the channel, leave the room, but infer only.

I never, even to myself, had used the *R* word.

Before I had a chance to think, The Post was booking me for a live on-camera interview and a still camera interview with two different photographers. They were coming to my house in the foothills of the San Gabriel Mountains, a little northeast of Los Angeles. I suddenly realized this was going to be important, not just to me, but to all women, to rape survivor's, to others who had not yet arrived at their tipping point. Beyond my early morning interviews, though, I could not have predicted what would happen next.

I remember waiting for the Washington Post videographer and their still photographer to arrive to record my interview breaking my silence for the very first time about my 1969 encounter with the now infamous, not-so-funny-anymore, comedian, Bill Cosby. This was the guy who I learned was being called *America's Dad*. I went into a zone. Once I had spoken the words out loud, some other energy force took control of me. It felt like the time when I prayed late at night in my Oregon barn while I was milking my goats back in 1979. I'm not sure where that prayer came from. *Let me be an instrument of healing.* Something outside of myself took over. It felt like whirling winds. I suddenly was offered a job in a nursing home as a nursing assistant and became certified. I discovered that caring for the dying gave me purpose and peace.

The Director of Nursing kept telling me, "*You should be an RN.*" As an artist, an art history and ceramics major, it was the last thing on my mind, but I kept hearing her voice in my head, and in the years to follow at thirty-nine, I returned to college and did – graduating with honors. It was the best decision for my life.

It felt like a destiny call of the same order this time, too. I felt that once I opened my mouth, I'd become a conduit for truth. It was for the support of only one woman who I didn't even know about and whom I had yet to meet - Andrea Constand. I knew nothing about her, nothing about the case. Barbara Bowman was the only survivor whose story I had read up to that point, before I contacted the Washington Post. It was educational. I met Sister Survivor Jewel Allison soon after that with Barbara on CNN, then Joan Tarshis and then I discovered there were many more speaking out after years of silence. Suddenly, I found myself on the same path amongst a group of women who became my sisters. After that my reason for speaking out changed, it became more than for myself and that one woman. It became about future generations, raising consciousness about sexual assault, changing laws and shining the light on *Rape Culture*.

I stood in the midst of my familiar things, lumbering stacks of books, *my addiction*, surrounded and warmed by framed photos of those I love. My Daddy's paintings on the walls, a candle lit, incense burning, my son's framed photo looking down on me with his soulful eyes - the one that I handed to Cosby at our first meeting. I waited and paced nervously. I wrapped my deep red, cobalt blue and gray paisley pashmina shawl, my security blanket, around my shoulders.

I looked up at my son's face and wondered what he would have thought about what I was getting ready to do. I wanted some kind of sign. I'd be speaking out publicly about an honored, wealthy, famous, beloved man in the black community - a powerful one at that. He practically owned NBC and William Morris Agency. He was extraordinarily wealthy. What if he sued me? I was on Social Security and teaching per diem at a small nursing school in the San Fernando Valley. I was gardening, reading a lot of books, walking my dogs, writing a musical about my circle of Playboy Bunny friends over the years. I was content, and after all my early life's traumas and pain, my life had become very peaceful. What was I thinking, stirring up ancient history?

Speaking out was a fearsome risk. I knew I'd be opening myself to a lot of racial slurs and personal attacks, but I had become used to it. Even with my own son looking unmistakably African in origin, my English, Scot-Irish genetics, I knew, would stir things up. It made me wonder how the black members of my own family of choice and chance, would respond to my blowing the whistle on someone the community revered. Cosby was someone who had spent most of his career promoting and uplifting black youth and providing them an example of professional possibility. Even though in his later years he was losing credibility with the younger generations of black youth, because he began railing at them from the podium like an angry, old grandpa establishing himself as a moral authority. His TV character, Dr. Huxtable, ironically a gynecologist, was for the first time in television history showed a black family being represented as educated, upscale professionals. He made a difference. That could not be denied. But he clearly had a shadow life. I had finally reached my tipping point. I couldn't worry about that then, because by that time, my choice was in the hands of a force greater than myself. I had to speak my truth.

When I saw that a black, male comedian had made a joke about Cosby being a rapist and everyone believed him, I was infuriated. Barbara Bowman's story of rape had been disbelieved for thirty plus years. I lost it. This hot, little rocket went off in my gut and ripped straight up into my brain and exploded! I was suddenly so pissed I could hardly see straight! I wasn't the only one who knew he had a shadow life.

At that time, around thirteen women had accused Bill Cosby of rape and Hannibal Burress was not going to let the public forget about it. He wasn't going to let Cosby off the hook. He'd been performing that bit for six months before it was filmed in a club in Philly and went viral.

The key phrases that hit me hard, and pulled my trigger, went something like this:

Burress, as Cosby: "*Pull your pants up black people, I was on TV in the 80s! I can talk down to you because I had a successful sitcom!*"

Burress: "*Yeah, but you rape women, Bill Cosby, so turn the crazy down a couple of notches.*"

During an interview with Howard Stern, Burress told him to Google "*Cosby Rape*" if he didn't believe him. It was a mind blower for me to hear all this. I had made a concerted effort all the years after he raped me to not know anything about him, his career, or his life. Nothing. I never wanted to see his face again. But, once I began speaking, the words came tumbling out of my mouth and I couldn't stop. My truth finally could no longer be contained.

I thought about that horrific year, 1969, when my son died and my life was shattered. It seemed as though nothing worse could ever occur. Yet, it was this lauded star who knew about my beloved son's death - and it was this man the Press was calling "*America's Dad,*" the man who callously drugged, kidnapped and raped me in the midst of the worst trauma any mother can ever experience.

This predatory 'mentor' used woman's vulnerabilities for his perverted and insatiable needs. He was to be exposed, perhaps, as the most prolific serial rapist of the 20th Century. I was soon to learn that I was just one unsuspecting victim in an unimaginable parade over a span of more than fifty years.

That one day's morning interview and photo shoot turned into an assembly line of interviews all in one day. I was being chauffeured from one studio to the next, CNN, Inside Edition, Al-Jazeera and so on. The UK Daily News walked up my street and stood in front of my garden hedge where I was still being photographed by the Washington Post to ask me about a Playboy Playmate who had committed suicide. I'd thought they were just neighbors out for a morning stroll. MSNBC arrived for their interview and after he left, I was rushed into the back of a black town car where I had hours on the road that day in between multiple interviews at major media studios all over Los Angeles County. It was a barrage. I was telling and retelling the story of that night.

I was forced to think about the thread of continuity throughout my life - the many rapes of body and soul; The emotional and psychological abuses; The dismissal, normalization of it and my family's rejection, several of whom were my abusers. It was all somehow being gathered together at once in this single swath of public revelation. It was as though this one loose thread of continuity was being tugged. My life's experiences were all being gathered up into a neatly defined, although sometimes messy, but acknowledged pouch made from the woven fabric of my life.

It was late in the evening before I was delivered back home. I'd had no food most of the day. There were quick tastes of tea and soup mid-morning at *Inside Edition*, arranged by correspondent and host, the very funny, brilliant and kind Jim Moret. That was pretty much it. I was famished and feeling faint by the time I arrived home. I walked into my house just in time to see myself on the late-night news. I always leave CNN on for the dogs while I'm gone because they like the soothing voices of Anderson Cooper and Don Lemon. My dog's ears perked up as soon as they heard my voice on TV. They kept looking at me as if they were wondering why my voice wasn't coming out of my mouth. I was emotionally drained, but at the same time exhilarated - finally speaking my truth - and most importantly, being heard. It truly was surreal.

The part I hadn't anticipated was having to recount the story of my little boy's death over and over. The stories were intrinsically connected. I had no choice.

I have been horrifically attacked for it. I've been called a liar, a gold digger, a white woman who wants to bring a good black man down to destroy his legacy. Behind my back, I have been called Norma Desmond, the fading mad actress in the old film Sunset Boulevard - *I'm ready for my close-up, Mr. Demille* - I was sent a version of the <u>Night Before Christmas</u> (<u>Victoria's Night Before Christmas</u>) - each line of the poem ending with, "*And her biracial son,*" and told that the reason my son died was because I was a terrible, negligent mother who left my son alone in the pool. My attorney sent a cease-and-desist on that one.

I have been criticized for repeatedly mentioning that my son was biracial. I always felt that because we have been accused of being a bunch of white women trying to bring a good black man down, that it was important for the public to understand who we really were. Many of us were in interracial families with racially mixed children. Many of his victims were women of color. We weren't racists at all, and he was an equal opportunity rapist.

There is no question that I will always feel guilty for trusting someone with my son's safety by the pool's edge no matter what anyone says to either attack or comfort me. I can beat myself up better than anyone. I was guilty for entrusting my son's safety to the wrong person and I felt that it was racially motivated. It became clear that Martin wanted to get rid of my son, "I was already starting to research military schools," he'd said. In the end he had his way - accident, deliberate neglect, passive neglect - I'll never know. He paid for it by losing me too.

For a long time, I bought the *"You left him alone"* story. I was unfriended by those I considered really good friends. I was blamed by family. And the *coup de grace* was that a family member let me know that Daddy supposedly told her *(and God knows who else)* that I left Tony alone in the pool while I was having sex with Martin in the bedroom! What kind of obsession did these people have with sex? I could have been praying in church and their spin would have been that I was screwing the priest - and the organist, too! It was sick. They were always adding one more stone to my sinking back. I flogged myself relentlessly anyway without their assistance. *Mea culpa! Mea culpa!*

Speaking out about my son's death so frequently, however, more things began to emerge from my suppressed memories. One day it hit me! Martin was with him! It was he who left him alone. It was Martin! It stunned me. I had to sit down. It was a sudden moment of realization with some relief. I hadn't just walked away from the pool uncaringly, leaving my precious son on his own. I left him with Martin. Though one never ever truly heals from the loss of a child, speaking out about Cosby would become, in some weird way, an inadvertent instrument in my healing over my child's death.

Chapter 72
A Movement
2016

I had no idea what I was opening myself to when I broke my silence, but after all my decades of silence it was too late for me to zip it now.

Yup! *In for a penny. In for a pound.* I just hadn't anticipated that by speaking out I was joining a movement!

All of the myriad events that occurred because of our speaking out in 2014 and into 2015 created a whirlwind of energy. Survivors were empowered to speak out, seek justice after breaking their silences of years. Not only Cosby's survivors but survivors of many other famous, powerful men; some not famous but always powerful after taking up residence in the psyches of their victims. By the end of 2015 we had been on almost every news show, a few talk shows, Dr. Phil, Dr. Oz, Exposed, A & E, Vanity Fair, TV7 News from Sydney, Australia and Kate Snow who hosted a multitude of us on NBC Dateline. We were in the newspapers, magazines and we were making noise. "*Good*" noise.

The New York Magazine *Empty Chair* cover in 2015 sat many of us survivors in straight backed chairs looking straight into the camera. There was an empty chair at the end of the last row - an invitation for those who had yet to find their voice. It blew the lid off the Cosby story.

In 2016 empowered women survivors banded together at the Jewish Women's Center in West Hollywood forming a group called ERSOL - End Rape Statute of Limitations - chaired by Ivy Bottini. The immortal Ivy Bottini was one of the original founders of the National Organization for Women along with Betty Freidan. Ivy was rapidly approaching 90 years old, and only had peripheral vision. She walked with a cane and required a caregiver. Ivy had been watching the television series, Law and Order, Special Victims Unit; she became infuriated and decided to do something about it. She called a meeting - and we showed up.

My old friend, Elaine Suranie, former Commissioner for the Commission on the Status of Women in Sacramento, California told me I had to be there and I never say 'no' to Elaine. I was joined by my friend, Kay; Cosby survivor, Lili Bernard with her son and many others ready to pick up the banner. Dr. Caroline Heldman, political science professor at Occidental College and former "*talking head*" at Fox News who filed a sexual harassment complaint against Bill O'Reilly, was Ivy's co-chair. There were many women and young men who showed up and were inspired to make a difference. It became the most essential meeting that could have transpired to abolish the ten-year statute of limitations on rape and sexual assault in California.

We met. We organized. We strategized. We created our own logo. We made our t-shirts and we rallied on the Cosby star on Hollywood Boulevard. I gave a rabble-rousing speech along with Lili, Caroline, and Ivy. We formed a coalition that became a movement and the Cosby "*Survivor Sisters*" were essential in changing laws in three states. We carpooled to Sacramento and testified, lobbied and rallied to support Senator Connie Leyva who wrote our bill - SB813.

The Justice for Victims Act, which successfully abolished the statute of limitations on rape and sexual assault in California. Governor Brown signed it into law on September 28th, 2017 and it went into effect on January 1st, 2017. From that day forward whenever a rape victim is able to speak about their assaults, they can seek justice through the legal system and prosecute their perpetrator. However, it is not retroactive. A new law has been written allowing rape survivors of childhood sexual assault to begin proceedings in a one-to-two-year window of time.

Cosby Survivor Lise-Lotte Lublin with her husband Ben, residents of Nevada, put forward their bill that expanded the statute in Nevada to twenty years. Cosby Survivors Heidi Thomas and Beth Ferrier-Tillo did the same thing in their state of residence, Colorado. We were truly making a difference. We were raising consciousness and educating the world on Rape Culture.

We, who could no longer seek justice for ourselves because our statute of limitations had long since expired, were making it possible for other survivors to find justice from that day forward.

We were filled with joy, energy, hope and determination fueled by the knowledge that we were empowering other survivors to come forward and see justice served. We were making changes for the future of women, for our daughters, our granddaughters, even for our sons and grandsons who have never been exempt from sexual assault, rape and incest. However, 1 in 4 rapists are prosecuted if the victim is a woman while 3 in 4 are brought to justice if the victim is male. Once again, we see the disparity between the worth of males and females in our society.

It was that year when the television mini-series, *The Hunting Grounds*, aired about rape on college campuses, the television special, *Spotlight*, shone its light on rape in the Catholic church. Johnna Janis' film, *Invisible Scars*, was premiered in Hollywood about her childhood incest. And, we opened the floodgates the Weinstein survivors came forward and broke their silence. We were on a roll.

Emboldened, we spoke at every opportunity. We testified at the West Hollywood City Council, the city in which I had been raped by Cosby in 1969. To be able to bring my story finally to West Hollywood was nothing short of miraculous. It would never have occurred to me when I was raped there in '69 to speak to the authorities, after all, who would believe me, a former Playboy Playmate, a Bunny, with a history of being sex-trafficked. I felt defeated before I even began the thought. But here I was testifying in West Hollywood where I Cosby had raped me so many decades before.

Women's Rights attorney Gloria Allred with whom I've had the honor to stand shoulder to shoulder through this journey of activism and empowerment joined us, along with two of my Sister Survivors, Lili Bernard and Linda Cooper Kirkpatrick. Last but not least, my good friend and playwright Gary LeGault who directed me in a three act play in Hollywood a couple of years before, called *Dial M for Marlene*, in which I starred as Marlene Dietrich also stood by me. The only thing missing was the champagne.

I always talk about karmic circles of healing. This particular moment at the West Hollywood City Council was one of those moments. In the lobby there were big-screen, closed circuit TVs in the lobby where what was said from the podium could also be seen and heard in the lobby. I addressed the Council making our pitch to support our State Bill 813 - Justice for Victims' Act. and we received a unanimous "*Aye!*" vote.

Feeling powerful and validated I strode up the center aisle and went through the glass doors out into the lobby. Standing just inside to my left was a beige-uniformed, gun-toting, female Sheriff. As I began to pass her, I noticed the corner of her mouth turn up. I smiled. She thrust her hand forward and as I started to take it, I said, *"I'd rather give you a hug but I don't know if it's legally appropriate."* She threw her arms around me. We embraced and rocked back and forth. This circle of healing, completed.

We petitioned to have Cosby's bronze bust removed from Disney World. We petitioned unsuccessfully to have his star removed from the Hollywood Boulevard Walk of Fame, but successfully petitioned to have many of his honorary doctorate degrees removed from various universities, including Temple University where Andrea Constand and he had met. Our voices were heard. In that summer of 2016 activism, I was finally able to stand tall and say for the first time out loud along with other survivors, *"I am a multi-rape survivor."* It was liberating.

During our road trip-activism to Sacramento I was also able to reveal for the first time that I had been sex trafficked for three devastating months when I was twenty-one. I hadn't told anyone before outside of people very close to me. I felt I was dissolving under the shameful memory of it. Everyone had different reactions. Some felt I was courageous in admitting it. Others with joyful relish wanted to hear all the prurient details. I was a furious, tearful mess.

No one truly understood how much it took out of me to reveal my decades of hidden pain.

Caroline Heldman on the road trip home framed my experience in a realistic way that I could live with more tolerably - and she was right. I was trafficked. I was victimized. I survived.

And I have the ruby red slippers to prove it.

We continue to speak out so others might find their voices. We speak for the future, for positive change in a time when women are once again being threatened with the imminent danger of being thrown back into the Dark Ages. Dark forces are afoot - as the patriarchy, the control-hungry, the misogynistic, paternalistic, power structure attempts to reclaim the territory of our bodies through any means necessary. Vigilance, voting and unwavering voices are our tools and we must use them effectively and persistently.

Chapter 73
Down to the Wire
April 2018

As we sat in Courtroom A in Montgomery County Courthouse in Norristown, Pennsylvania, we waited for Andrew Wyatt, the jocular, blowhard publicist to escort Cosby up the aisle. Cosby was so anxious to get out of that courtroom, he almost forgot he was supposed to act crippled and blind. He did a jokey little dance step backwards as Denise, the court administrator, held him back, while the hallway was cleared for him to exit. I sat and watched this monster walk past me. I felt nothing but disdain. He was a bad actor. I was past feeling fear from standing up to him; I was standing up for myself at last.

It was cold, gray, and raining the previous three days in Montgomery County, but that day, the sun was shining. It was glorious outside. I hadn't had to white knuckle it through blinding rain, making huge waves as I plowed through the streets to get to court that morning. It was a huge relief. But it was cold inside the courthouse. Sitting on marble benches against the hallway walls was dreary, and artificial light made it feel even colder. This was the second day of jury deliberation. For those of us who had been at the mistrial the year before, we were prepared to hunker down for another long siege.

We were an interesting mix: survivors of Cosby's drugging and raping from decades before, activists, Cosby supporters, and the gathering of familiar journalists. The journalists wandered into the media room to plug-in their laptops, but were keeping an eye on our locations just in case there were statements to grab if there was a verdict. We were all looking for available plugins in the hallways, wherever we could find them. Laptops were open, entries were being written, everyone was staying close in case we were called back into the courtroom for another defining question by the jury. And so, we waited...

Because of my previous speaking commitment at UMD's sexual assault symposium, I'd missed hearing my five sister survivors testify. It was disappointing but I was being given the eyewitness reports. The five - Janice Baker-Kinney, Chelan Lasha, Janice Dickinson, Lise-Lotte Lublin and Heidi Thomas were powerful, emotional and searingly truthful. But I was back now for the duration. I would be there for the verdict.

Chapter 74
The Worth of a Woman

It seems that no matter how we prepare, we will never prevent rape and sexual assault without changing the culture first. Rape culture has been prevalent in society for millennia and is still alive and well all over the world. It is a weapon of war. Child brides are still being sold for little more than *two goats, ten chickens and a pig - and that's probably a hefty price for some*. Girls are dying from being impregnated before their bodies are mature enough to carry a baby and give birth. Girls still remain bartering chips just like so much produce in so many places in the world.

Rape culture is endemic and a pandemic. We must raise consciousness until it is eradicated.

But it will never be enough just to teach women how to protect themselves against rape. We must also teach boys as they grow up to become men of honor and respect - and to honor and respect the women who bore them and those who would bear their children. We must teach our boys that women are not possessions, not property and not their servants. Women are the people who gave them life, who loved them and protected them, nurtured and nourished them, who taught them how to walk and dreamed their future with them. As boys need to be taught to respect and honor women, women must, as well, be taught to feel entitled to being treated with respect and honor. Girls must respect and honor themselves, recognizing their true value, setting healthy boundaries and educating themselves. They must be inspired to aspire, achieve and accomplish.

Women are reinventing themselves every day, finding their voices. More women are entering politics, becoming physicians, scientists and advocates for change. We are not content to be patronized as the "weaker sex." We know we are strong, capable and resilient; multitasking queens with immeasurable worth. We must not allow ourselves to ever be diminished.

When we stand up for ourselves, when we consistently refuse to accept archaic perceptions of our place in society, we all thrive - men and women alike as co-equal partners on this journey called life. Times are changing, just not fast enough. There are still dark forces daily promoting our demise as powerful partners.

While we as women are making significant progress, there are still institutional stumbling blocks along the way. Some states are ramping up their efforts to throw us back into the Dark Ages, insisting our bodies and futures should be controlled by our male dominated government - generally, old white men with the exception of, perhaps, Justice Clarence Thomas. Laws must be passed to ensure our autonomy. It must be codified that women are equal under the Constitution of the United States across the board, not just state by state at the whim of primarily white male lawmakers. There are those women who have aligned themselves with the white male power structure and patriarchal religious systems. It is a sad observation to see these women subvert other women's rights. We must be vigilant and we must stand our ground. We must use our voices and our vote. We fought long and hard for the right to vote and by not using our vote we become authors of our own demise.

We must demand control over our own bodies in every state - and in every country. Being held hostage by our biology, our anatomy is just another form of cruelty, of slavery and an attempt to control other human beings. We do not need to allow ourselves to be defined as incubators or serial brood mares. Our careers must not be derailed, redefined, nor redirected by strangers. It is not for a distant government to determine our identity, nor our destiny.

Making choices for one's own life, one's own future is the act of an adult citizen. It is *our* right. Men in government try to keep women in line like children instead of the co-equals that we are. A legal system that is not influenced by theology nor misogyny must be supported and upheld. We have had the rug ripped out from under us time and again and it must stop. Increased numbers of progressive women legislators, female professionals and women in the media sharing their stories are essential to continue moving the needle in the direction of legal and social equality. Speaking out, freeing our voices from the fear of retribution is just the beginning. Reaching out and embracing others in their truth, supporting other women's voices, opening wide our arms in empathy, in compassion, as a mother takes her babe to the breast, is a very good start, but only as it is coupled with a spine of steel, a focused eye, strength of purpose and a very loud chorus of voices.

Men have not done such a good job keeping our world at peace, keeping our people off the streets, nor feeding our babies. They seem to be very good at trying to control other people's territories, resources, economies and killing their families in other countries though. Women who are skilled at maintaining and sustaining life know how to share, stock pantries, multitask and prepare for future needs; to assert their expertise and bring the world into a more stable and sustainable future.

The question has to be asked - Why are men so afraid to let women own and control their own bodies? Why must women have to swim against the current to do the things that come so naturally. Women know how to use collaborative and nurturing skills to protect and grow the world for the long game - for the generations to come. If our global society is to survive, progressive-thinking women - and men who support women - in positions of power who will effect positive change must take the reins, write laws and continue to enlighten the world with their brilliant visions for the future.

Better Times: Saying "Yes!" to Life

My Girls, My Strength, My Legacy, My Diamonds

L-R Erinbrooke, Mama and Meaganlark: As we reflect on our lives, our children hold up the mirror. Holding the future.

Chapter 75
Cameos

Floating cameo images drift through my mind at times when I walk alone in the hills, dig in the garden, crochet or work on my art pieces - my *buddha boxes*. Some memories carry more weight than others, some things I'd forgotten entirely until speaking out about my past life. Buried traumas were dredged back up to the surface. Writing this memoir has forced me to confront the depths of trauma I thought I'd moved on from but hadn't completely. But in order to tell my '*woman's story*' in the most authentic way possible I have had to face things again in the light of a new day. It has been a purging, a cleansing, a deeper lesson on the transformation of pain into passionate advocacy. Healing requires transforming pain into empathic service to others. We have each been given gifts - *our diamonds* - our best service to the world is to shine - and inspire each other to shine.

I have been trying to focus more on the good friends along the way that had a grounding effect on my life. From my earliest memories, through my troubled youth, I treasure the salvation of those hands offered to me through the deep, dark waters submerging my soul - those who saved me when I was drowning.

Harry Drinkwater used to call those times, "*our times of trouble.*" It put things into perspective for me when he said that. I could see it as a season that would pass - or a chapter in a book. I could finally turn the page and when I reached resolution - the satisfying conclusion - I could close that book and put it up on a high shelf out of reach - out of my misery.

If we refocus our vision on the brighter moments, they will be our touchstones in our *times of trouble*. There will be those who will stand out in our memories for their calm acceptance of us as we were, and as we are becoming.

I have listened to the stories from all sides. I have heard the stories that have been whispered trustingly in my ear for the very first time, with tears and hugs. Some of those stories were about Cosby, but most were stories from people by whom I am deeply humbled, people whose trust I inadvertently earned through putting my own neck on the line and speaking my personal truth so publicly. When I broke my silence it broke the padlock on many other silenced voices, as well.

By finding my voice, I am bringing my own circle of healing to closure.

By finding my voice I am transforming my years of pain into creative action and activism.

By finding my voice, I have become an advocate for change, and for the future of those who will stand on my strengthened shoulders.

Through service we are healed.

Chapter 76
Lines in the Sand

Yes, these are the moments in life that clearly define us. Speaking publicly about sexual abuse as a Cosby, multi-rape, sex-trafficking and domestic and child abuse survivor, has been that line in the sand for me. A line once crossed, there is no return possible.

I can't help but think about the *what ifs*. *What if* my birth father had survived the war? *What if* he had been alive and heard what had happened to me? His generation, the Great Generation, was the *Silent Generation* when it came to the rape of a daughter, wife or sister. It was a hush-hush, shameful kind of thing. Talking about sex in open honest terms was considered inappropriate, impolite - inferences only. S.E.X. was considered a dirty word in most households not to be spoken aloud. To put it in context when I was growing up, *heck* and *darn* were considered swear words. Women obeyed and women were not yet allowed to have credit of their own nor buy a house without their husband's or father's signature.

As a child of the Forties and Fifties, I was dominated by adult authority. It's all we knew. It was the social structure and climate of the day. *"Father Knows Best,"* was everybody's favorite TV show. I was acclimated to suppress and repress my feelings, my thoughts, my needs. *"Ladies never show anger in public. Ladies are always polite. Ladies speak in modulated tones. Ladies always write an elegant hand. Ladies always cross their ankles and fold their hands in their laps. Ladies don't chew gum in public. Ladies don't slouch.*" And we ladies were groomed by old movies to yearn after the "Frankly, I don't give a damn," kind of guys - the emotionally and sometimes, physically unavailable men with the simmering eyes that undressed us as we restrained our natural passions. Ladies were never allowed to acknowledge, or own, their sexuality.

Mom hated closed doors in the house, so I had no entitlement to privacy either. If she came upstairs and found my door closed, she'd throw it open and look in suspiciously, as if I was doing something nasty. I was usually communing with the cicadas up our hill at twilight or writing *haiku*, or doing homework. If I disobeyed or spoke my mind I was ignored. I learned early that I had no rights at all, nor was I entitled to any. This was my training. This was the soil from which I grew.

My lifelong journey has been learning to claim what is mine - my voice, my rights, my self-determined boundaries, my personal safe space - my own island in the goddam storm. Just knowing I could say, no! Or - YES!

But I think my father, had he lived, would have been proud of me. He, the aspiring writer, on duty as a young forestry ranger, writing in his fire tower before he was drafted. He might have been surprised, then gratified to discover that this little girl of his mustered the courage to speak out against an insidious blight on our society. I believe that he might have been proud that I had found my voice - my calling. I believe he would have been proud that by doing so, I had found myself in the company of people he would have loved to have known - journalists and news correspondents - people who put their necks on the line for what is right. People who every day stand for truth. I try to imagine him standing a little taller knowing his little girl had found her voice and that her words carried weight. I know he would have been proud that my words were valued in such esteemed circles and that I was no longer disregarded and silenced. But, then, a wry thought crossed my mind that had he lived, maybe none of this would have happened at all.

Chapter 77
Montgomery County Courthouse
2018 April

"Oh, oh, I can tell something's happening!" Reporters and others camped out in the courthouse hallways were rushing toward the open door of the Courtroom. Denise was holding her clipboard as she checked us off while we filed into Courtroom A.

"What is it? Do we have a verdict?"

We looked from face to face. No. The jury had a question. We sighed a sigh of disappointment and decided we were in for another very long siege as we were the year before when the jury finally came back with a mistrial. We settled in for the duration.

Michael Case, who with straight-backed formal dignity, proceeded down the center aisle as though he was Sergeant at Arms, carrying his ceremonial mace in Queen Elizabeth's Parliamentary opening ceremony. He turned facing the assembly, commanding everyone's attention without a word. He informed us again of the rules. Cell phones, not only off, but out of sight. No internet transmission. If any of us were caught with a phone ringing or our mobile devices transmitting, we would be escorted out of the courtroom and may not be allowed back in for the rest of the day. We prudently made sure that none of that happened to us.

Ironically, Gloria Allred forgot. Her phone rang. She, the illustrious, women's rights attorney in whose presence, abusive men quailed, was unceremoniously escorted out of the courtroom just like any of the rest of us commoners. She was humble, held her dignity and did not get indignant. I held my breath, because I, as an R.N. managing my then ninety-six-year-old friend's care, was on 24/7 call. At her age, my directions to the nursing assistants were critical should anything untoward happen and my instructions were required. It was a risk I had no choice but to take. I surreptitiously slid my hand under my thigh where my phone was hidden on vibrate to double check. I had to make sure the ringer was off.

We sat as the new defense attorneys, Tom Messereau and Kathleen Bliss, meandered down the center aisle. They were the ones Cosby finally got to take his case for the second trial after Mr. McMonagle wisely resigned. They were followed by the publicist, Andrew Wyatt, with Cosby on his arm sporting his *blind man* prop cane. He couldn't hurt us now.

Judge O'Neill entered. We stood, then sat. The jury filed in, one by one. We had this choreography down pat by now. The attorneys stood for the jury. We read their faces. I made eye contact with a juror on the end row and quickly looked away. I did not want to be perceived as potentially trying to influence the jury. We had to be careful. We were not allowed to wear our *"Stand in Truth"* buttons, or anything that might indicate whose side we were on as we had the previous year. Anyone who watched the news coverage over the previous three years or so knew our faces well.

We listened expectantly. Was the jury going to pore over more discrepancies in Andrea's phone records again? Would they weigh in on her frequent calls to Cosby's myriad telephone numbers after his alleged assault? Were they going to question the three blue pills again? Was it three whole pills or one and another one broken in half? Did they want to hear again in Cosby's own voice admitting under oath that he acquired Quaaludes to give to women so he could have sex with them? We wondered.

We'd been through all this before in the first trial. Was this jury going to be swayed by the "bait and switch and dazzle?" Were these jurors going to fall for the attorneys' attempts to confuse and distract? Since Cosby had new attorneys, they may not repeat the former attorneys' strategies, but in our minds, there was so little to grab onto. For us since we knew his M.O. 'up close and personal,' it was cut and dried.

Cosby had hired Tom Messereau for this trial. He was the attorney with the long white hair, whose defense resulted in Michael Jackson's acquittal. We worried we might be in trouble. Oddly he was rather silent a lot of the time. He let his associates present their case. Would we have a hung jury again? The questions swirled in our brains. We steeled ourselves for another mistrial. We prepared ourselves emotionally as best we could, to be let down one more time.

The prosecution called their first witness, an energetic bright forensic psychiatrist, Dr. Barbara Ziv, who outlined the post-assault behaviors of rape survivors, clarifying and demystifying post-rape symptomology versus mythology. They systematically brought forth one sister survivor after another to show prior bad acts. Their strategy was to clearly define Cosby's consistent *modus operandi*, his specific fetishes and to illustrate his many decades' long history as a sexual predator. We were more encouraged moment by moment. The prosecution's strategy in the second trial was proving to be more effective than the first.

The jury's question was, *"What is the legal definition of consent?"* Wow, well, this was different. "Should we be encouraged?" we questioned.

The judge's answer was that there is no legal definition of consent. We rolled our eyes at each other in disbelief. Shouldn't there be? Everyone left the courtroom in reverse order. We prepared for another long day of deliberation. We went to the cafeteria, but didn't stay long because there was no cell phone reception there. We plugged in our phones at any available outlet. We sat. We chatted. We wrote. We checked our email. We smiled at passing journalists who were pinning our location just in case, so they could find us for any first reactions to a possible early verdict. I was beginning to feel claustrophobic. I was not feeling mentally prepared to be in this cold mausoleum for hours to come. We had been blessed with glorious sunshine after the gray gloom, the torrential rain and the insidious damp that had seeped into my Southern California bones over the last few days.

Desperate for fresh air and without telling a soul, I decided to take a chance. I bolted outside to a bench adjacent to the courthouse plaza where all the media tents were set up. I inhaled the warm air deeply. The fragrant masses of blooming daffodils surrounded me and I gratefully opened my little Trader Joe's Lemon Basil Pasta Salad that I'd been hungering for all morning. Car noises and birds surrounded me. The fresh lemon juice I squeezed on my *penne* was life-giving and I savored every succulent bite as I basked in the sun's heat. Casually, I thought I should head back inside. I tried to see my cell phone, but the sun was blinding me. I'd forgotten to take it off 'vibrate.' I thought maybe I'd save some bites for the next break, but the flavor was irresistible, so I sat for a few extra minutes while I finished it.

I tossed my trash in the rubbish bin and slowly strolled back towards the plaza luxuriating in the warmth of the sun. I stepped carefully over massive cables leading to big TV cameras and lights, but then I noticed TV crews hurriedly beginning to ready their equipment. I sensed an air of anticipation and started to hurry. I saw a sight that I'd never seen before. On the office building's terrace across the street from the courthouse there were crowds of people amassed. They were looking expectantly at the front door of the courthouse. Something serious was happening and I began rushing. I hurried through security and was blocked by a familiar sheriff at the bottom of the great marble staircase.

"What's going on?"

"I don't know, but they told me not to let anyone up."

"But, I'm one of his victims. You know me! I have to be up there!" I said in a panic.

"Take that back elevator to the upstairs hallway. Hurry!" I ran like a crazy woman.

The elevator was not fast enough. I was chomping at the bit. I got out on the second floor and ran down the hallway into a crowd gathered at the far end of the hallway. Everyone was being held back from anywhere close to the front hallway of Courtroom A. A female Sheriff with muscled, tattooed biceps and a bleached blonde crew cut looking an awful lot like a Warrior Avatar stood at attention. I pleaded with her to let me pass, but to no avail. The jury was already filing in one by one into the narrow side hallway leading into the courtroom. Denise, the courtroom administrator, was just closing the door. I wanted to yell, *"Hey Denise! It's me, Victoria! Please can you let me in?"* But it was too late.

I felt defeated, deflated. I couldn't believe that I wasn't going to be in the courtroom with my Sister Survivors at what was clearly something very heavy duty. This had to be the moment we'd been waiting for, the very moment we'd lived for through our years of activism, hoping to see him suffer the consequences of his actions.

Crowds of courthouse employees gathered in clusters. There was a static electricity of anticipation in the air.

I said to the woman next to me, *"Question or Verdict?"*

She said, *"Verdict..."*

I just simply could not believe that after three and a half years, I would not be in the courtroom for this moment, whatever the outcome. Then, the blonde woman next to me looked down at her phone. I said, *"What?!"*

"Guilty! Guilty! Guilty! On ALL three counts!!! Guilty!"

"Oh, my god!!! Oh! My! GOD!!!"

Cheers broke out in the hallway and everyone was looking at each other in disbelief and joy.
Good old Sheriff Carl! He had texted out to her as soon as transmission was allowed.

"He's GUILTY!"

I think I shrieked in disbelief, tears welling up stinging my eyes and I was separated from my sisters in this overwhelming historic moment.

Chapter 78
This Man

Kristen Feden, the brilliant prosecution attorney, the only woman, the only black attorney on any of the legal teams, had given closing arguments. She had raced back and forth across the courtroom in her crisp black skirt suit in high heels, commanding everyone's attention. Our eyes had been riveted on her. She stood behind Cosby pointing down at his head.

"This man!" she said, "This man!"

We were mesmerized, caught in her spell. If the jury wasn't lured by her words, we'd have been lost. But they were, and we weren't.

Guilty! Guilty! Guilty! On ALL three counts!

After the mistrial the year before, it was hard to believe this word would ever be said aloud.

Guilty!

And this was the moment after three dismal days of bone-chilling rain that I chose to slip out into the glorious sunshine to eat my salad, and not hear NBC's Marianne Haggerty frantically texting me to hurry back inside. I'm still kicking myself. Later Marianne would say, *"Didn't you hear me texting you?"*

Just then, the courtroom doors burst open. Escorted through it were my Sister Survivors in tears - Therese Serignese, my last year's Airbnb roommate; Lili Bernard - Afro Cuban artist and actress who had been on Cosby's show with her powerhouse voice; her friend, our ERSOL co-chair and strategist, Caroline Heldman, Ph.D., political analyst - all sobbing.

Sheriff Avatar smiled and motioned me forward. I ran with arms outstretched in tears. We embraced, comforted each other and held each other in disbelief, joy and pent-up release. Was it really true?

The sheriffs began clearing the hallway, pushing everyone back to the furthest hallway, because Cosby would be walking out with his entourage. He had to enter a side office to sign paperwork. We hadn't thought about that. Would he be in handcuffs? Would we get to see?

As we were herded back and blocked off by tape, I heard tears behind me. I remembered my pledge to myself three and a half years before that Cosby would never see me cry, nor have the chance to feel satisfaction in my weakness and vulnerability ever again. I shook myself and dried my eyes quickly. I straightened the black suit jacket that had been my uniform through both trials. I liked to think of it as my *Johnny Cash-until-there's-peace-and-justice-suit.* I moved to the front of the crowd with my chin up, shoulders back, just like Mama taught me. I stood front and center as Cosby was guided by his ashen-faced PR guy, the formerly arrogant Andrew Wyatt. They were followed by their stricken flock. The Perp Walk.

I stood tall and proud. I was expressionless but emboldened. I stood triumphantly. I knew they saw me. I saw their eyes glaze over when they came up to where we were standing before they had to hang a left. They looked stunned; their faces blanched in disbelief. They thought they had this one. They couldn't have missed me as they hung a sharp left turn into the narrow hallway, leading into the side office where signing documents would make it even more real.

At that point, we really didn't know what to do next, so we headed down the massive white marble staircase, a little off balance, steadying ourselves with trembling hands on the banisters. We forged our way into the sunlight amid "Congratulations!" and "Well done's!" We greeted the lineup of cameras and microphones thrust into our faces and stopped to answer the insistent cacophony of questions as best we could.

"How do you feel?" "Whaddya think?" they ask, thrusting mics and cameras into our faces. Oh God! We couldn't yet believe it was really real! We had yet to process our feelings. Maybe, some meaningful words came out of my mouth. How would I know? I was still in shock. My cell phone was exploding with forty-seven texts, twenty-three phone calls and endless emails in ten minutes.

We made our way to the podium where Gloria Allred was preparing to speak. Lili Bernard and Caroline Heldman were to her right. I grabbed the hand of Shari Botwin, LCSW, rape survivor, author, and trauma-informed therapist, and brought her in with us. She was to my left. I spoke after Gloria. I had no prepared speech, but I had overflowing gratitude in my heart. *"Thank you, thank you, thank you, for believing in us! We are not going away! So, get over it!"* Gloria smiled a little smile. *"The work must and shall go on!"*

The media feeding frenzy was just beginning. We were all being approached for interviews later, here in front of the Montgomery County Courthouse. I said *"Yes!"* to everyone. I finally looked at my phone and saw endless numbers with no attached names. I had no idea who I booked with by then. I knew I had to be back by 9:30 that night to be interviewed by Chris Hayes on MSNBC, followed by CNN's Don Lemon, whom I hadn't spoken with since our Don Lemon Special that aired in January of 2015. We'd come a long way. The BBC wanted my interview at the same time as CNN for their Morning Show in London. I wondered how I could cram it all in. I couldn't. They had to move on and Lili took that one.

After the guilty verdict, our mass media interviews and speaking at the podium, I was left with only two hours to get back to my activist friend and hostess Diana's apartment in Paoli. Too excited to eat, I tossed back a quick snifter of Courvoisier while I randomly threw stuff in my overnight-case. I raised my glass in a little private toast to victory, justice and to my Sisters.

I heard a beep from a car horn outside my window and rushed out the door. My dear amazing Bird Milliken was waiting to drive me back to the courthouse plaza - and the MSNBC and CNN tents.

Waiting to go LIVE, Don Lemon said into my earpiece, "Remember when you were on my show back in the beginning? We had all those big pictures of Cosby on the wall behind us and you were all upset and hugging?"

"Yeah! How could I ever forget?"

He said, "And, can you believe where we are tonight 3 1/2 years later?"

"Crazy, right?"

Then, after my MSNBC interview, Chris Hayes murmured, "Rachel Maddow just told me, 'She's good.'" I was honored...

Chapter 79
The Journey After the Verdict

NBC News producer, Marianne Haggerty, had ordered a car to pick me up in front of the courthouse at 11 p.m. They were to take me to New York after I finished my last interview with Don Lemon. I was to be interviewed the following morning on the Today Show with Hoda and Savannah. Gloria Allred, Lili and I would be their guests. CNN producer, Ellie, stood with me on the courthouse steps with my suitcase waiting and waiting. The car never showed. Finally, after multiple midnight calls to already sleeping Marianne, she straightened it out, but I was worried she might not ever speak to me again. She finally sent the car to the CNN producer's hotel in Conshohocken. We piled into Ellie's small rental car with another journalist I didn't know and we plowed on through the late night, down very dark narrow winding roads to the next town. I still hadn't eaten since the verdict.

Almost as soon as we got back to the Conshohocken Marriott I plugged my dying phone into an outlet, and the town car arrived. I was unceremoniously loaded into the back seat obviously fatigued and groggy by then. Mohammed, the driver hovered over me, very kindly offering to take care of me as if I was his own mother. In fact, I did feel old enough that night to be his mother. He offered to stop and get me anything I might need. *"I need sleep,"* I mumbled.

Though I tried, I couldn't get comfortable, but more than that, I couldn't shut off my brain. I tried and tried without success. My brain was buzzing as if I'd drunk a pot of double espresso.

I closed my eyes trying to get into the zone, but my thoughts kept drifting into random places. *"Would I be here if I had done everything people told me not to do?"*

Everything counselors ever told the traumatized and grieving not to do in a crisis, I did. If I hadn't left Los Angeles in January of 1970, and then California altogether in '71 walking away from everything I knew, I was convinced I never would have survived. Sometimes, removing ourselves entirely from a toxic situation like surgically excising a malignant tumor is the only way to begin life anew, even if it isn't the prescribed treatment.

The driver interrupted my reverie with, *"Ma'am, I have to stop and get gas. Do you want anything?"* As beyond hungry as I was, the thought of Qwik Stop hot dogs or pepperoni sticks curdled my stomach. I said, *"No thanks."* and returned to my drifting thoughts. I shifted positions, tried to curl up, close my eyes and ears to the passing lights and highway truck noises but I just couldn't get there. There was a beehive buzzing in my bloodstream. I finally gave up, opened my eyes and stared out of the back of the shiny black town car. I wondered if I had slept at all. I tried to decide how close we were to Manhattan and wondered if I could power through the TV talk show circuit in the morning and make any sense at all without some shut-eye or food.

Mohammad handed me a bottle of water and asked if I'd like a little music, then told me the story of his years in this country as a Pakistani immigrant. I closed my eyes and began drifting back again thinking of the odd chain of events that led me to these moments - like dominos falling.

Chapter 80
"Breathe!" She Said

I was jolted out of my *'rememberings,'* the ones I'll take with me to my grave, the ones I needed to make peace with still, and the ones I had laid to rest.

We were now weaving through the streets of a dark predawn Manhattan morning. People were purposefully rushing to their destinations with heads into the wind, their hands clutching their collars against the chill. Streets were shiny-slick and wet. Yellow cabs with ticking meters, discrete black and gunmetal gray town cars wove slowly through the traffic with a sense of importance. I remember when I was a young girl yearning to be part of the intense, sophisticated energy of this city before the rapes, before my dreams were shattered.

There were streamers of neon, minute squares of light peeking from dark silhouetted skyscrapers. We pulled up to the curb. *The Baccarat* awaited. I only had two hours before my car picked me up for the *Today Show.* After a hot shower I was dressed and ready to go, with no time for sleep. I laid down and waited for my car. It was now over twenty-four hours since I'd eaten or slept. Somehow, I made it through *The Today Show*, then an HLN interview before Gloria grabbed me and said, *"Come with me."* We landed at CNN for New Day. Alisyn Camerota and I hadn't seen each other since my very first interview with her in December of 2014, when CNN had arranged a first surprise meeting with

Barbara Bowman and Jewel Allison. We had come full circle.

After lunch at the Friar's Club on Gloria's invitation, Lili, Caroline, Gloria and I left quickly to get to CBS and *Inside Edition* for our final interview of the day. We were greeted by the warm and lovely Deborah Norville, who had interviewed me for the pilot of her new series *Exposed* a couple of years prior. Once the interviews were over, I was returned to my friend's place in Paoli, which had become home during the trial. I stood quietly for a moment before going inside and took a deep breath. The air was crisp and clean, fresh and regenerating. I looked down the hill to the deep grasses in the woodsy glen below the house. I felt life surging back into my spirit with every breath. I inhaled the beauty and savored our victory.

"Guilty!" Guilty!" Guilty!" I repeated quietly to myself. I threw my arms up to the sky and did a little *pirouette* in the muddy driveway. I laughed out loud, exuberantly and didn't care if anybody saw me. Daffodils were blooming as triumphantly as I felt. Through the deep, patchouli layers of soggy leaves, there were mounds of lush green grass and bare branched trees expectantly awaiting the cotton-candy-pink Spring. It was a time for the rebirth of us all.

Cosby was now a registered, violent, sex offender and we had triumphed against all odds. We triumphed for Andrea Constand, for us, and for all women who had not yet seen justice. We triumphed for the innocents that we may have saved from any of his future predatory pursuits. We did good. Now we had to await the court schedule for his sentencing. *"I'll be there,"* I promised myself. *"I'll be there,"* I said to the wind.

I was grateful for the women who had become sisters on this journey, and the activists who I was sure I would see again in September once the exact date was established. But now, it was time to celebrate.

Returning to Capone's, my favorite Italian restaurant and sports bar out on Germantown Pike for a goodbye drink, I now easily navigated the familiar back roads of Norristown. It had become a second home thanks to the great gals I met there, Angel and Heather. Along with my balls-out activist-protester, badass friend, Bird Milliken, my author, talk show host friend, Elona Washington, we had an impromptu celebration and lifted a glass to Andrea Constand before I hit the road again. Justice for Dre was justice for us all.

I decided to drive down to North Carolina to decompress with my daughters and their families on their five lush-green acres in their big, old, historic, two-story, colonial house before returning home. Something normal. Something real. I loved to feel the hum of the open highway beneath me with its gradually changing landscape - the last gasps of winter as I drove South towards the renewal of a healing Spring.

Chapter 81
Back to Real

I rose before dawn with a sense of excitement and anticipation of my next adventure. I had my Irish Breakfast tea, my morning yogurt and even took my vitamins and herbs. I looked back wistfully at my serene sanctuary and tiptoed past Diana's sleeping form. We had connected at the first trial where she was standing in front of the courthouse holding her homemade sign with all of our names written on it. She had invited me to stay with her during the second trial. As I pulled my wheeled suitcases past her on the couch, she murmurs, *"Safe trip."* I whisper *"See ya in September for the sentencing! Thank you!"* Thank you for the gift of this sanctuary you have freely offered me, and the gift of friendship. One more survivor in the fold. One more woman who has found her voice. One more Sister.

I dug the root of a lovely blue wildflower to take with me in hopes of transplanting it in my daughter's garden. The cobalt-colored petals vibrated within my soul. I pulled out into the crisp, clear, early morning air with just a rosy blush of dawn. The traffic was light and I felt so excited to be taking a road trip by myself. The feeling of freedom on top of our victory was exhilarating. I headed south to North Carolina and couldn't help but break into song. *"Well, I'm going to Carolina in my mind…"* James Taylor - thank you! I thought if all went well, I'd be there before dinnertime. I was jubilant. The scenery became greener the farther south I drove. Cherry blossoms were bursting out everywhere. Trees along the highways were welcoming me deeper into their bosom.

Somewhere around noon I got a call from TMZ. They wanted an interview. Could I do it, they wanted to know? I told them I was on the highway driving, but if we could work it out, I'd be game. They gave me a time and would warn me a half an hour beforehand so I could find a turn-out and get myself settled in somewhere. We'd FaceTime. I was in a good mood and enjoyed the prospect of FaceTiming with the media while on the road. Everything felt possible suddenly. Justice had been ours!

TMZ gave me the heads up and I started scanning for a likely spot to pull off the highway. I took the exit and saw a little country Qwik Stop, a small dirt turn-out, surrounded by trees I could back into for a bit of privacy. I found myself nestled under a cozy leaf overhang and I opened my sunroof. I propped my phone and I checked my lipstick. As I waited for my cue, I listened to the breeze gently rustling the leaves of the trees above me. I heard the occasional chirping of birds and the distant sound of trucks lumbering down the highway.

We're on. Harvey asked me all the usual questions. I gave him the usual answers, but then he asked me if I thought Cosby would get special treatment in prison and if so what kind of special treatment would I like to see. I replied, tartly, *"I hope he gets the same special treatment that he gave us!"* By the time I arrived at my daughter's house, the headlines read, *"Victoria Valentino wants to see Cosby raped in prison."*

My daughter, Meaganlark, said, *"Mama you should have known better. TMZ always spins people's words to make them as sensationalized as possible."* So, when they called the next day for another comment about Mrs. Cosby's public statement, I said, *"No!"*

My eldest granddaughter, who was about nine at the time asked about what her Nana, was doing after apparently seeing some of my media coverage. Meagan explained and she exclaimed, *"Mama, that's for women!"* At that point, I knew for sure that I was on the right path.

After a couple of weeks savoring the company of my grandchildren, enjoying being in my daughter's home, doing normal things, I bid them all big smoochie goodbyes and returned home to my other reality.

I returned to my sanctuary in the foothills of the San Gabriel mountains to renew my spirit and gain some objectivity before I headed back to Montgomery County Courthouse towards the end of September when the sentencing would occur. There would be more Sisters flying into Norristown to join hearts and hands. There would be many survivors, activists, supporters and the press there. The usual array of Cosby apologists we all knew by now would also be congregating in front of the courthouse. We'd be there in the early morning darkness to see justice served, to see our rapist in handcuffs led off to prison. We just didn't know for how long.

Of course, we would all stay in touch. We were a Sisterhood. A family drawn together because we had a common denominator. We shared our rapist. We had our private conversation group on Facebook where we kept up on any news. We supported each other and some of us got together for any opportunity, activism, birthdays, other individual endeavors. We did not share the same backgrounds or lifestyles. We were not even in the same age group, but we were almost umbilically connected from then on. We knew each other's sorrows and vulnerabilities. We knew what fed each other's spirit and we knew each other's bullshit, too. The press made much of our Sisterhood, but it was not all rainbows and butterflies. We had all bounced off walls around each other. PTSD'd with each other. We'd been pissed at each other. But in the end, those of us who bonded over the years, and those who had yet to be welcomed into the fold, knew that under any condition, we would be there for each other at the drop of a hat if needed, no questions asked. We had faced a monster together.

Joseph Campbell, my favorite mystic said, "The thing in the cave, the monster that you think will kill you, you must face and slay even if it costs you your life. That is what will save the village. When we face our fears, we find our greatest strength."

Chapter 82
The Sentencing
September 2018

The summer flew by. We received the court date, September 25th. When I arrived in Philly for the sentencing, I spent the week as a guest in my new friend Elona's three story townhome which was walking distance from the courthouse. I could see the it from my third-floor bedroom window.

That week began with a flurry of news from the Victim Advocate Division and D.A. Kevin Steele whose delightful father, attorney Rodman Steele, was there. He attended every court session. Rod was an attorney from Florida committed to investigating Jeffrey Epstein and Trump's connection to him. He was a tall, slender, white haired, craggy-featured statesman, and a father deeply proud of his son. We stayed in touch. He often texted me to keep me apprised of any updates. He was diagnosed with lung cancer sometime in the midst of the trials, yet even with a portion of his lung removed, he devotedly arrived in court to support his son. Sadly, he passed away in the late summer of 2020. I know that I am not alone in grieving his loss.

Everyday there was some new tidbit of information shared by Victims' Advocacy. It occurred to me that I should be sharing the updates with my social media followers while I had time on my hands. I walked over to the courthouse plaza every evening around twilight and I would livestream. Sometimes when Bird Milliken was free, she'd do the camera work, but often I was on my own. It seemed important to share our journey with the world since all the media outlets presented the edited version, but no one heard directly from the dragon's mouth. We had all been bashed, attacked, received death threats, been spat upon, accused of being gold diggers, liars, racists even though approximately a third of us who spoke out were women of color - you name it. So, I did it. I looked forward to walking around the courthouse plaza in the dying light talking intimately to my Facebook followers.

Many of the Sisters who had not been at court for the two previous trials began arriving. Our Sisters who had been at every trial were there as well. All of our favorite journalists and some we had yet to meet were gathering. This was our moment.

Tamara Green, the earliest known accuser from the mid-Sixties. Sarita Butterfield flew in from Rio de Janeiro. Cindra Ladd, the ex-wife of the late Alan Ladd, Jr., Oscar winner for his film, *Braveheart*, was there. Cindra made a statement in which she was quoted many times. *"We are only as sick as the secrets we keep."*

Barbara Bowman was there. Therese Serignese, one of the first Jane Does from 2005 who had accused Cosby when Andrea had first spoken out, who had just lost her daughter to an opioid overdose, was there. Lise-lotte Lublin and her husband, Ben, whom I first met on the Dr. Phil Show in January 2015 arrived. Lili Bernard, Afro-Cuban artist and actress was there, she who is now able to pursue justice because the laws were changed in New Jersey, the State in which Cosby drugged and raped her. Linda Cooper Kirkpatrick, who met Cosby on the tennis court and a member of our ERSOL coalition joined us again. She who had the dubious distinction of being the most enthusiastic carpool Karaoke voice on our long drives to lobby in Sacramento.

Stacey Peterson, talk show host on Radio Europe flew in from Spain where she had fled out of fear after Cosby raped her many years before. There were many of our supporters there - Bird Milliken, childhood rape survivor Susie Q Spite, Diana McBryan, my survivor hostess from Trial #2, trauma therapist and author Shari Botwin. Francesca Rizzo, standup comedienne and *"We Support the Survivors"* admin on Facebook, Lisa Talmadge, a loyal and longstanding advocate arrived on the scene. Mary Noel, who had driven every day during the trials from Hershey, Pennsylvania with her pockets stuffed with Tic Tacs for us all, showed up. We were finally going to meet many of the women in person who had been strong researchers and supporters of our cause, women whom we had only previously known virtually. I watched the lights on the courthouse plaza that night from my bedroom window. It was too exciting and sleep evaded me.

Cindra swung by Elona's to pick me up in the early morning rain and darkness. It was good to have a friend to arrive with after a nerve-wracking night. There was great anticipation and lots of anxiety building within us all. When we gathered in front of the courthouse early in the pre-dawn morning of the sentencing, it was still dark as night, cold and raining. We had been instructed to arrive very early around 6 a.m. due to the potential for danger; the chaos of the crowd and intense media coverage. Everyone needed to be seated in the thirty seats of the back two or three rows reserved for the public. The apologists had been in the habit of trying to get there first throughout the trials. Victims Advocacy led by the solid, deeply caring Jennifer Storm, were all committed to making sure we were not harassed or hurt.

They had posted Security around us as we were being mercilessly heckled by the apologists. They were jumping in front of the cameras when we were being interviewed and yelling slogans. It became more of a circus than we had experienced in the first trial - a different kind of wild, but a wild scene nonetheless.

Once we made it through the interviews, we were surrounded by the crushing noisy crowd in the cold insistent rain on the courthouse plaza. We were jostled by the crowds of onlookers, media cameras and boom mics, but protected by the cops and other Security. Finally, we were shepherded up onto the courthouse veranda under the overhanging roof out of the rain. Freezing in line, we were all huddled together, waiting for the doors to open at 7 a.m.

We were overjoyed to be reunited - Sisters and activists, supporters and friends, arrived one by one clutching their raised collars, juggling umbrellas, shivering and hugging each other.

Andrea Constand, with her attorneys, Bebe Kivitz and Dolores Troiani, PAVE founder Angela Rose, and the various journalists who attended to her closely were ushered into the building through the side doors into their holding rooms until the court was in session. We would not get to see Dre until she made her subdued, dignified and much anticipated entrance once we were seated.

Finally, the courthouse doors were opened and we all filed inside. We listened once again to all the familiar courtroom rules and regulations - and Judge O'Neill's recitations. It was a long lead-up to Dre's moment - and to ours.

And, then we waited expectantly for the grand entrance of the one person who tied us all together - our common denominator - Bill Cosby.

We sat side by side, squeezed in together. I was bookended by Cindra and Susie Q clutching each other's' hands and feeling shivery. We weren't sure if it was the weather outside or our nerves. We knew that Cosby could be sentenced to ten years for each of his three guilty charges, but what would Judge O'Neill deem just? We had no clue.

Cosby's defense team challenged the Judge this past summer trying to force him to recuse himself. He was essentially being blackmailed because years before when he and his wife had been separated, he had an *affaire* with a woman who would later become a judge in her own right. They also tried to say his judgements would be compromised because his wife was a professor specializing in women's issues. He withstood their pressure. He was a seemingly low-key kind of guy not prone to theatrics, although he was known to whistle melodically as he strode nonchalantly through the courthouse hallways.

The sound transmission in Courtroom A was so poor throughout all the trials that, because we were confined to the back rows, we always strained to hear. We kept asking, *"What did he say?"* What really struck us was Stewart Ryan, the Assistant D.A. recitations of all the restrictions that were to be placed on Cosby once he was sentenced. He explained that Cosby would have to register as a violent sex offender in any town he visited for the rest of his life. Bizarrely, Cosby asked, "*Does that mean even if I'm there for only one night?*" He still somehow delusionally thought that he was going to walk out of that courtroom a free man.

When the judge finally pronounced the sentence, it was so lacking in courtroom drama that we didn't even realize what had happened. Once we women conferred, we finally realized that the judge had indeed pronounced Cosby's sentence, but it was in so much the same volume and monotonality of everything he had already said, that we weren't sure what had just happened. It was anticlimactic.

We wanted trumpets and heraldic pages in red tunics emblazoned with rampant lions. We needed fanfare! But we still saw justice served. He still got three to ten years in total. It could have been more but at his age we figured it may as well be a life sentence. We hugged and wept. We waited to see what would happen next. Would he be led out of the courtroom in handcuffs so we could, see? We craned our necks.

There was a low buzz in the courtroom. Police officers along with Detective Wittenberger and Detective Reape moved in and surrounded him. We saw them stand Cosby up but then their bodies obscured our view. We struggled to see. We stretched our necks higher to see if we could get a better view of what was going on. Detective Reape, who had visited and interviewed each one of us all over the country, must have intuited our need to see Cosby in custody. He stepped back a bit leaving an opening. He knew the horror of all of our stories. He knew how important this moment was for us. We saw Cosby hand his suit jacket over to someone as he stood there looking a little discombobulated in his big white shirt, baggy black trousers held up by suspenders.

At that point, we were all herded out of the courtroom. We were pushed into the side walkway surrounding the grand marble colonnaded stairwell. There was an undeniable sense of exhilaration. It was over!

The area in front of the courtroom door was cleared of bystanders and the area was cordoned off by yellow crime scene tape. We jostled for position at the front of the crowd. Each of us entitled to be front and center to witness this moment. We lost in our reverie - our past moments in time that linked us all to each other. He was no longer in control of the events to follow and we needed to see that. He could no longer exert his twisted power over us ever again. It was our right. We waited - and waited again. The air of anticipation was thick in the crowd. Our moment had arrived.

The courtroom doors opened and we held our collective breath. There he was - Bill Cosby - shuffling out into the vestibule heading down the hallway. Each of us in our own mind's isolation, yet conjoined by our common experiences, we'd waited. Each of us as different as grains of sand, yet this man, this predator, this formerly beloved comedian was our common denominator; the thread that wove our memories and our pain together.

When he shuffled out of the courtroom with his hands cuffed in front of him, I had a brief moment of pity - more pity than he ever had for me. He looked like such a pathetic frail old man. The moment was fleeting, because I saw his miniscule almost imperceptible smirk. I realized that he still thought he was just playing a role. We saw a photo of him later when he was at the police station getting booked. His expression had adjusted to his new reality. This was not a sitcom.

Justice had been served. Three to ten years in state prison! He wouldn't be up for parole until September 25th, 2021. I kept repeating it over and over to myself. Who, in 1969, could have imagined Bill Cosby in state prison? Certainly, not him. He, who believed himself to be above the law.

Once he was out of sight, we all rushed down the staircase out onto the rain-slick courthouse steps. My phone once again began to explode. The Press was lined up in a crush sticking out their mics, cameras and vying for our reactions, our sound bytes. The atmosphere felt very different from the last two trials. It was like Judge O'Neill's pronouncement - anticlimactic. There was almost a sense of apathy - maybe it was the rain bleeding from the gray mottled skies - maybe it was just the comedown after a four year high.

I chose to wear my mother's shoes that day for a reason. For all the times when she had no voice, no words, no control over her own finances, her own life's direction, her own body - I wanted to bring her with me in spirit - to share the moment seeing my rapist in handcuffs.

For all of my conflicted feelings about my mother, her malicious lies -- for my enduring love, compassion and devoted care of her - even after her ultimate betrayals of me from beyond the grave - I stood in her black suede high heels in pouring-down puddling rain on this alluvial plain of justice. *"See Mommy?! See? I stand for you, too."*

Chapter 83
Manhattan, My City of Firsts

Motion, movement, motors humming, wheels turning... gray skies shedding their tears. We were on the highway heading towards Manhattan where I experienced my first loves, my first traumas - and finally my renewal.

I was whisked away once again trodding through puddles in the pouring-down rain, weather unfit for this moment, from the post-sentencing press conference and the string of media interviews. The sun should have been blazing in celebration. For a change, I was not in the back seat of a sleek shiny black town car staring at the back of a chauffeur's head. I was riding shotgun with a friendly female CBS producer driving. We were feeling lighthearted and a bit giddy on our way from Norristown, Pennsylvania, Montgomery County Courthouse, to New York City to be interviewed in the morning on *CBS This Morning*, then *Inside Edition*, one-on-one with Deborah Norville, a midnight phone interview with *The Project* in Melbourne, Australia, *Victoria Derbyshire* in London at 5 a.m. - I broke down sobbing in that interview and apologized, *"I don't know why I'm being so emotional."* Next was *All Things Considered* on NPR - all before my car arrived to carry me through the morning crush to CBS.

Circles of healing close in upon themselves as new circles are born - new circles growing in new ways, blossoming into a unique and eclectic unknown - one of liberation, empowerment and healing. Vindication and validation. Victim no longer.

Chapter 84
In The Final Stretch

In the morning I was booked for CBS *This Morning* with Gayle King. Once the stylists finished my hair and makeup, I was escorted to the Green Room. It was surrounded by glass walls and I was able to see everyone on set. Every magazine that was displayed on the coffee table had the recent Bill Cosby sentencing story on the front cover. It was a big story. *"America's Dad..."* in handcuffs.

Gayle King entered and greeted me. Holding up one of the magazines, I commented, *"He wasn't America's Dad to me!"* She said, *"That's your first line."* I was tempted to bring up the fact that her best friend, Oprah, never reached out to us in support. She waited till after the survivors of Harvey Weinstein came out publicly about his abuse. She spoke at the Oscars that year, eloquently and movingly about empowering women in our industry and beyond, whose lives and careers were derailed by sexual harassment. It was beautiful and inspiring. And as a woman's advocate it was the right thing to do.

After my interview I was rushed across the street for a quickie interview with Deborah Norville at the *Inside Edition* studio. I was pretty sure I saw the back of Oprah in the hallway speaking to a couple of people. I stopped and turned, thinking about rushing over for a burning question, but I was steered quickly out the door.

Deborah had come in early to do a fly-by instead of the later afternoon taping because CBS had already made my plane reservations to wherever I wanted to go. I, of course, chose North Carolina to be in time for dinner with my daughters and my grandkids - a quick flight. The thought of that warm reception with hugs and cries of *"Nana!"* was too good to pass up.

Chapter 85
Ruminations and Rants

The media asked me why I spoke out after holding my silence for so long, and all I could say was - *"If not now, when?"* How does one explain - the shame, the self-blame and the fear of exposing such an intimate degrading experience to someone - or the world - who has never experienced it? It takes a long time to call it by its name, to speak that word - the **R** word - **Rape**. It's a word we cushion and couch in less harsh terms, fearful of those who hear it from our lips. Have we overstepped? Improper topic?

We apologize as if we were to blame. We apologize for bringing up an unsavory topic and spoiling our companions' day. When we share our experiences, we often feel people pull away. We ask ourselves, "Have I revealed too much?" Do we now have some mark on our forehead that excludes us from polite society? Do we have an offensive smell?

The missing piece in my puzzle was finally found through Andrea Constand's courage to step forward again to confront her rapist in a public forum. I finally reached my tipping point. It made me confront the thread of continuity throughout my life - sexual assault, emotional, physical and psychological abuse - and unspeakable grief - the residual damage I'd suffered alone over many decades. Without forethought or expectation, I found my voice. I found a community of people with shared experience - a Sisterhood that ultimately validated my own journey of the assaults on my body, heart, life path and soul. *The Healing After* was a journey unto itself. Each survivor's journey has its own unique flavor, its own distinctive style, but the post-rape symptomology has predictable hallmarks.

Sexual crimes are the ones that are the least prosecuted because the boundaries are different - squishy. If someone steals your car it's pretty clear cut. If someone murders your neighbor it's straightforward. No one questions what you were wearing or why you were there - nor if you're telling the truth and you really *"wanted it"* in a baaaad way.

This is a crime that is more disputed than not - a crime where the victim is too often revictimized by the system that was set in place to Protect and Serve. This is a crime we absorb into our own cellular memory, which lives forever as a subliminal presence in every relationship from that moment forward. It is a crime that the justice system too often dismisses lightly with a cavalier nonchalance. It is a crime where that which is stolen and damaged cannot ever be replaced.

Too often those victimized just suck it up and get on with life - silently suffering and alone. The burden falls on us, affecting us regardless. We live in fear that we will be exposed, rejected, made to feel dirtier than we already feel. We keep an emotional suit of armor invisibly encasing our nightmares, so that they don't seep out and stain someone else. We create stories to gloss over the uncomfortable truths. We try to make ourselves socially acceptable. We fill in the awkward gaps in time when we suffered from the callous destruction of our dreams by those with insatiable black holes instead of good souls. We make up socially acceptable stories to not shock when others are recounting their fun college days - or their white wedding.

Every aspect of our future lives is impacted. Then there is the generational trickle-down, the way we relate to our children - then they to theirs - and on it goes from generation to generation with no one really knowing or understanding where these dysfunctional patterns originated.

It becomes part of the family DNA. The conversations are never easy in any survivor's family. But once we acknowledge the need to communicate, the need to sort out the tangle of emotions and reactions, we're opening the window to the healing light. I have had to address and try to resolve my past traumas with my own children. It is ongoing.

When a society is still trying to drag women back into the Dark Ages of womanhood; where Roe v Wade has been overturned, women must still fight to have autonomy over their own bodies. The never-ending rhetorical question will always be, *"What is the worth of a woman in today's society"*

Thank the goddesses that we can stir a pot of gumbo with one hand, hold a baby on our hip and run a corporation - simultaneously! Thank the goddesses that we are capable of more facilely accessing both hemispheres of our brains than men who tend to be mostly limited to one hemisphere - the linear, black and white one. We are multitasking queens! We have logic AND empathy, critical thinking **and** artistic sensibilities. We can drive and cry at the same time! Ain't we cool?

We have to remind others - and remind ourselves - that there is a vast difference between being a victim - and being victimized. Had I not removed myself from city life I would most likely be dead. Nature's seasonal lushness and amazing grace took me to places where I found myself again. I was led to authentic people who liked me for the person I was. It was astonishing. It was a tentative acceptance of trust when I discovered no one wanted anything from me except to join in with the family activities - peel an onion, grab a beer, learn to make a *roux*. I found crusty protective layers of armor peeling away from my vulnerable, cynical self. I found myself getting back to my sacred core.

I understand now that I am not alone. I am entitled to set healthy boundaries. It's ok to say no. We are entitled to say no! But more importantly we are entitled to say "Yes!" Underneath the public smile and *panache* there might be a very angry person. We discover we are also entitled to our anger.

Forgiveness is a concept I still struggle with. It almost seems that we're giving permission to the perpetrator to do it again without suffering consequences. It says, "Awwww it wasn't that bad. I know you didn't mean to eff up my life. It's ok. Go say a few Hail Marys and all is well. Go eff up more women's lives." "Oh, I'm sorry." NO! It's *not* ok. I can let it go for my own health, but I still expect to see perpetrators suffer the consequences of their own actions - as we have suffered the consequences of their actions.

After my encounter with Cosby when I had walked away from everything and seen my life redirected, I, would never have thought in my wildest imaginings that I would find this validity, this strength of purpose. Crossing the *finish line* in 2018 after a four-and-a-half-year marathon since breaking my silence in 2014 was life-affirming.

Justice for Andrea Constand was the only justice for those of us for whom the statute of limitations on rape and sexual assault had long expired. Seeing Dre' achieving justice in a tangible way gave us our lives back. We had been given a voice. We had been believed.

We had rallied, testified, interviewed and lobbied, changed laws and minds. We had said, *"Silent No More."* We had said, *"We Stand in Truth."* Our supporters had said, *"Believe Women"* and *"We Support the Survivors."* We had chosen not to just survive, but to thrive! We had broken our silence and we saw justice served.

We opened the floodgates through which other victims of sexual assault by rich, powerful men had sought justice and found their voices. We had given courage to other survivors so they sought their own paths to justice. We had shown that by speaking out, by becoming a powerful chorus, we were not executed or eviscerated in the public square. We were, and are, the mothers and grandmothers of the future. Our voices were strong and we are relevant, as long as there is one person on this earth who is being sexually victimized... as long as Rape Culture persists!

We have to grow into our truth. When something happens that triggers us in such a way that our whole life's purpose hits us in the face, we must say 'YES!' It takes us by force. There is no time to question. The fire ignites within us. We explode with all that has simmered within us for a lifetime and finally comes to a boil. No time to think about consequences when the spark of truth and justice takes the lead and inhabits every fiber of our consciousness.

When at last that happens - we MUST say, "Yes!"
There is no other choice.

And, at my age - at any age - *nothing to lose.*

"And the day came when the risk to remain tight in
the bud was more painful than the risk it took to
blossom."
--Anais Nin

I think back to that time when I hit the 101 north -
when I followed my own *"Yellow Brick Road"* against
everyone's protestations, because at last, I listened to my
inner voice, my intuition. It took me back to peer at the
person I'd lost and it gave me a hint of who I was yet to
become. I just had to follow the breadcrumbs. It admonished
me to trust my instincts, my gut, my spirit.

It showed me I had a choice. I could live - or I could
die. And I chose life.

In January 1971 when I left Topanga Canyon
weaving the next chapter of my life's tapestry on my
'walkabout' leaving everything I knew, it was against
everyone's protests. I hit the road once more with a crazy
guitar pickin' songwriter, Jay "Bobby" Willis, and his good
dog, Moby. I knew I had no choice but to go.

Brother Moe McEndree said, *"What are you doing?*
He's a jerk!" Yet, that "jerk" was the messenger who took
me back to myself - who took me home to his Mamom. She
was the mother I never had, but needed. She was the mother
who gave me unconditional love - and as a bonus, taught me
how to make a good Cajun gumbo. That jerk gave me a

loving family with six nieces for whom I crocheted. He gave me a new baby of my own to sing to - and I found myself becoming whole. Even as I questioned my own truth, I journeyed forth.

I said... *"Nothing left to lose..."*

It was that jerk who gave me a life that allowed me to live to write another song. You see, when we follow our own truth, no matter where it leads, no matter what anyone tells us, it takes us on our own road home... home to our Self...

Finding Our Voices

The early days as we spoke out and discovered we weren't alone.

The Empty Chair. 2014 - 2015

"A woman can be not believed for 30 years? But it takes one man?"

– Victoria Valentino
on Hannibal Buress'
Bill Cosby jokes
Year of alleged assault
by Bill Cosby: 1969

NEW YORK

71.

72.

73.

74

75.

The Gathering, Montgomery County Courthouse,
Norristown, Pennsylvania.
71. Diana McBryan at Trial 1, 2017 with all our names
handwritten.
72. Jane Manning's Coalition, Equal Justice for Women.
73. Sporting my buttons.
74. Rally Sacramento 2016 Abolishing the Statute of
Limitations on Rape & Sexual Assault in California.
75. Meeting the media after the mistrial - 2017.

76.

77.

78.

79.

80.

76. In Solidarity.
77. On the courthouse steps.
78. NBC's Kate Snow and I returning to court after lunch.
79. Bird Milliken welcoming me to Philly.

80. Bird, Lili and I protesting in front of Montgomery County Courthouse - 2017.

81.

82.

VERDICT RENDERED Caroline Heldman, Lili Bernard and Victoria Valentino, three of the dozens of women who have accused Bill Cosby of sexual assault, embrace after a jury in Norristown, Pa., found him guilty on April 26 of drugging and sexually assaulting Andrea Constand. The case was one of the first high profile sexual assault trials to take place since the #MeToo movement began.

in 2014.

18   TIME May 14, 2018

will read the party to a bright political future.
—KATE SAMUELSON

83.

81. Waiting to go LIVE on courthouse plaza with CNN's Don Lemon and MSNBC's Chris Hayes.
82. Guilty! Guilty! Guilty!
83. Hugging and weeping in disbelief after the guilty verdict.

The Journey After the Verdict

84.

85.

86.

87.

84. At the podium and in the news celebrating justice.
85. Sisters gather: "The Sentencing," September 25, 2018.
L-R Top, Lili, Linda, Tamara Green. Bottom: Cindra Ladd,
Me, Therese Serignese.
86. Friar's Club, NYC, hosted by Gloria Allred. Lili,
Caroline and I, 2018.
87. *Today Show*, Lili, Gloria and I with Savannah & Hoda.

88.

89.   90.

91.

88. Speaker at Rally on
Hollywood Blvd. 89. Red
Carpet, TRUTH, Cory
Feldman's film.
90. Awareness into Action &
PAVE against sexual
harrassment & violence in
the film industry.
91. Lili Bernard, Me, the late Sister Sunni Welles.

92.   93.

94.   95.

96

92. Vigil: Independence Square, Philadelphia, July 2021 after Cosby's release from prison. Preparing to speak.
93. Definition of Consent. Make it legal!
94. Bird protesting at Cosby's Cheltenham Mansion during Civil Trial of Judy Huth v Cosby, Santa Monica Courthouse, California June, 2022.
95. The Sisters gather again in support & solidarity for Judy: Lili, Susie Q, Caroline & I.
96. More Survivor Family picnic on Courthouse lawn for lunch including Lise-lotte & Ben Lublin

Hollywood Critics Association Awards:

Lili & I Walk the Red Carpet 2022 for Award Winning
Showtime series, *We Need to Talk About Cosby,*

Produced by W. Kamau Bell, Katie King, Erik Adolphson.
Production Supervisor, Grady C. Kelly.

EPILOGUE
June 30, 2021

Just when you think your work is done and you've moved on, the rug is ripped out from under you once again. It was a Wednesday morning and I was having a self-care day. I was determined to stay in my nightgown and do nourishing things for my soul when the phone rang. I saw that it was ABC calling. It occurred to me that because we had just received a letter from the Victims Advocacy Division at Montgomery County Courthouse in Pennsylvania preemptively denying Cosby's request for parole prior to his three-year minimum sentence, that the media must want a comment. He had consistently refused to participate in programs for sexual assault abusers and showed no remorse. We had all taken a collective sigh.

I answered the call.

"Whaddya think about Cosby getting out of prison?"

"Excuse me?"

"He just got out of prison today!"

"But, but… we just got a letter…"

"Yeah. The Superior Court overturned his verdict because the prior District Attorney Bruce Castor, (the bumbling attorney in Donald Trump's impeachment hearing,) told him if he confessed under oath he would never be prosecuted."

"Oh, shit! But we heard him on tape confess in court to buying drugs to give to women so he could have sex with them! This is outrageous! I'm stunned! I had no idea!"

And then it dawned on me. I remembered the Appeal Hearing on December 1st of 2020. Their verdict was to be revealed in the Spring of 2021. So, this was it. Son of a bitch!

At the time of Cosby's appeal hearing, I was throwing stuff in my suitcase at my daughter's house in North Carolina preparing to race off to the airport after a month away. It was a Superior Court hearing on Zoom. They were trying to dispute, invalidate, discount and throw-out the testimony of the five prior bad act witnesses, my Sister Survivors - the women I knew to be truthful. These were women I knew to have suffered PTSD from their awful encounters with Cosby. Their testimonies under oath were necessary to establish that Cosby was a serial offender. How else could they do it? The current D.A. Kevin Steele had to establish that Cosby had a pattern of behavior, a *modus operandi* - an M.O. - and he clearly, indisputably did.

The thing that deeply disturbed me the most during the appeal hearing was on a real atavistic level. It was one of the Justices - a woman - who said, "*I just don't see a pattern here.*"

There was a thread of continuity in every assault that we knew about with all of Cosby's victims. We learned during our activism that it is a psych disorder called somnophilia - "*Sleeping Beauty Syndrome.*" He needed to position women facing away from him so he couldn't see their faces - or perhaps so they couldn't see his. They had to be unconscious. Even in consensual relationships he had to face his partners away from his view. This was stated by one of the Sisters who had a two year relationship with him but was only drugged when they reunited after a break-up. He had fetishes about eyes, too, and he liked slicking down his victims' hair.

There were definite patterns, enough to establish him as a serial offender. Sixty-two victims came forward, and many of us knew at least one or two more who were afraid to go public for a variety of reasons. So many stories came flooding in from people I'd always known and people I'd never met with the same refrain, "Me, too!"

As the day progressed with one media call after another and sometimes two or three at a time, I never had a chance to get dressed. I just threw a scarf around my shoulders. Many of the interviews were Zoomed or FaceTimed, so I was glad I'd had the good sense to at least put on makeup and brush my hair that morning. I sat in my closet where my computer desk is nestled amongst my vintage clothing collection. *"Welcome to my closet!"* I jested.

The adrenaline was surging through my system. - We had all been in the doldrums with the pandemic and suddenly there was a new infusion of energy and purpose again. It was a whirlwind of non-stop media interviews for the next three days. And by Friday night I was on a *red-eye* to Philly for a vigil to join up again with many of my Sisters. We'd be doing what we did best - raising the flag of truth and justice.

As ever I was enthusiastically greeted at the airport by Bird's wiry, joyfully grinning self, dancing to "I am WOMAN!" with bubbles filling the air and holding her big sign.

"Victoria Valentino! Philly Welcomes You! And any other badass bitches! This way!"
I have never felt in my life ever so welcomed by anyone anywhere!

We stayed with Bird in her ancient stone watermill house. And as she drove us out into the country, we felt like we were on *Mr. Toad's Wild Ride*. Filled with the joy and excitement of being together again doing The Work made driving through winding, woodsy roads, through the long deep dark tunnel she called *The Vortex* into the deep green leafy foliage on the other side, even more thrilling. We arrived at her two-story pop-art decorated stone home. She lugged my suitcase past the white grand piano, the naked guy store dummy wearing a lampshade over his lightbulb head and up the staircase holding onto the hand carved wooden snake banister. It was an ever-evolving artistic delight. The cherry on top was my room - *The Victoria Valentino Suite,* with my framed, autographed Centerfold hanging on the wall. Best of all, I got the one bedroom with the shower in the bathroom! This was going to be quite a reunion.

The vigil was an incredible event - a gathering of the clans - a survivor of the Catholic church, a Weinstein survivor, Stewart Ryan the assistant D.A. who so brilliantly shared the closing remarks with Kristin Feden at the Cosby trial. Jennifer Storm, the former head of Victims Advocacy in Norristown during our multiple sojourns - all were there. There were many advocates and lots of local media. Katie King, the producer of Kamau Bell's brilliant four-part Showtime Critic's Choice Award series and four Emmy Award nominated series, "*We Need to Talk About Cosby*," in which many of us were interviewed, was there with her film crew. Sister Susie Q, my back seat carpool lobbying pal flew in from California. Sister Stacey Petersen flew in from Spain via Arkansas. Sisters Lili and Caroline choreographed the event. Joyce Short was there to promote her Consent

Awareness Network - CAN - and her A6540A bill to establish a legal definition of consent in New York. *"Freely given, Knowledgeable & Informed Agreement."* Filmmaker Roger Schulte had begun filming our journey during the trials and was with us chronicling our vigil and reunion for his documentary, Love *is All Around.*

Lili, Susie and Caroline wearing long white dresses were setting the stage with Lili's handcrafted *luminarias* - white candle-lit paper bags with our names artistically cut out and placed in an arc at the front of the plaza area. The three girls were blindfolded with scales of justice held high. The dancing began to an Afro-Cuban beat and the speeches ensued. How fitting that the Liberty Bell was our backdrop.

When I spoke, I made the point that no matter whatever our achievements were in life, we would always go down in history for our common denominator, Cosby. Our names would always be entwined with our rapist's. Our careers were derailed as Cosby's star soared. We lost income, careers, friends, family, home towns and countries. We lost our health all the while his fame and net worth skyrocketed. For each of us the damage manifested differently but our common experience irrevocably modified our lives. Rape is murder of the soul - a life sentence. Should the perpetrator receive any less?

Cosby's status as a violent sexual predator was expunged completely from his record. All of our testimonies in court, and out, were completely erased. The Supreme Court rejected D.A. Kevin Steele's attempt to reopen the prosecution. Yet while Cosby's star remains on Hollywood Boulevard's Walk of Fame, it is often shat upon - that is some consolation.

Gloria Allred successfully prosecuted a civil suit against Bill Cosby in California in June 2022, for drugging and assaulting Judy Huth, now in her sixties, at the Playboy Mansion when she was sixteen. The laws have changed in California providing a one-to-two-year window of time for people who were raped when they were minors to seek justice. We came together again in solidarity to support Judy. As the statutes of limitation have changed in some states, justice for some of us is still within reach. We have been part of the solution.

It is important to remember that Cosby was not found innocent. He was found liable. Cosby will go down in history as a serial rapist. This will be his legacy.

We have boldly spoken our truth. We have been heard and we are no longer victims. We have given encouragement and strength of purpose to other survivors so they might pursue justice. We have inspired others to find their voices and we have opened doors for survivors to walk through boldly without fear to speak their truths. We mobilized, changed laws and our work will go on. The silent will be heard and I believe we shall prevail. This will be *OUR* legacy.

And, so, Sisters *and Brothers*. Chin up, shoulders back, stand straight and proud. Keep your eyes on the goal. Speak out and hold your torches high for truth and justice. Remember to breathe! We have changed *HER*story for future generations and we will continue to stand in solidarity.

"And still, I rise…"
--Maya Angelou

51.

52

53.

54.

51. Daddy Nino in his art studio.
52. Mom and Daddy.
53. Mom and I.
54. Mom at 86.

55.   56.

57.   58.

55. Mom and I.

56. Mom enjoying her 90th Birthday party. Sat sitting behind her.

57. Mom's 90th in frontof her fireplace.

58. Aunt Pat, Daddy Jim's sister, who said, "Kid, you've got brains leaking out your ears. You're going to make it."

59.   60

61.   62.

59. Santa Fe vacation sun.
60. Fanzine cover by Maurice Rinaldi. 1998.
61. Hard Copy interview, Playboy Mansion West. 1996.
62. Registered Nurse. 1986 - present.

63.

64.

65.

66.

63. Hugh Hefner and I, NYE 2000 Playboy Mansion West.
64. Montreal 2004 *Cavalcade d'Etoiles*.
65. Glam photo by Maurice Rinaldi.
66. Accepting Public Service Award from V.A. on behalf of Playboy holding my father Jim's Purple Heart.

67.   68.

69.   70.

67. Gifting Hef with Daddy Nino's serigraph of the making of Frankenstein's monster, Halloween Movie Night at Playboy Mansion West.

68. Francesca and I, Bunny Reunion, Las Vegas 2005.

69. Officiating at Playmate Sister Cynthia Myers' Memorial Service.

70. Reconnecting with Robert Morse for the first time since 1966 when we filmed *How to Succeed in Business Without Really Trying.*

High on a mountaintop breathing free on the Greek island
of Delos.

ACKNOWLEDGEMENTS

The writing of this book has been the trial of my lifetime and would never have come to fruition without the unconditional love, encouragement and support of my beloved friend, Amy Victoria Wall Lerman, who insisted that I must continue to put my journey in print. She has struggled along with me since I first read its first scribblings to her from my handwritten journal as we sat in my rental car in pouring rain in the juror's parking lot in Norristown, Pennsylvania in 2017. I can't thank her enough for living with me through this Herculean task over the years and not giving up on me. *You, Amy, have truly been the wind beneath my wings.*

I am deeply grateful to so many friends, old and new, who held me up spiritually if not physically throughout my doubts, tears and complaints of sleepless nights wrestling with shadows from the past and wondering why I should voluntarily open old wounds. It has been therapy, a necessary purging, a spiritual cleansing and self-exploration to relive the most difficult time of my life - my first twenty-six years. At very nearly eighty, I am grateful to have lived to tell the tale, and find some clarity.

I give thanks daily for so many people that I will never have room to include you all, but you know who you are and that you have my endless love. Lee Brainerd, thanks for the em dashes and such, and taking me on as a family project. To Kim Heath who gave hours of her time translating my scribbles into Google docs and making this project decipherable, thanks for your commitment and tolerance. Thanks to Courtney Scrabec who, when I thought my book was finished and was asked for an objective read-through, rearranged everything in proper order saying, "Don't hate me. I love you" and showed up with wine.

So grateful to Jeni and Paul whose comforting voices over the hedge makes me feel safe and who through all the years have kept watch over my garden, my fur babies and my sanctuary while I travel, and me when I've been ill, just because they're the best kind of neighbor ever. Thanks for letting me have the privilege of watching Clara and Alex grow up to be the finest big people I know... (outside my own kids and baby grands, of course!)

Endless gratitude to my funny, beautiful, unique and brilliant daughters, my best friends and most trustworthy critics, who gifted me with my precious six grandchildren, the jewels in my crown. They have put up with my absences and will have to read these stories that they really may wish they never knew. As cautionary tales, I hope they pass down the message that listening with their hearts and unconditional love are the mainstays of life that will never fail them. I hope the lessons derived from my journey are that throughout all the trials in life there are lessons to be learned to hone us into more empathic beings - and that kindness and patience are the balm for all wounds. To my biological father's side of the family who always gave me unconditional love and encouragement, and to my Cajun family who never let me go, I love you and am deeply humbled that you have stood by me always without judgement through all my incarnations and liked me just the way I was. Indescribable gratitude to Francesca Emerson who opened her home and lifelong friendship to me, nonjudgmentally, after my son died and as a result, saved my life. And the blessings next to the wounds have been reconnecting with Mandy Sue who let me mother her when she was four and adorable, who has come back into my life in her sixties, because she saw me speaking out in the media. Reconnecting with Tony's half siblings has been a closure of circles in the last few years as well, knowing what happened to them and who they've become. My love for them has never diminished.

Gratitude to my editor, publisher, Marissa F. Cohen, for taking on the task of attempting to control my run-on sentences, limiting my way too many stories, myriad cast members and stream of consciousness ramblings, so it all might make sense for the reader. To my favorite photographer, Maurice Rinaldi whose photo of me graces this book cover and who always makes me look good.

I think it only fair to thank the men in my life - the abusers, the good guys, the benevolent friends, as well as, the interesting and eclectic women in my family who taught me endurance, courage, fortitude and the awareness of the awesome healing beauty of nature. They showed me that I had to be my own hero - chin up, shoulders back. To my mother who was a sensitive, damaged soul and yet a magnificent example of keeping herself beautifully put-together and showing the world her undaunted spirit throughout her many trials. I love you Mama Diva, in spite of yourself. Thanks to Auntie Te who taught me to crochet and write poetry which helped to sustain my sanity; to Grandma Refa and Grandma Grace who showed me that any obstacle can be overcome with a little gumption. Eternally grateful to Auntie Nor Nor without whom I would not have known that someone cared and remembered that I was still alive. To Uncle Al, and Sat Nomura in Buddha heaven, the only men in my young life who never betrayed my trust. And for the many great recipes I gleaned from so many along the way that have enriched my culinary repertoire, revived my palate and appetite for life, *Bon appetit*! Humbled by the healing salvation of growing up in the woods of Ridgefield, Connecticut, and the enduring friendships, Linda, Lavi, Tamia and Dawn, that have affirmed my existence. To my friend, Tikoes, who always leaves me good books, loving cards of gratitude and fresh greens from her garden on my porch chair during her early morning hikes, and who shows up with a good salad and a cold beer when we both need a close woman friend to share the nourishing day to day stuff of life - and our troubles - deep thanks.

Deeply grateful to the amazing journalists, correspondents and talk show hosts whom I've been fortunate enough to meet and who thought I had something of worth to contribute - Jim Moret, Alisyn Camerota, Deborah Norville, Don Lemon, Chris Hayes, Kate Snow, Gayle King, Michael Smerconish, Denham Hitchcock of Australia's TV7, amongst many many others. Deep gratitude to Scott Higham and Manuel Roig Franzia for breaking my story in the Washington Post in 2014, and truly caring.

Humbled to have stood side by side with Gloria Allred and my dear Sister Survivors in our quest for truth and justice as we used our voices to speak truth to power, raise consciousness, change laws and shine the light on Rape Culture in hopes we might one day make it an outdated concept. Cheers to Andrea

Constand and Kevin Steele for bringing us all together for a righteous and just cause.

Many thanks to my dogs, YuYu and Gigi, and my big orange cat, Billy, for keeping me grounded in the truly important things of life - belly rubs and treats.

To my son, Tony, who made a decent woman out of me - in life and in death - you are my conscience in everything I do. Always in my heart. Always my guiding light. I hope that in this book I have done you justice.

ABOUT THE AUTHOR

Victoria Valentino was a serious acting student in New York, born in Hollywood during WWII, raised in Connecticut in an artistic family. But when she became Playboy's Miss September 1963, it radically redirected her life and career. A multi-rape, child and domestic abuse, sex trafficking survivor, she became a folksinger songwriter and single mother. In 1969, on the very day she celebrated the signing of her recording contract with Capitol Records, her six-year-old son drowned. Several weeks later, she was drugged, kidnapped, and raped by Bill Cosby. Ms. Valentino, now a media personality, keynote speaker, activist and mentor to other sexual assault survivors, shares her eclectic journey of survival and transformational healing.

Made in the USA
Columbia, SC
26 September 2022

67726804R00274